MEDITERRANEAN SEA

S⋯

⋯ascus

Tyre

PHOENICIA

Caesarea
Philippi

TETRARCHY
of
PHILIP

GALILEE

Capernaum •Bethsaida

• Gergesa (?)

Cana

•Nazareth

Nain

SEA of GALILEE

TETRARCHY

DECAPOLIS

•Caesarea

of

HEROD

Samaria

ANTIPAS

(?)
•Sychar

Jordan River

SAMARIA
(under Pontius Pilate)

PEREA

•Joppa

Jericho

Emmaus

Bethany
beyond
Jordan ?

Jerusalem• •Bethany

Bethlehem•

(directly under the
legate of Syria)

JUDEA

DEAD SEA

•Machaerus

Gaza•

IDUMEA

N

W   E

S

0 5 10 15 20 25 miles

HARLAN HUBBARD

Toward understanding
JESUS

ELWYN E. TILDEN, Jr. *Professor of Religion*
Lafayette College

Toward understanding
JESUS

PRENTICE-HALL Inc.   **Englewood Cliffs, N. J.**
1956

Preface

THIS BOOK is an introduction to the life and teachings of Jesus. It is designed for readers who, having no special interest in ancient history or literature as such, recognize Jesus as one of the great figures in man's religions, and wish to understand him.

Many people who feel this way are, of course, found within the Christian movement, and are to some degree already familiar with the life and teachings of Jesus. I invite them, through this book, to enrich their faith. Other readers who may be unfamiliar with either the Bible or Christianity will find, I trust, that what I have written is reasonably clear and useful in forming an understanding of Jesus.

This is an "introduction" in the practical sense of making the reader acquainted with Jesus. Perhaps, in seeking to make clear to men of today what Jesus was like, I have left out more historical material than I have included. This is desirable when acquaintance is first being formed. Understanding Jesus is different from understanding all the problems that exist concerning him. From time to time I have pointed beyond the limits of this introduction, so that readers who have a continuing interest in Jesus may follow further the matters they have encountered here.

Always I have had in mind those people who turn to the study of Jesus with two reasons for gaining understanding of him more prominent in their thinking than any others:

First, as a matter of intellectual enlargement, they wish to see Jesus as he saw himself, and fit him into the rest of their knowledge. His presence in human life rouses their interest. I have tried to aid this purpose by guiding the reader in accumulating for himself the biographical facts about Jesus.

Second, many readers turn to the study of Jesus because they look for help in forming a satisfactory religious viewpoint for themselves or in better understanding the faith they have. The fact that the study of Jesus aids personal religious growth should be distinguished from the explanation of why this is so. On the latter point readers' opinions may differ. I have tried always to remember that, although I was writing an academically disciplined book on the life and teachings of Jesus, its value would be increased beyond the stated purpose if it helped a reader understand himself a little better. The quest for individual religious understanding is often characteristic of a person's formative years, but I hope this book may be stimulating and helpful to any serious reader who would know Jesus better and see more clearly the scope of his own faith.

The plan by which this introduction to Jesus has been arranged centers on the four Gospels in the New Testament. There are many books about Jesus that could be read, but the most important are the four oldest. I have tried to give sufficient guidance so that readers may make sense out of the story of Jesus' life as the Gospels record it. I believe I have done this without turning my introduction to Jesus into an introduction to the books about him. I have treated separately the career of Jesus and his teachings. In connection with each chapter I have given a few suggestions for further study; these include supplementary readings that cover the texts of the four Gospels systematically.

The Gospels, which alone record the story of Jesus, cannot be understood without an appreciation of the history and religion that produced them in the first Christian century. In the first section of this book I have tried, without burying the reader in details, to describe Jewish religion and conditions in early Christianity in such a way as to make the Gospels more understandable in their historical setting than they are in isolation.

The discussion of Jewish religion and Christian origins calls for an awareness on the part of the reader of what religion is and what it does. Hence this book begins, seemingly at a great distance from Jesus, with the problems of understanding man's religious nature and the ways it has expressed itself in historic religions. The chapter on the other religions suggests brief comparisons between Jesus and the non-Christian faiths.

Most introductory books on the life of Jesus seem to have been written on the tacit assumption that we can understand Jesus without understanding religion, or that the reader understands the problems of religion already. The first assumption is so clearly wrong that probably it is not often intended. How can we understand the life and thinking of a person who was devoted entirely to religious issues until we see something of the problems with which men as religious beings have wrestled, and which Jesus claimed to resolve? As for the other assumption—that readers of the Gospels understand religion already—I write for those of us who are working toward an understanding of religious truth, and who welcome help.

Thus it comes about that *in practice* an intellectual interest in understanding Jesus is often accompanied by a search for individual religious faith. In my own judgment, however, this association is not merely coincidental. Whatever other origins it has, it comes partly from the nature of the effort to understand Jesus. Understanding him is a very profound thing. It unites the intellectual and the religious in us in ways we cannot avoid. The whole of our personal life is involved, either when we accept as true the message about him, or not agreeing with what we hear, examine again our own most significant attachments. The study of Jesus leads us through the tussle of reflection and decision, just as he himself led men in his own time. How this bears on understanding Jesus, I have tried to show here and there throughout the book.

I wish to say explicitly that though I am an evangelical Christian, I have tried to make this book a usable introduction to Jesus for all readers, whatever their individual religious viewpoints are, who will make the effort to use it. I have tried to point to the important questions, and distinguish between them and the answers that may be given. I have suggested for consideration problems that will, I hope, touch all of us in new ways. I have sought to describe the issues that all modern people face in understanding Jesus; for I feel that through facing these issues and fixing our own attitude toward them we grow toward intellectual and personal maturity.

I have not intended to dictate my reader's own religious decision for him. Constantly I have tried to keep in mind not only my own convictions about Jesus, but the needs of readers who are seeking an understanding of him that may or may not be similar to mine, but in any case is sincerely their own.

Acknowledgments

This book is the product of many minds that have worked together, even though the responsibility is that of the one whose name appears. Many books, colleagues, and teachers have helped, their contributions now lost beyond recognition. I believe that all specific indebtednesses are properly identified.

If I may be pardoned for singling out two men to whom

my debt is large, I acknowledge in this public way my gratitude to two professors of the faculty of the Princeton Theological Seminary, Henry S. Gehman (Old Testament Literature) and "my professor," Otto A. Piper (New Testament Literature and Exegesis). This expression of regard is proffered not to involve them in responsibility that is mine, but in appreciation for work which, as men and scholars, they prepared me to do.

I am grateful to the students in the classes in Religion at Lafayette from 1949-55. Even more am I under obligation to the members of the staff of the Department of Religion during those years, who will recognize on these pages fruits of long fellowship and discussion.

Mrs. Donald Riddagh, of Easton, gave generously of her time and skill in preparing the manuscript copy, making its completion possible when such seemed an impossibility.

The end-paper map is the work of Mr. Harlan Hubbard. I am grateful to him for including my project in his artistic activities.

Mr. Ron Lewton, of the staff of Prentice-Hall, Inc., has not only contributed generously of his editorial skill in the preparation of this book, but by his sympathetic and imaginative approach has increased its usefulness to every reader.

My wife not only worked over the manuscript but, by her encouragement and cooperation, made its preparation a joint enterprise.

The Scripture quotations in this publication are from the *Revised Standard Version of the Holy Bible,* copyrighted 1946 and 1952 by the Division of Christian Education, National Council of the Churches of Christ in the United States of America, and are used by permission.

E. E. T.

Contents

Steps preliminary to understanding Jesus

I

Beginning the study

*W*HEN we study the life and teachings of Jesus, we are studying events and ideas that have had, and still have, great meaning in the sphere of life called "religion." In fact, it is in religion that Jesus' greatest importance lies. This is because his own personal interests were entirely within the religious sphere, and because he has become the most influential figure in the Christian religion.

Jesus himself was primarily concerned for men's lives in relation to God and God's will, an interest that lies at the heart of religion. Although he was deeply concerned about all the problems people have, whether personal ones or those that involve the individual and society, his approach to the solution of these problems was through religion rather than through the use of methods developed by rational investigation. For him, the starting point in solving all problems is the fact that God is supreme in the universe. He held that individuals should concern themselves first with establishing the proper relations with God, and he offered help toward that end. He taught that out of a man's relationship with God, duties of a definite sort follow in his relations with his fellow men. One of the important things in understanding Jesus is to appreciate the vital union in his

3

thinking between a man's duty to God and toward his
fellows.

Jesus' first followers maintained, in their presentation of
him, his primary emphasis on living in full and proper relation with God. In fact, they went a step further. Because of
his death and resurrection they regarded him as having supreme importance in *their* relation with God. They stressed
in their reports of him what seemed to them important in
this religious sense, preserving only bits of his daily doings
and family background. To this day little is known about
the personal or private life of Jesus, and for that reason it
is impossible to write a biography of him in the usual form.

As the activities of his first followers crystallized into a
religious "movement," and then into the religion known as
"Christianity," he was acknowledged to be the historic
founder. Christian interest in him continued to show a motivation that was predominantly religious. By hundreds of
millions of his followers he has been considered a unique
being, the divine Lord and Saviour. His ideas and his own
person underlie that portion of the Christian Bible called
the "New Testament," though he directly composed no part
of it himself. The lives of his followers in human society
were guided ideally by the conviction that faith in him
should be the master of all of man's activities. His followers
looked to him for a religious relationship in which they
might approach all the problems of their lives. They did
not directly consider the relation of Jesus to political
thought, or art, or economics, as something to be studied
apart from faith.

Accordingly, it is through the important place Jesus has
in the Christian religion that he has exercised great influence in Western culture. His teachings, preserved for
religious reasons, have left many marks on literature and
other forms of artistic expression. The efforts of his followers
to interpret the nature of human experience, in the light of

what they have believed about his nature and experiences, have, in turn, affected philosophical and religious thinking outside the Christian movement. The practices of Christians in celebrating events in his life such as his birth (Christmas), his death (Good Friday), his resurrection (Sunday, Easter) have had a lot to do with setting the pattern for life in Europe and the Americas. Of course, the present calendar, with his birth as its reckoning point, dividing history into dates before Christ (B.C.), and after Christ (A.D.[1]), is a particularly clear case of his influence.

Hence it is that although Jesus was primarily concerned with religious issues and solutions, and within the Christian religion is regarded first of all with religious concern, his influences may be traced far afield. Probably no one in the last two thousand years has influenced the lives of as many people as has Jesus. It is not known how many books have been published about him.

Describing the approach

Because the life and the continuing influence of Jesus are centered within the sphere of the religious, it follows that he can be fully understood only in relation to the religious aspirations and experiences of the human race as a whole. This fact raises many problems, some of which relate to the background and experience of the individual reader, while others are broader in scope and more academic in content.

I shall discuss three matters relating to personal experience, since readers seeking to understand Jesus can make a good beginning by carefully observing their own religious situations.

(1) In general, I have had in mind the needs of readers who may be first coming alive to the intensity of religious

---

[1] Anno Domini, that is, "in the year of our Lord . . ."

problems, and just beginning to fashion a truly individual faith. They may feel inclined to challenge the whole range of truths accepted earlier. They are learning to think for themselves, to accept commitments that are their own, and to grant the right of others to hold commitments that differ. It is accordingly helpful to recognize that when we study the life and teachings of Jesus, we may be raising for settlement certain individual problems in the sphere of religion. Often definite decisions regarding the meaning of Jesus and the meaning of one's own problems come simultaneously.

(2) Some readers of this book may come to the study of Jesus for the first time, and as a first venture into the study of religion. It may well be that they also come to the study of religion and of Jesus without any contact either with the inner life of modern Christianity or with religious thinking in other faiths. Through their lively interest in modern natural science and technology, they may not have given serious thought to the issues with which religion deals, namely, the sense of man's limited existence and his dependence on powers outside himself.

Such a reader will need to keep in mind the fact that religion as an area of human concern has developed its own technical aspects. It has its own approach to human problems, and in the person of a leader such as Jesus, it speaks in a mature way. Accordingly, such readers should consider their own religious feelings and judgments in comparison with other religious thinking. This comparison will help them see what in themselves is "religious" though they may have thought that they had nothing religious about them. As they seek to understand Jesus in a rational way, they will also come to understand something of the great problems in life for which men's solutions always involve religious attitudes—decisions about life's meaning and its finiteness.

Furthermore, religion as a field of human activity has its

"experts," men who in ways we need not consider now have developed special knowledge and skills in the matter of men's relations with God. Such people should be reckoned with in the study of religion, just as experts are respected in other phases of human life.

Jesus was such an "expert," and it is characteristic of the Christian position, of course, to believe that Jesus, above all other figures in men's religions, should be considered as any person shapes his own religious life.

Perhaps we can make clearer the importance of Jesus as an expert in religion if we think of our relations to a medical doctor, whom we consult about some sickness. Here we are dealing with a man who has spent much time on his subject, has developed certain skills, and accepts responsibility for making judgments. Although we know our own pains and the meaning of some of our symptoms, we lack the knowledge and the experience to be sure of our own conclusions, and to find a remedy.

In the terms of this illustration, Jesus appears in human religion as an "expert," speaking out of serious reflection and with a mature acceptance of responsibility. He knows his subject, and on occasion uses the technical language belonging to it. One may not wish to accept Jesus' diagnosis or his remedies, just as one may reject the advice of a particular doctor, but the seriousness of intent and the capacity to speak should be recognized in either case.

(3) Although the reader who comes to the study of religion with little or no personal participation in any of the religious traditions has a certain handicap, the person who brings to his study a familiarity with the life and teachings of Jesus gained through home and church often has problems of his own. In many instances, such readers, though acquainted with the traditional Christian vocabulary, have not dug into the underlying issues of Jesus' life and teaching. They have been instructed, perhaps, but often they

have not thought for themselves as if seeking truth on which
great issues depend. This condition is normal in the growth
of American young people, and should not be taken as a
cause for self-reproach. When we recognize it in ourselves,
the recognition should remind us that the time has come
for serious thought about our own faith. It should suggest
that a mature understanding of Jesus includes new facts
and issues, and new questions, which have gone unmen-
tioned and unnoticed hitherto.

However, it is not only the individual reader and his religious concerns that must be reckoned with in the study
of Jesus. Jesus' achievements, his claims, and his meaning
must finally be viewed against the experiences of mankind. In
more definite terms, he must be understood: (1) in relation
to religion as a human phenomenon; (2) in comparison and
contrast with the living religions; and (3) in his relations of
dependence on, and of freedom from, ancient Judaism.
Respectively, these are the academic disciplines of the
Philosophy of Religion, the History of Religions (or "Com-
parative Religions"), and the History and Religion of the
Jews (or "Ancient Judaism").

PHILOSOPHY OF RELIGION. Because of our interest
in Jesus as a religious figure, we find ourselves asking: What
is religion? How is the word "religion" to be defined? What
is meant by the words "being religious"? What is the relation of religion to other aspects of human life and activity?

We shall discuss these questions, and the way in which
they apply to an understanding of Jesus, in Chapter II.

HISTORY OF RELIGIONS. Such questions as these stir
the interest of readers: What are the major religions of the
world? What may be said about similarities between the
religions alive today? What are the differences? What may
be said about the character of Jesus as compared with other
religious leaders? Are his teachings like the teachings of
others?

A presentation of these matters is a long and detailed business, but the essence of the answers, from a Christian point of view, is set down in Chapter III.

HISTORY AND RELIGION OF THE JEWS. The study of ancient Judaism and the sacred writings of the Jews is intimately associated with the study of Jesus because of the facts of history. Jesus was born a Jew and was part of the history and religion of his people. There can be no serious effort to understand him that does not reckon with that relationship, and distinguish all that was distinctive in Jesus' own point of view.

As far as the Jewish background bears on the general problem of understanding Jesus, we shall take it up in Chapter IV, though I shall reserve the discussion of specific details in the relation of Jesus' ideas to his background for treatment in Section Three (Chapters XV-XXIII).

It is not for a moment being proposed that the beginning student of the life of Jesus must become in any way expert in these fields before he can understand Jesus for himself. The point is more one of the need for orientation than for information. We must see how the study of Jesus fits into this broad setting, and how these other fields of religious knowledge and experience make a contribution to our understanding. Inevitably, the study of Jesus touches all religion, and probably everything else in human life.

Outlining the study

The study of the life and teachings of Jesus may be divided into a number of parts along both logical and practical lines. It will be helpful to the reader to go over the outline of the following material thoughtfully in order to familiarize himself with the conventional divisions and the approach of this book. It would be helpful to review this outline several times in the course of reading so as to maintain a sense of the whole of the subject in relation to the detailed discussions.

Putting the matter in general terms, we must divide our study of Jesus into three main parts: (1) We must inquire into the nature of our sources of knowledge of the life and teachings of Jesus. (2) We must reconstruct the story of Jesus, first in outline, considering the problem of dates; then in detail, rehearsing the story. (3) We must describe his major teachings and their implications.

THE BIBLICAL SOURCES. It is possible to come to a measure of understanding of Jesus solely by reading the surviving accounts of his life known as the Gospels of Matthew, Mark, Luke, and John, the names being those of the traditional authors. Serious students, however, need to inquire about the origins of these records, and the way in which they are related to the beginnings of Christianity in the first Christian century. The answers to these inquiries have much to do with the views one finally holds about the value of the Gospels. This is a highly technical discussion which we shall not try to follow in its details, but shall summarize for the general reader in Chapters V, VI, and VII.

THE STORY OF JESUS. For most Christians today, the course of Jesus' life seems very blurred. We probably have little feeling for time intervals or changes of place in the story. This fact in modern Christian understanding rests in part on a lack of interest by the first Christians in biographical details. The material with which a full and clear biography of Jesus could be written has been lost. Yet in part these silences, which seem to modern Christians much like serious omissions, are based on the view that the important thing in the story concerns who Jesus was and what he accomplished in his death. We shall study this Christian view of Jesus later in connection with our reading of *Mark*, and in Chapter XXIV. The problem of dates and the course of Jesus' life story, we shall consider in Chapter VIII.

Since the story of Jesus has existed, from the first century onward, told in four ways, no single detailed narrative may be considered the *only* possible presentation. Writers on the life of Jesus usually do one of two things. They may *piece together* the materials of the four Gospels in such a way as to provide a single continuous account. This process is called "harmonization." It assumes the historical trustworthiness of everything that has survived, and further assumes that enough is known about the life of Jesus to fit the pieces together. Neither assumption commends itself to many modern scholars for scientific purposes, though the knowledge of Jesus that most Christian believers have in connection with their religious faith is harmonistically formed.

If the harmonizing procedure be rejected, the modern scholar may attempt to *reconstruct* the story, using whatever parts of the Gospels seem to him historically trustworthy. That is, he applies what he believes to be valid historical tests to the materials in the Gospels, and uses the parts of the story that satisfy his requirements. The crucial issue here, of course, lies in the principles of evaluation or tests to be applied. What underlying philosophical and historical principles are to determine our tests of the written records? Naturally, this question is answered today in a number of ways, which lead, as we shall see, to different views about Jesus.

Each of the approaches to the life of Jesus has reason behind it. The first seeks to satisfy the Christian desire to tell all about Jesus that can be told. The second seeks to satisfy the individual scholar's sense of what is dependable, on a historical basis. Each method has serious weakness in it if we depend upon it alone for our knowledge of Jesus.

In this book we shall follow a third approach to the life of Jesus, one more closely in line with the first Christian pattern than either of the above methods. We shall take the

oldest extant Gospel, *Mark,* and concern ourselves with this
first known presentation of Jesus. The careful reader should
read *Mark* several times, and with the help of the following
chapters prepare an outline of that Gospel for his own use.
In Chapter IX we shall discuss the opening of the Gospel
and the significance of John the Baptist, so that Mark's
approach to the story of Jesus will be clear. In Chapter X
are helps to an appreciation of the story of Jesus' life in
Galilee, and in Chapter XI is similar assistance with respect
to the closing events of Jesus' life during the last week
("Passion Week") in Jerusalem. It is not intended, however,
that these chapters shall be a substitute for a careful, analyti-
cal reading of the text of *Mark.*

After we have explored Mark's Gospel, we shall relate
to that account the major biographical additions of the other
Gospels. In Chapter XII the Christmas story and its implications will be considered. In Chapter XIII we shall discuss
the meaning of the stories of Jesus' temptation in *Matthew*
and *Luke.* These are of considerable importance in appre-
ciating the point of view about Jesus that runs through the
Gospels. In Chapter XIV we shall consider possible additions
to our biographical knowledge of Jesus in John's Gospel.

THE TEACHINGS OF JESUS. Each Gospel stresses the
activity of Jesus as a teacher. He committed nothing to writing himself, but probably worked intensively with a small
group of friends who memorized his teachings. He also addressed large crowds of people. Summaries of both his
private and his public discussions have been preserved.

In Chapter XV we shall describe Jesus as a teacher, taking account of his methods and the problems related to
them. There is today some difference of opinion about the
meaning of Jesus' teachings. We shall try to gain an understanding of features of his methods that may underlie some
of these differences.

After this general discussion, we shall outline in a series

of chapters Jesus' main ideas: The Kingly Rule of God (XVI), Sin and Repentance (XVII), Agape (Love) (XVIII), Jesus and his Disciples (XIX), Family Life (XX), The Practices of Religion (XXI), Human Destiny (XXII), and Jesus' Teaching about Himself (XXIII).

Alternative views about Jesus

The story of Jesus is one that leads readers to form conclusions about him. Men in the past have decided in various ways, and in differing degrees of intensity, for him or against him. Even in our earliest sources, varieties of Christian decision and emphasis respecting Jesus are preserved. In Chapter XXIV we shall study the particular points of view of each Gospel, and discuss the bearing of this fourfold presentation of Jesus' life upon our knowledge of him historically.

In Chapter XXV typical modern views of Jesus are described, including the older, orthodox view of the Christian faith, and the opposing "liberal" view, which in one form or another is found today both within and without the Christian fellowship. Without doubt, it is between these alternative positions that the modern reader must make his choice in understanding Jesus.

. . . . for further study and discussion

1. Prepare an outline of Chapter I.
2. Make a list of words that seem to have special meaning in the study of religion. Include words that are used in describing the study or that appear in the sub-headings of this chapter. Look these up in a good dictionary.
3. If your list does not include the following words, look these up also: *religion, biography, Christianity, Bible, faith, rational, conventional, philosophy, worship, history.*

II

The nature of religion

$\mathcal{T}$ HERE is no widely accepted definition of the word *religion*. This fact remains true notwithstanding the very considerable number of definitions that have been proposed. There are several reasons for this failure of scholars to agree on what religion is. For one thing, in human life religion exists only in concrete form. It cannot be isolated and examined by itself, but may be seen only in action, as it were. Religion also appears in an unknown number of *religions,* each of which has its own story. Furthermore, religion, as it exists in men's religions, makes many emphases and declares many different messages. This variety raises the question, "How shall we determine which emphasis and which message is most revealing of the nature of this thing we call 'religion'?"

All these facts about religion today are impediments in the way of stating what religion is, but it may be that there is an even more weighty problem which makes a completely satisfactory definition impossible. Religion is one of those tremendous realities in experience about which every man feels himself informed to some extent, but about which he finds it difficult to speak with precision. Such conceptions as "love," "democracy," or possibly "life" itself pose similar difficulties. We feel that we *know* what these are, yet find it hard to *say* what they are. It may be, therefore, that simply

14

because religion is a living reality, existing not only in external forms but also in the hearts and minds of men, it is beyond definition. Whatever the reasons, however, why "religion" is hard to define, Jesus is one of the key figures in its history. We shall see his importance a little more clearly if we ask, in this chapter, "What *is* religion, within which he made his great contribution?" and, in Chapter III, "What are the major religions of today, with which the teachings of Jesus and the Christian movement as a whole are to be compared?"

When we look at religion

There are two broad divisions of religion. These are interconnected. We may distinguish them in our thinking even though we should not separate them entirely from each other. One division relates to forms or ways in which a group of adherents expresses its faith. The other division covers basic religious ideas and the expression of these in words. In each of these divisions men's religions show amazing variety together with recurrent similarities.

Under the heading of *form* I refer, for example, to the ways in which men worship God. We may mention the posture of the worshippers; the acts of the leaders of worship; the kinds of music, and possibly dancing, used; the physical conditions surrounding worship; and so on, through all human acts connected with the expression of religion.

The reader will notice that such acts as standing, sitting, walking about, speaking or maintaining silence are not of themselves religious. They are simply parts of man's physical activity employed in this instance in the expression of his thinking and feelings. It is when men begin to put these actions together, as an author joins words to express thought, that the religious *forms* of one faith come to differ from the forms of another, and to have meaning for the under-

standing of man's religious experience. Thus, though other
influences also bear on these religious forms, one potent
force contributing to the wide variation among them is the
differences in religious ideas which they express.

A second major division of religion pertains to *content*—
the basic ideas or faith that is held by a group of people. We
can speak of these ideas in the most general kind of language as treating the three realities with which man has
contact. That is, all of men's religions one way or another
reckon with: (1) the meaning of the world of nature, *and
man's place in it;* (2) the purpose and nature of deity either
as part of the world of nature or somehow distinct from it,
and man's relation to this unseen force; (3) the nature of
man, *and his relations both with himself as an individual
man, and with other men.*

It is a mistake, however, to suppose that religion is concerned primarily with *knowledge about things.* Although
it is true that many of man's faiths make assertions about
what the world, or God, or man *is like in nature* (and so
represent a form of natural science or philosophy), the characteristic feature of religion is *its concern with man's relation to these things about him.* Thus religions may differ
in content in two ways. They may differ in what they have
to say about men and their world, and in *what they assert
about the necessary or desirable relationship between* men
and the other realities of their experience.

Defining religion

When we try to define religion both *as it is prac-
ticed* and *as it seeks to state man's relation to everything
around him,* I suggest that we look for a statement that
reckons with the great variety of both form and faith. I prefer the following: "Religion is the *sum-total of beliefs, sentiments, and practices, individual or social, which have for*

their object a power which man recognizes as supreme, on which he depends, and with which he can enter (or has entered) into relation." [1]

This definition, comprehensive though it is, leaves untouched *the inner nature of religion*. What is the *real nature of man's approach* to whatever power he recognizes as supreme?

I believe that one way of arriving at an answer is to start with the limited (finite) character of our human existence. All the religions, as far, at least, as I know them, are deeply affected by man's limitations and his dependence on other realities beyond himself. Religions take account of the fact that we as individuals do not cause our own existence, and that we cannot perpetuate our experience indefinitely in a world that seems hostile to physical life. Religions recognize that we as a race, and for the most part as individuals, cannot live indefinitely cut off from our fellows, and cannot remove ourselves, save by death, from this world of time and space.

It is men's reactions to our finiteness that in two contrasting ways have molded human religions. Men may show *fear* (sometimes in the sense of terror) before a limitless universe which seems to bring man into existence in order to crush him. Men may also show a *yearning for an individual relationship* with the superior forces in life on which our existence is seen to depend. Men may fear, but they do not always cower before, the Unseen.

These two elements, fear and desire for individual association, are explainable, I suggest, when taken as aspects of something else, namely man's desire to fulfill himself, to *live* in the fullest possible sense of the word. Negatively,

---

[1] Léonce de Grandmaison, "The Study of Religions," in *Lectures on the History of Religions* (London: Catholic Truth Society; St. Louis: B. Herder, 1910), I, 3. Reprinted by permission. I first saw this definition in Edmund Soper's *The Religions of Mankind* (New York: Abingdon-Cokesbury Press, 3d ed., 1951), pp. 19-20.

therefore, he fears the powers that can and do crush his life.
He seeks to arrange his living so as to avoid catastrophe.
Affirmatively, he reaches out beyond himself for the life
he hopes to find. His religion, viewed thus, is all those acts
and attitudes which in intent are devoted to the fostering
of life through resources of power beyond the self.

On being religious

We can sharpen our understanding of the nature
of religion by applying our definition to a confusion of ideas
that is widespread in our time. I refer to the confusion of
religion and ethics.

Not infrequently a thoughtful person will say, "I don't
have any religion, but I believe in treating people right."
Of similar meaning seems the statement, "My religion is
the religion of the Golden Rule."

In terms of our discussion of the nature of religion, let
us ask what a person has in mind when he says things like
these. Then let us see if, again in terms of our definition,
he really is saying what he supposes he is.

When a person says (in various ways of speaking), "I
don't have any religion, but I believe in treating my neighbor right," we naturally look around for the kind of *religion*
he has in mind and which he *does not* follow. In the case of
someone in America or Europe, that faith is chiefly Christianity in one or another of its branches. The speaker is deliberately and consciously rejecting Christian belief and any
claims of Christian organization over him. He wants us
to see his separation from the "sum-total of beliefs, sentiments and practices" that constitute the *form* of Christianity.
He also wishes to state that he does not accept the *relationship* to God that Christianity teaches.

However, in this declaration of freedom, our speaker
wishes to make one exception. He recognizes that there are

among the beliefs and practices of Christianity certain important ways of thinking and acting toward one's neighbors. He asserts that he too has practices that show regard for others. At that point, he says, he will recognize kinship with the traditional faith. In terms of Grandmaison's definition of religion which I have been using, our speaker identifies his religion with a certain kind of ethical *practice*. He declares his independence of *beliefs* and sentiments of the Christian sort.

But the question is this: "Is such independence from all belief and feeling possible for human beings? Has not the person who so declares his freedom from one 'sum-total of beliefs, sentiments, and practices' failed to note his adoption of another?" The answer, I believe, to the former question is "No," and to the latter, "Yes."

The line of reasoning is as follows: No healthy man lives without making some sort of relationship with the world around him. In some way he accepts life. He arranges his way of living to find the greatest satisfaction for himself that is possible. If he rejects faith in God as his way of reckoning with life's most important values and power, he adopts *something else* as most valuable in guiding life or as most worth living for. This alternate center of meaning may be any of many things. The type of person we are discussing may speak of "luck," "fate," "nature," "pleasure," "success," or something else. It is conceivable that his center of reference really is an altruism that could be summed up in the Golden Rule. On the other hand it is much more likely (no matter what he *says*) that he puts *himself* in the center, giving first importance to his own desire for pleasure or achievement.

The point to be observed, however, is that whatever a man's highest value may be, he recognizes *something at the center of life* that determines the meaning of his experience and points the direction for his activities. In our speaker's case, he thinks that this "something" (the nature of which he may not be able to specify, even to himself) requires of him a certain favorable attitude toward other people.

Thus, though he says he has no religion, his relationship to life, taken all together, comes out a complete match for the parts of the definition of religion we discussed above. His attachment has no organization, of course, and no recognized status among men's religions; but this lack is irrelevant to our discussion. Like his fathers in faiths which had a name, our speaker is also a believer! He has chosen his life-center and committed himself to it. Such a person often finds the term annoying, but it fits: he is *religious*.

The religious attitude is so pervasive in human life that Professor Vergilius Ferm prefers to reverse the order of discussion I have been following, and defines "religion" in terms of "being religious." He puts it this way: *"To be religious* is to effect in some way and in some measure a vital adjustment (however tentative and incomplete) to whatever is reacted to or regarded implicitly or explicitly as worthy of serious and ulterior concern." [2] Based on this definition, Ferm says that *"religion"* is "a generic term referring to all conceivable religions," and *"a religion"* is "a set of meanings and behaviors having reference to individuals who are or were or could *be religious."* [3] The reader may compare these with the definition offered above.

Because religion appears, even when unrecognized, in the lives of all normal people, Jesus, one of the great in the history of religions (Christians see him as the greatest of all), becomes important to the thinking of everyone. His character and his teachings raise questions not only about the faith of his followers but of all men.

---

[2] *Encyclopedia of Religion* (New York: Philosophical Library, Inc., 1945), p. 647. Reprinted by permission.
[3] *Ibid.*

. . . . for further study and discussion

1. Restate Grandmaison's definition of religion (pp. 16-17) in your own words, using synonyms or phrases of similar meaning.

2. What does Grandmaison mean by the "power which men recognize as supreme"? Could this power be either a conscious being (a deity), or a thing, or an idea? Explain your answer.

3. What might the religion of an "atheist" be?

4. Write a definition of Christianity, following the pattern of Grandmaison's definition of religion, but adapting it so that it fits Christianity alone (e.g., "Christianity is the sum-total of the beliefs, sentiments . . .").

5. Analyze carefully the meaning of the words "My religion is the Golden Rule." (a) What specifically does the speaker reject (See Mk. 12:30)? (b) What does he accept as the center of life? Explain your answer carefully. (c) Suggest other possible answers to *b*.

III
Religions today

*I*N THE preceding chapter we have seen that *religion* is defined by reference to ideas and practices in human life that revolve around an individual's choice of some supreme reality. These ideas and practices are *religious* as men express through them the attachment of their individual lives to whatever, for them, matters most.

Men call the collections of religious ideas and practices, as followed in separate human groups, *religions*. There are many religions. It is common to point to about eleven that are significant today as "major," "living" religions, but there have been many others which, being now without adherents, are called "dead" religions. Of course, in defining religion we must reckon with the dead religions, too. When we ask how Jesus' ideas and his movement fit into the religious scene today, we may limit our perspective to the living eleven. Marxian Communism, however, represents one important omission from any discussion limited to the traditional religions; I shall comment on this problem at the end of the chapter.

It is not possible in this book to describe men's living faiths, yet I believe it is desirable for our own understanding to associate in a general way our study of Jesus with those major movements and ideas to which he is naturally to be compared. I propose, therefore, to present as briefly as possible the following matters, shaping each one to our main objective, the study of the life and teaching of Jesus: (1) the distribution of the living religions today; (2) the question of similar features in the living religions; (3) the distinctiveness of Jesus among the religions of the world; (4) the range of choice today between competing religions.[1]

The distribution of the living religions

Were a visitor from another planet to come to our Earth and seek to learn the ways of human beings, undoubtedly he would be obliged to spend much time in the study of our religions. Almost from the first he would see that people, as they are, include religious thinking and actions in their daily lives. He would also discover geographical and historical order within the abundance of religious variations. Let us, for a moment, try to imagine how things might look to him.

He might notice, for example, that each of the major religions of mankind has (and has had) a sort of geographical center of gravity. It is not difficult to describe these localities, if we keep in mind the obvious fact that individual followers of the major religions are found in most parts of the world.

In the Far East, our hypothetical visitor would see in China three religions woven together: Confucianism and Taoism, both seemingly indigenous, and Buddhism, imported from India. In the islands of the Pacific he would

---

[1] I am under obligation especially to the following surveys of men's religions: John B. Noss, *Man's Religions* (New York: The Macmillan Company, 1949); an extended presentation of the history and beliefs of the major faiths. Edmund D. Soper, *The Religions of Mankind;* covers the same materials as Noss but more briefly. (Either of these books would serve the thoughtful reader who wished basic material for studying Jesus in relation to other religions.) Robert E. Hume, *The World's Living Religions* (New York: Charles Scribner's Sons, revised); older than the above, but in its outline form, compactness, and summarizing sections not yet superseded.

commonly find Buddhism in strength. The chief exceptions
are Japan, where Shinto prevails, and Indonesia, where
Islam is strong. In India the chief religion is Hinduism, although two numerically small Indian faiths, Jainism and
Sikhism, have maintained their independence for centuries.

Islam runs like a belt across the Eastern Hemisphere.
Though it had its origin in Arabia, it is now found from
Indonesia, China, and Pakistan westward across the des-
erts of the Arab countries to the Atlantic Ocean.

The largest single faith, the Christian, though cradled in
Palestine, is now in strength elsewhere, chiefly in Europe
and the Western Hemisphere. Christianity, of course, like
most of the other of man's religions, has many divisions.

Judaism and Parsiism originated in the Middle East, and
in a limited way still survive there. The numerical strength
of each has moved elsewhere, however, Judaism turning
west and becoming strongest in Europe and the United
States, while Parsiism migrated eastward and survives chiefly
in India.

In his visit our traveller would notice certain family resemblances among our religions. At least they exist to be
noticed. In China these resemblances are due not to a common origin apparently, but to a sort of osmosis, or gradual
intermingling within the life of the common people of elements from Taoism, Confucianism, and Buddhism. In India,
on the other hand, the relations are clearly those of a family,
with Hinduism fathering (or mothering) Buddhism, Jainism
and Sikhism, as well as being, through its many variations,
nearly all things religiously and philosophically to all men.
The varieties of religious thought and practice that somehow
are able to exist together within Hinduism astonish most
Westerners. In the Middle East are family relationships
between Judaism, Christianity, and Islam. The connections
between the first two are intimate and direct, and they are
sources from which Islam borrowed freely. The resem-

blances between religions, however, go deeper than the similarities resulting from "family" connections, and we shall look at these more basic things in the next section of this chapter.

If our visitor remarked that only about three-fourths of the Earth's inhabitants are included, even by name, in the major religions, we should introduce him to the other, smaller living religions. Since these do not embrace all the rest of mankind, we should need to describe for him the religions of millions of people who live in the wild places of the world. These aboriginal people are often referred to as "primitive," though the term is inexact because they have long centuries behind them. Their religious outlook is surprisingly similar around the world, and though it does not constitute a single religion, is referred to by scholars as "Animism." At the opposite intellectual and religious extreme from Animism are the secular attitudes by which many men in Europe and the United States are guiding their lives. For them the old ways of the traditional faiths, or the even older ways of Animism, are dead. But religion is always in the making. The tale is endless.

How alike are religions?

In this great human panorama, it is evident that a few major movements exist bearing traditional names. Among these is Christianity, with Jesus of Nazareth as its chief figure. I should not care to propose when our hypothetical visitor would notice Jesus in a special way; but there can be no doubt that the complexity and variety of man's religions, intermingling as they do points of similarity to other religions with differences from the others, would catch his attention, almost as soon as he began his tour. These differences and similarities, which are both of *form* and of *content*, are probably likewise matters of interest to most readers of this book. In seeking to understand Jesus our problem is partly one of perspective. To what extent, in studying him, are we studying all religion? To what extent is he distinct?

We may begin a process of orderly thinking about this problem by listing the agreements between religions that our definition of religion has indicated:

(1) Religions agree in sensing some kind of need for man to associate himself with something bigger than himself. Men need something to fulfill their lives.

(2) Religions also agree that some one, or some idea, or something material exists that is worthy of man's regard. This reality rises to the place of first importance in a man's life. It comes to have power over him. He relates his life to it.

(3) Religions agree in seeking to remove man's distance from what, for him, matters most. They propose to establish some sort of association between him and the chief object of his concern.

(4) Religions may also be said to agree in the use they make of certain common actions and words. Though all the possible postures of the human body are probably not used in the major religions, certain common ones recur frequently. There is likewise a common religious vocabulary. Words like *faith, sin, soul, spirit, prayer, God* appear frequently. These are similarities indeed, but we have already noted that the various actions may express different ways of religion. Though the forms are the same, the faiths are different. The same distinction holds for the vocabulary of religion.

For example, all the living religions have sacred books, but the books differ greatly. A number talk about "salvation," but the nature and meaning of the deliverance in view differ. "Sin" is a frequent term, but again the character of the offense differs from one religious point of view to another.

Without detailing our description further, we may say as a generalization that there is some significance in the superficial similarities of form and of language in religions. These similarities, however, for proper discussion, involve underlying conceptions which may or may not seem alike, but which, at any rate, must be understood more thoroughly than is possible by means of the forms or words that express them.

Our question now is, "Apart from the general agreements between religions, what more basic likenesses may be described?"

Hume, in his book *The World's Living Religions,* lists ten points of "similarity and dissimilarity" in the eleven living religions, and discusses each with supporting evidence.[2] These points are as follows:

(1) The Belief in One Supreme Being
(2) The Claim of Divine Incarnation
(3) The Claim of a Supernatural Origin of the Founder
(4) The Claim of Divine Revelation
(5) The Claim of an Inspired Scripture
(6) The Report of Miracles Wrought
(7) The Principle of the "Golden Rule"
(8) The Recognition of an Especially Sacred Community
(9) The Hope of a Universal Religion
(10) The Hopes and Fears of a Future Life

In these terms Hume points to some of the great realities of belief and practice in modern religions. The reader who is anxious to discover what religion "is all about" would do well to memorize this list of topics.

---

[2] Pages 258-271. The ten points of similarity and dissimilarity are reprinted by permission. Hume gives detailed material from the eleven living religions on which the comments of this section are largely based. The permission of the copyright owner for the use of this material is gratefully acknowledged.

We should not assume, however, that we can make a mechanical comparison between the eleven living religions. The relations between them are very varied, and a rather easy illustration of the situation is the fact that the similarities listed by Hume do not appear equally in all faiths. Only five appear in all eleven religions:

> The Claim of Divine Revelation
> The Claim of an Inspired Scripture
> The Report of Miracles Wrought
> The Recognition of an Especially Sacred Community
> The Hopes and Fears of a Future Life

Here are, indeed, certain points of likeness running across all eleven major religions, but, as Hume puts it, here is dissimilarity, too. Not only is each sacred scripture distinct from every other, the sacred community of each religion is separate unto itself. The deity who reveals himself is usually not to be identified with the god of the other faiths (Christianity and Judaism are an obvious exception here). There are differences as well in the character of reported miracles, and in the hopes and fears for the future that the various religions entertain.

The other topics in Hume's list appear in fewer of the major religions. Hume, for example, reports that the *Principle of the "Golden Rule"* appears in seven of the eleven. Six non-Christian religions approximate the substance of Jesus' thought, but only two religious teachers (both Chinese) put it in a positive form, as Jesus did. Only one of them (Lao-Tzu) gave the principle a universal application, as Jesus did. Only Jesus based this fundamental rule of human behavior on the idea that God himself acts according to it (Mt. 5:44-45).

In five of the eleven appears the *Claim of a Supernatural Origin of the Founder.* Except for Christianity, Hume's evidence shows that the claim of supernatural origin was not a central issue in the religions that have it, nor was it part of the original movement. In the Christian religion, although Christian scholars are divided in their judgment, there are grounds for asserting that Jesus, from the earliest stages of Christianity known to us, has been peculiarly "the Son of God." Again, though the conclusion is debated, it is possible to argue from the texts of the Gospels that Jesus himself thought in terms of a unique relation between himself and God (Chapter (XXIII).

The Belief in One Supreme Being is clearly found in only four of the eleven living religions, and all of these are related to each other. They are the form of Judaism after the Babylonian Exile (see below, p. 45), Christianity, Islam, and Sikhism. The character of the god is different in each, however. The other religions have many gods, the count running into the thousands in Hinduism, although two religions in their original form (Buddhism and Jainism) seem to have had no belief at all in a single personal deity. Jesus' view of God as king and father stands alone here (see below, pp. 213-15).

Several religions of mankind have held the *Hope of* becoming *a Universal Religion,* but the hope is held vigorously and propagated only in Islam and Christianity. The contrast between these two religions on this point should be studied with care. Islam, which is growing rapidly, seems to many non-Moslems to put limits on its own universalism by the rejection in most of its sects of the use of reason in seeking religious truth. Its inherited doctrine also restricts women in ways that are hampering the work of its more liberal leaders. Of all eleven living religions, only Christianity has within its faith a living sense of mission as large as humanity.

From these materials in Hume we can illustrate the fact that important similarities of content exist between the major religions. Even the process of describing these, however, reveals that clear differences exist as well. Whether

these differences lead men to decide that one religion is
more meaningful than another, or superior to others, is a
matter we cannot investigate here and are not discussing.
The answer to the question with which we started, "How
alike are religions?" seems to be this: religions have similarities of intent (when that intent is broadly stated). They
show similarities in outward practices, and also in a number
of points of content. Though the likenesses between religions are most apparent when there is some sort of historical
relationship (as is the case between Hinduism and Buddhism, Judaism and Christianity), they also appear in religions that have been quite separated from each other.
However, as we examine religions closely, we see that each
is distinct from each other. Each one in its central faith
and in its practices has elements that are peculiarly its own.

The distinctiveness of Jesus

In our discussion up to this point we have been
thinking of traditional Christianity (rather than any special
form of it) as one among the major living religions; and
Jesus himself has not been particularly in view. He, however,
is distinguishable from the non-Christian religions, and,
in a lesser degree, from the form of Christianity that grew
up after his death. Opinions differ as to whether Jesus and
the later Christians held religious views that were, or were
not, in harmony. A reading of the New Testament, however,
will make plain that even first-century disciples such as
Paul spoke in different ways, and about somewhat different
topics. Jesus stands by himself, and can be distinguished
from all other forms of man's religions.

We might state his distinctiveness in three ways: Biographically he was a distinct historical figure. He was distinct from all others in his religious ideas. He was distinct
in his unique message to men.

(1) Jesus stands alone among the great of man's religions in his first-century birth in Palestine, and his inherited membership in the religion of the Jews. These are facts of secondary importance, no doubt, but we shall need to know something about them in order to understand Jesus. I shall lay the groundwork for this in the next chapter. Jesus was not influenced, so far as we know, by any non-Jewish religion.

(2) In the realm of religious ideas we may speak of Jesus' distinctiveness in two ways. First, he may be distinguished from nine other faiths by the fact that he was very closely linked in his thinking with ancient Jewish belief. (Later Christianity and Islam, the remaining two of the eleven, were, of course, influenced by Judaism also.) Jesus clearly believed that God had acted in the historical affairs of the Jews, making himself and his will known to chosen leaders. The result was that Jesus accepted completely the authority of the Scriptures which recorded this activity. His teachings, down to the words themselves, can usually be paralleled from the older text. I shall describe important illustrations of this theological relationship in our study of Jesus' teachings.

At the same time, his contemporaries, who also used the same Scriptures, felt a difference between themselves and him. This difference has been stated in a number of ways that appeal to modern readers. It has been said that Jesus emphasized the place of the individual in religion against the claim of the community. It has been noted that he minimized ritual aspects of religion and emphasized communion with God. It has been said that his important contribution was his idea of the fatherhood of God with respect to individuals. These ideas, noteworthy as they are, do not set Jesus off from his contemporaries in a distinctive way. They are found in Jewish Scriptures, even though they were minimized in the usual Jewish practice. Jesus' peculiarity lay not in any emphasis on some older teaching as such, but in his insistence that *God who had acted redemptively in days gone by in the history of the Jews was at work in a climactic way to complete his purpose for human life.*

On Jesus' part this was a claim to know what God was about in first-century Palestine. It was also the claim to understand God's saving program in the past. As a result of this conviction Jesus felt he understood God's intentions *behind the events* recorded in the Jewish Scriptures. He interpreted the letter of the text by his claim to knowledge of the spirit behind the context. He identified himself with the carrying out of God's purposes, asserting that through his own activities and in his teachings he was giving to the Biblical words a fuller interpretation than had ever been given to them before. This attitude that he understood God's plan more intimately and participated in it more fully than any other person was the religious idea that completely distinguished Jesus from the Jews of his time.

(3) Thus we may describe Jesus as unique in his *message to men*. He offered a *new* word about God's purpose and man's needs. His message was that the unseen, loving, heavenly father, who had been working through the human past, and in a special way through the descendants of a Semite named Abraham, *was now beginning a new development*. This was taking place in human life. God was in fact setting up his Rule of Righteousness (the "Kingdom of God") in the world. Men, said Jesus, should repent and yield to God's Rule. He promised them that as they did so, the energy of God would flood their lives, and enable them to live in fellowship with God.

We may speak of this as Jesus' *teaching*, of course, because it is what he taught his disciples. It was indeed the central stuff of all his thinking, as we shall see in discussing his teachings in detail. It molded everything he drew from the religion of his fathers. At the same time, this is more

than a teaching, because it is a message about God's actions
and purposes that men could not discover for themselves.
It is Jesus' assertion about new divine events and new human
possibilities. These come to men from outside their ordinary
lives.

It is this message that sets Jesus apart from all other
teachers of men's religions. If one breaks it into parts one
will find limited parallels to it in the hopes and fears of
other faiths. Taken as a whole, this message stands alone,
offered by Jesus as the fulfillment of God's purpose. It may
or it may not be true; but it is unique.

Religious choices today

Individuals of Europe and the Western Hemisphere do not face real choices, as might be inferred from
the foregoing discussion, between all the historical religions.
For example, modern men in the West do not normally decide between Christianity or Jainism, or Confucianism, or
Islam. Many people, in fact, never make a conscious selection of a religious faith, but passively remain in the group
in which they were raised. Many others choose only between the various groups *within* Christianity, and move
from one denomination to another, sometimes for religious
reasons but often for practical considerations.

When people in the West do choose between different
religions, they usually face what we may describe as a trio
of religious possibilities. Of these, one member is the Christian faith (in any of its divisions); the second is a formless
secularism, that is, a "practical" way of life without special
reference to God; and the third, dynamic and organized, is
Marxian Communism. Neither secularism nor Marxian Communism seems a religion in the traditional sense, but each
offers basic religious satisfactions and makes demands that
are in part religious. Each holds before men some supreme

value; each points to a way of life that will—it pledges—be more beneficial than any other; each calls men to exclusive loyalty. Although the intensity of the religious issues varies, being stronger in some geographical and social settings than in others, no one can neglect the fact that Communism these days is offering itself as a substitute for any of the other eleven living religions, or for disorganized secular attitudes.

Since the invitation of Communism is a fact of modern life in most parts of the world, our discussion of the traditional religions does not show the tensions that actually exist due to the Communist evangel and sword. In central Africa, for example, where the various tribal religions are weakening before the coming of modern technology, the religiously dynamic forces are Christianity, Islam, and Communism. In large reaches of Asia the issue may involve only the ancient faiths and Communism, or it may pit one of the ancient Far Eastern religions against Islam.

The effect of these conditions is that in many places the social and political divisions run along lines of religious division, and Communism is seeking to gather to itself the religious loyalties and enthusiasms of which men are capable. Political leaders face their most serious problems across *religious* barriers. Religious decision has become one of the powerful forces of our time.

. . . . for further study and discussion

1. Look up the approximate size of the major living religions of the world. Statistics may be found in the *Britannica Book of the Year* or the *World Almanac*, for example. Which religions are larger and which are smaller than the population of the United States?

2. Describe one of the major living religions of the world, other than your own. If possible, base this description on your own observations as well as a reference book. In your description

be sure to include important beliefs, the prominent ways of worship, and important applications to everyday life.

3. Compare Hume's points of similarity and difference among the living religions (p. 27) with Grandmaison's definition of religion (pp. 16-17). Under what parts of Grandmaison's definition do Hume's points fit?

4. Do you see clearly the meaning of the following words: *distinctive, superior, better, different?* What grouping of words would be necessary if you were asked to place these four words in two pairs, the two most nearly alike in each pair? Explain why any other pairing of words is possible but not demanded by the meaning of the words. Apply your observations to the problem of discussing differences between religions.

IV

Ancient Judaism:
Jesus' religious inheritance

$\mathcal{T}$HE ancestral religion of the Jews is known as Judaism. Through a piece of scholarly convenience this name is frequently applied to Jewish religion after about 500 B.C. For the earlier phase of the story, during the preceding millennium and a half, the term *Hebrew religion* or something similar is employed. The nouns *Jew* and *Hebrew* may follow the same pattern of use.

This distinction in terms is not only convenient but represents a major distinction in Jewish religion, and generalizations such as are proposed in this chapter frequently break over it, unless caution is observed. The sixth century before Christ, when the shift from "Hebrew" to "Jewish" life may be located for practical purposes, saw the destruction of Jerusalem (the capital city), the loss of self-government, and the burning of the ancient temple of Solomon. Though these losses were in a measure restored later on, the effects were not erased. They had led to new insights born of pain and suffering.

The aim of this chapter is to say enough about the ancestors of Jesus and their religion so as to make plain most of his references to the past, and prepare the way for more detailed comment on certain selected problems.

36

The story of the Hebrews

The story of the Hebrews, from the early beginnings, is one of the great narratives of literature. It is preserved for us in sacred writings known in Judaism as the *Holy Scriptures* and in Christianity as the *Old Testament*. The story is populated with saints and sinners, heroes and common folk. Its famous episodes remain a part of the Western cultural tradition quite apart from the matter of its place in modern religion.

In the study of the Old Testament we face a paradoxical situation. We seek to reconstruct history in a literature that only to a limited extent was intended to preserve historical facts. The Old Testament is largely made up of writings that have a *religious* purpose. These were part of a larger Hebrew literature that once existed, but the strictly secular material in that literature has all but vanished. What has survived was meant to summarize and describe *from a religious point of view* the men and the events which the secular historian once recorded.

As a result, the modern student seeking to retell the story of the Hebrews finds many perplexing omissions in the narrative of the centuries. He finds events described not for their own sake but to illustrate the Hebrew philosophy of history. He finds materials that served religious purposes, such as songs, hymns, sermons, and ceremonial requirements. He deals, in a word, with a collection of writings in Hebrew (and Jewish) religion which, asserting the belief that the unseen God has especially revealed himself in the affairs of certain men and nations, has contented itself with quite limited excerpts from the story as helps to faith.

The Old Testament, then, was not written to tell the modern reader all that he would like to know about the origins of the Hebrew, and Christian, faiths. It contains, however, much of the stuff of which religious, economic, and social histories can be written. To this literary deposit the archaeologist and the historian of the ancient Middle East are adding much new knowledge; here and there across the sweep of two thousand years of Old Testament life, we see things with astonishing clarity and intimacy.[1] We look back into this particular segment of the past somewhat as we look toward a modern skyscraper after dark: here and there, at random, lights are lit. Elsewhere the rooms are dark, and the outline of the building itself may be only partially discernible.

The traditional story of the Hebrews told in the Old Testament is naturally the one cited by Jesus in his teachings. Acquaintance with it is accordingly necessary in order to understand him and essential Christian teaching. It is the story that is surveyed and summarized here. The reader, however, will bear in mind that scientific reconstructions of this story vary among themselves, especially for the period before 1200 B.C.

The story begins about 1900 B.C. with Abraham (or Abram as he was also called), a wealthy sheik who migrated with his family westward to Palestine from the territory of present-day Iraq. His wealth was based on the breeding of cattle and sheep. His culture was that of the lower Mesopotamian valley at the end of the third millennium before Christ, about which we know a great deal. His language was Aramaic. We do not know when he or his family adopted Hebrew, which was the local dialect of Canaan, the section of Palestine in which the emigrants settled.

We are similarly without information regarding the origin of Abraham's worship of one God. There is preserved a Hebrew tradition that in the days before Abraham his ancestors

---

[1] Albert E. Bailey, *Daily Life in Bible Times* (New York: Charles Scribner's Sons, 1943) illustrates the Old Testament stories for the general reader.

had worshipped many gods (*Joshua* 24:2), as indeed the
city of Ur, whence he emigrated, did in his own time. Abraham's acceptance of loyalty to only one God may have been
an independent step resting on some sort of individual experience. We know nothing as to whether Abraham denied
the existence of other gods—there is no reason to suppose
that he did in theory—but he left in his family a tradition of
worship that affected all subsequent thinking. The point of
this thinking was that God, the creator of all, had "called"
Abraham and had a unique purpose for him and for his
descendants.

Abraham, together with his son Isaac and his grandson
Jacob (also called Israel), lived a semi-nomadic life. Stories
out of their lives became the basis of Hebrew national consciousness and religious faith. These are now preserved in
Genesis, the first book of the Bible, and still show traces of
the time when, like the sagas of other peoples, they were
told and retold by word of mouth at many an oasis campfire.

In the sons of Jacob the family of Abraham proliferated
into the twelve tribes of the Hebrews. The tribal growth took
place during the middle of the second millennium, in Egypt,
after an emigration that, according to tradition, was caused
by famine. Although the details of this period are obscure,
the evidence we now have points to around 1300 B.C. as the
time, when, according to the account in *Genesis* and *Exodus*,
Moses led the escape from Egypt. This event is known as
"the Exodus." It is one of the formative facts in Hebrew
religion, and aspects of it are constantly mentioned in the
Old Testament. God's saving power, for example, never had
a more vivid illustration than here.

Under Moses, the various families and tribal units made
a loose confederation based on religion, but, unfortunately,
the historical reconstruction of this period is as much in dispute as is anything in Old Testament studies. In a compact
called "the covenant" the tribes pledged themselves to the

worship of God under the name *Yahweh* (poorly spelled in
English *Jehovah*).

The significance of this covenant was that it was formed
with God. It was to constitute the basis of the religion of
the confederated tribes. It was to be applied to all aspects
of Hebrew life. The Ten Commandments (*Exodus* 20:1-17)
were a summary of the great moral-spiritual principles of
the covenant. These are framed in a legal style of the time.
They differ from contemporary religions in their prohibi-
tion of polytheism and idolatry, and in their lofty moral
standard.

A large body of religious and social legislation associated
with Moses and the establishing of the covenant relation has
survived in the Biblical books of *Exodus, Leviticus, Num-
bers,* and *Deuteronomy.* These volumes, together with *Genesis,* form the "Law of Moses" to which constant reference
is made in the New Testament. The five books themselves
are referred to as the *Pentateuch,* or "Fivefold Volume." In
Judaism both the books and the content are known as the
Torah, that is, "the Teaching."

The way in which these books were composed and preserved is obscure and is reconstructed in a number of ways.
According to the traditional teaching Moses wrote them all.
If that was the case, it is obvious from such books as *Judges*
or *1 Samuel* that they had little influence during the centuries immediately after Moses' death. The Old Testament
itself indicates that the process of accepting the teachings
of the Torah was a natural one, and a part of the maturing
of Hebrew faith. For this and other reasons modern scholarly
views connect the actual preparing of the Torah *in its present form* with religious developments in the fifth century
and afterward, which I shall mention later (pp. 45-46).

In the latter part of the thirteenth century there is archae-
ological evidence to show that Hebrew tribes were invading
Palestine. A majority of them established themselves there,

chiefly in the hill country between modern Galilee in the north and the desert lying south and west of the Dead Sea. Just to the east of the major Hebrew settlement lay the deep gorge of the Jordan River valley, and a few miles westward the land sloped down to the Mediterranean. The Hebrews never held the coast in force and never became a nation of sailors.

Until the eleventh century, the Hebrews lived in a Bronze Age culture. They were held together more by religious and family ties than by political cohesiveness. With a mastery of the processing of iron, however, and with changes in the political situation, Hebrew power began to grow, under a king named Saul, in the mid-eleventh century. Prosperous conditions continued under David and Solomon, producing what later generations looked back on as a Golden Age. In David's day, the indications are that the population numbered two or three millions.

The period between the occupation of the mountain range in Palestine and the death of Solomon about 926 B.C. was important in the religious history of the Hebrews, although its details need not concern us here. One point that illustrates a particularly important feature of Jewish religion is worth noting, namely the influence in the community of religiously-minded men who were not in any sense "professional" religious people. Moses himself was one of these; for that matter so was Jesus.

In the twelfth and eleventh centuries there were local leaders who, through force of arms and personal qualities of leadership, led in the defense of scattered Hebrew villages. These men were called "judges." The full number is unknown. Each seems to have exercised leadership in his own way; but in many cases the leadership was partly religious, and in defense not only of the hearths of the Hebrews but of their altars as well. The famous names here are Deborah (a woman), Gideon, Samson, and Samuel.

These judges did not inherit their position but seem to have acted partly by popular request and partly through an inner compulsion. They existed, therefore, in some sort of working relationship with the priests of Yahweh who held hereditary office in a system of priesthood (the details of which are obscure for this period). With the establishing of a central political power under Saul, and later David, the military and legal circumstances that had created leadership of this sort ceased. The spirit of free leadership in the community, nonetheless, continued to manifest itself in men known as "prophets," who stood in public protest in the name of Yahweh against the organized priesthood of Yahweh, priests of foreign cults, and other violators of the ancient covenant with the Hebrew God, whether king or commoner. Since the influence of the prophets came to its height in the period after Solomon, we shall return to them momentarily.

The policies of Solomon led to severe economic difficulties and to a revolution which divided the kingdom into unequal parts. Religious factors entered in also, the smaller division lying around Jerusalem and called "Judah" remaining loyal to the house of David. It also tended to stay close to the older religious teaching, stemming from Moses, of the worship of the God of Abraham. In the north the rebellious "ten tribes," or "Israel," were more open geographically to foreign influences; and popular religious practices blended together the worship of Yahweh with that of local deities.

This division between Israel and Judah took place about 926 B.C., and the destinies of the two small states, though occasionally prosperous, were increasingly threatened from without, by Egypt to the south and by Assyria and Babylonia to the east. Gradually both states became tributaries of foreign kings. Against the counsel of the prophets, they rebelled and were destroyed.

The Northern Kingdom was sacked in 721 B.C. Its inhabitants were either butchered or scattered by the Assyrian conquerors, whose cruelty was a byword in those days and has not often been surpassed since. The Southern Kingdom came to its end in the burning of Jerusalem in 587 B.C., and its population was removed forcibly to exile in Babylonia. This deportation marked the beginning of the Babylonian Exile.

Throughout the period of the Hebrew monarchies, the major religious spokesmen were the prophets. Their influence continued through the Exile, and for a short time thereafter. For practical purposes, we may think of these men as representing the voice of Hebrew conscience speaking aloud. But Hebrew prophecy claimed to be more than the voice of conscience and prudence. It represented itself as God's word of judgment, counsel and assurance, as the tides of history swirled through the valleys and round the mountains of Palestine. The words "Thus says the Lord" probably form the most frequently repeated phrase in the writings of the prophets, or, in fact, in the whole of the Old Testament.

Quite the contrary to what the term *prophet* means in English, the prophets were preachers of righteousness rather than visionaries. They spoke to the point that God's righteous will is the standard for Hebrew life, and the measure by which God will judge all nations. Their main theme was the certainty that God's righteousness will prevail over evil men and nations. It was in the working out of this theme that the predictive element enters their words. It should be noted, however, that their concern was directly with their contemporaries; they spoke publicly, and often in the presence of those whom they denounced. There is nothing quite like them and the prophetic movement in other major religions.

After the prophetic tendencies disappeared in the fifth century, the writings of certain of the prophets came to be regarded as of divine authority, and were included in re-

ligious instruction. The summaries of the prophets' lives and
their words have had great influence in both Judaism and
Christianity. Among the great names are those of Samuel
(11th cent.), Elijah (9th cent.), and Isaiah (8th cent.).
There are also references in the Gospels to Elisha (9th
cent.), Micah (8th cent.), Malachi (5th cent.), and others.

The prophets themselves often claimed God's guidance
and asserted that events in history would vindicate their
words. They refer to various modes of what is called "in-
spiration," including dreams, visions, mystical experiences,
and events in human affairs. They also show regard for the
words of earlier prophets, an attitude that developed excep-
tional strength in later Judaism. It will be understood that
each prophet is an *individual* illustration of a religious
movement most of which went unrecorded, though it was
influential in its own time.

The Babylonian Exile of the sixth century ended after the
Persians had destroyed the last great Semitic empire of
antiquity with its capital in Babylon. Relatively small groups
of Hebrews, now called Jews, returned to rebuild Jewish life
in southern Palestine. Though the history of the next five
centuries was troubled, it was important both religiously
and politically. The Jews remained under Persian rule until
the conquests of Alexander the Great in the fourth century.
After periods of Greek and Egyptian rule, Jewish leaders
known as the Maccabees set up for a time, in the second and
first centuries before the Christian era, an independent
Jewish kingdom. This became part of the expanding Roman
empire in 63 B.C., never to regain its freedom from non-
Jewish masters until the founding of modern Israel in 1948.

In the religious life of the Jews great changes took place
after 587 B.C. which served to fix the form of Judaism for
centuries. In practical life, conditions of the Exile forced
a creating of new patterns of instruction and worship. This
activity, aimed at continuing love for Yahweh, the God of

the fathers, seems to have led to the local institution later known as the synagogue.

In the realm of faith the discussion of changes brought about by the Exile is too complex for treatment here, and not especially pertinent, except that this may be said: the older Hebrew faith stressed especially the place of the individual in the whole people of the covenant. In the Exile profound thought went on about the meaning of individual life and individual guilt, and more was said than in previous centuries about the relations of individuals, as individuals, to God.

While scholars differ as to the kind and intensity of foreign influences that may have worked on Jewish religion during the Exile and afterward, there is little question that there was a revival of concern among the Jews for the traditional words and teachings of Moses. The books *Ezra* and *Nehemiah,* in the Old Testament, describe a religious revival in Jerusalem in the fifth century. In this the writings of Moses played an important part; many modern scholars agree in the general conclusion that at about this time a collection of Mosaic traditions was made and put into general circulation as the written basis of Jewish faith and practice. Some scholars, it must be said, insist that Moses had nothing but a traditional connection with the parts of the Bible now bearing his name. At the opposite extreme is the traditional view of Jews and Christians that Moses wrote the entire Pentateuch with his own hand.

There is nowadays a significant trend of thought toward a mediating view. A number of historians seem more disposed than the experts formerly were to see in the Torah a codification of words and teachings of Moses that were kept alive by popular use. Whatever the truth may be of the mediating view in general and its details in particular, it seems apparent that, in the history of Judaism, the teachings attributed to Moses became influential during the Exile and afterward. So strongly, indeed, did Jewish religion turn to feed upon its own past that in Jesus' day the "Law of Moses" was the most important portion of Holy Scripture.

The Hebrew faith

Insofar as the religion of the Old Testament concerns the study of the life and teachings of Jesus, certain major ideas stand out. In a brief description we are freed from the necessity of studying these in relation to developments in Hebrew religion and in the neighboring religions. Whether Moses authored the Pentateuch or not, men in Jesus' day believed that he did; and their references must be taken from that point of view. Whether God, indeed, spoke to and through Moses, is a matter that will be judged differently by different readers. There will be no comprehension of the attitude of any part of the New Testament, however, if we forget that Jesus and his contemporaries could refer to the Pentateuch in alternate sentences as the Law of Moses and the Word of God (Mk. 7:8,9,10,13).

For present purposes the significant points of faith may be stated as follows:

(1) God is personal and righteous. He is creator of heaven and earth. He is at work in human affairs.

(2) God cannot be controlled by men. Even more, he cannot be "found" by men unless, of his own will, he reveals himself.

(3) God reveals himself through events in human history but shows his concern for men chiefly in events connected with Hebrew history. He gives understanding to chosen individuals (prophets) to see his meaning in these events and to communicate that meaning to men.

(4) Mankind is in a state of rebellion against God's righteous will. Symptomatic of this rebellion is the worship of "other gods" than Yahweh. Yet God is acting through the channels of human history to overcome this rebellion and fully establish his righteous will over the wills of his creatures.

(5) Abraham and his family form the human group to whom

God has chosen to reveal himself in his redemptive concern, and through whom he proposes to reach mankind.

(6) There is a body of sacred literature, reaching back into the past, enshrining the heart of Hebrew religion: the Law of God, the great redemptive acts of God, the words of the prophets, and the records of the experiences of faithful men in this life.

(7) There is a goal to man's life, the Rule (Kingdom) of Righteousness, which God will establish in the future, but to which he seeks the allegiance of men now.

(8) There are ritual acts that God requires of his people. These include circumcision, the keeping of the weekly Sabbath, and the observance of the prescribed sacrifices. A number of things need to be said about this important side of Hebrew-Jewish religion by way of introduction to the Gospels.

These ceremonial practices, such as circumcision, animal sacrifices, washings, fasting, and so on, came from ancient religious rites that existed long before Abraham. A number of the *forms* of sacrificing and giving offerings were borrowed—*so far as form went*—by the Hebrews. The scope of this borrowing, however, should be carefully observed. It is not being said here that the *meaning* the Hebrews saw in the forms was the same as the meanings in earlier religions, or in other religions contemporary to the Hebrew. All that is said is that the forms were borrowed from older ways of worship. The meaning within the Hebrew tribes was expressive of Hebrew faith in Yahweh. In some cases, in fact, the form as well as the meaning underwent changes. In Hebrew ritual, for example, human sacrifice was forbidden entirely, and the flesh of sacrificial animals was devoted to God, being expressly forbidden as food.

These two aspects of the ritual of sacrifice (form and meaning) suggest a tendency in Hebrew religion to view the ritual as symbolic. That is, the sacrifices were taken to be meaningful as material expressions of faith in the Unseen, but were not viewed as serving the needs of man's physical life, or functioning in a magical way of themselves.

This view was stressed by the prophets, who recognized

the antiquity of the ritual and had harsh things to say about men's abuse of it. In some cases, in fact, the prophets appear to go to the extent of denouncing ritual sacrifices as such. However, when we examine such passages closely, we see that the speaker is condemning worshippers who sacrifice insincerely, rather than the ritual itself. The prophets thought that when a man claims merit with God for the *act of worship alone,* he is abusing the ritual. They were willing to recognize the use of an elaborate ritual for common worship, as long as faith and moral obedience to God's will were the prerequisites.

Though Jesus took the same position, he showed a freedom from ritual which led his followers to drop ceremonial practices almost entirely (see Chapter XXI).

A further word is necessary regarding the *intention* that was expressed in sacrifices in the Hebrew-Jewish religion. This is difficult to describe briefly, and scholarly opinions vary somewhat. In a sentence, sacrifices were the system, based on sincere use, whereby a man (or the nation) restored his broken relation with God, the break having occurred through sin. We can clarify the meaning of the animal sacrifices at least for our understanding of Jesus' thought by viewing them, as the Old Testament commonly does, within the frame of the relationship between the nation and God (i.e., the covenant relation). This perspective suggests that the sacrifices were intended to be *propitiatory, expiatory,* and *substitutionary.*

Propitiatory. Apart from other considerations, God required sacrifices when men sinned, and accepted these as ground for forgiveness. In the ritual to regain God's favor the sacrifices do not so much *solicit* favor as express the worshipper's recognition of God's requirements and his desire to maintain his relation with God's people, and hence with God.

Expiatory. Sacrifices, however, as a system, raise more profound questions. *How* do they restore a man's broken relation with God? Do they do this only because he *accepts* them? Or do they in some way accomplish something, or point beyond themselves to the accomplishment of something, that makes satisfaction for wrongs and therefore makes possible a return to fellowship with God?

Without going into a discussion of the details of this problem, one possible conclusion is that in the Old Testament sacrifice accomplishes something, or points to the doing of something, on behalf of the worshipper.

Substitutionary. In the sacrifices the animal was a substitute for the one who offered it. Its death was symbolic, being the only possible way to atone for certain violations of God's Law, according to the ritual. This taking of life was understood to be in place of the death of the worshipper, and illustrated the Hebrew faith that sin, particularly unintentional sin for which the sacrifices were largely designed, broke man's life-giving relation with God. Hence the one who offered the animal offered its life in place of his own. He gained no material benefits from the sacrifice since the flesh was either burned or given to the priest. The value of his act was spiritual. It maintained for him the satisfactory relation with God which had been threatened by his sin. Therefore, the death at the altar marked at the same time the ultimate reparation for sin and the loss of fellowship that sin causes with God's people and with God.

The basic mystery still remains, namely: how are we to understand the working of the sacrifice? How is it actually efficacious? The Hebrew prophets recognized that the divine forgiveness lay deeper than the visible death of sacrificial victims (*Micah* 6:6-8). Without going into the details of their thought at this point, we may say that the climax of the prophetic vision is found in *Isaiah* 53 where the "suf-

fering servant of Yahweh" (not clearly identified) suffers
for men and achieves their reconciliation with God (compare this idea with Mk. 10:45).

Institutional and popular religion
in the first Christian century

In the days of Jesus, Jewish religion had developed
a number of features that are constantly appearing in the
Gospels. The most important of these are discussed here.

BUILDINGS. The Jewish *temple*, the only one and
the sole center of Jewish animal sacrifices in Jesus' time, was
in Jerusalem. The particular structure is sometimes referred
to as the "third Temple," and was under construction for
some decades after Jesus' death. Its inmost room, called the
"Holy of Holies," was without furniture, and was entered
by the high priest once yearly. The Holy of Holies was surrounded by an elaborate structure consisting of rooms,
courts and porticoes, the outside portico, which surrounded
the whole, being three-fourths of a mile in circuit. Jewish
males in Palestine were expected to visit the temple three
times a year. It was supported by gifts and special taxes. It
was managed by a corps of priests under the control of the
"High Priest."

The *synagogues* were centers of local worship in the towns
and villages of Palestine. The Holy Scriptures were the
central fact in the synagogues, as the sacrifices were in the
temple. Religious services were held each Sabbath; these
included readings from the Old Testament, set prayers and
responses, a sermon, and a benediction. The leaders of the
synagogue were not priests but laymen entrusted with various duties. This synagogue system, functioning as local
school and law court, was the center of Jewish life in the
various Jewish communities, whether inside or outside Palestine. From the incidental references in the New Testa-

ment, we infer that the first Christian churches were organized like the Jewish synagogues.

The synagogue structures of which we have knowledge were rectangular, with several rows of interior columns supporting the roof. A chest containing the scrolls of the Scriptures was set at the front of the room, flanked on either side by the "chief seats" of the leaders of the synagogue and the community. These men sat facing the worshippers, who were divided, the men sitting on the main floor, the women in a balcony. The preacher read and spoke from a desk placed somewhere in the middle of the room. He was seated while preaching.

PARTY GROUPS. Judaism, in the first century, included a number of religious-social movements within itself. These were not, for the most part, organized parties, though a few did exist, nor were they comparable to modern Christian "denominations." Rather, they represented types of thinking recognized and tolerated within the common Jewish life. The most important for our purpose here were the Pharisees, the Sadducees, and the Zealots.

In Jesus' day, the *Pharisees* were the spiritual leaders of Jews who were concerned for the religious aspects of Jewish life. They were marked by great zeal for the observance of the laws of Holy Scripture, and distinguished from other Jews by the insistence that these laws were to be observed in the light of "the tradition of the elders." This tradition, they asserted, had descended by word of mouth from Moses, just as the Torah had come down in written form.

Notwithstanding this zeal for the traditions of the past, the Pharisees displayed a liberal attitude as well, for in their love for the Law of Moses they eagerly sought to find applications of it to new historical circumstances. This shows a flexibility not always found among religious people, and is noteworthy on that account.

The Pharisees have left a deep impression on Judaism and

Christianity. They are the only movement in Judaism that has maintained its viewpoint from Roman to modern times. In Christianity, most of the early followers of Jesus were Pharisees in outlook, and Saul (Paul) of Tarsus was a Pharisaic scholar. Jesus shows sympathy for certain Pharisaic points of view, and, to judge from *Luke*, chapters 1 and 2, this sympathy ran through his family background as well.

It is unfortunate that, for the English reader at least, the true character of Pharisaism has been obscured by the excesses condemned in the Gospels. Jesus' most bitter recorded words are against a hollow religious practice that cares only about form and reputation. The Pharisees, who claimed to seek the highest, were, therefore, able to fall the farthest, and "pharisaical" has come to mean "outwardly but not inwardly religious," "hypocritical." The Christian reader does well to remind himself that the sincerely pious and religiously concerned people of Jesus' day in Palestine were largely Pharisees.

The *Sadducees,* a group smaller in number than the Pharisees, were those Jews who sought to develop a cosmopolitan life and culture. In this they were bitterly opposed by the Pharisees. In religious beliefs they professed to adhere to the text of the Law of Moses more closely than did the Pharisees with their tradition, but in practice the Sadducees moved away from Judaism in the direction of the Greco-Roman culture of the time. They were willing to have social and governmental associations with the Gentiles, as the Pharisees were not. The families from which the high priests were chosen were of the Sadducaic point of view, though most of the lesser priests were Pharisees.

Among the tensions of day-to-day life in Palestine were those created by a secret revolutionary movement of patriotic Jews called *Zealots.* Their existence is understandable when it is recalled that ancient Palestine was under Roman occupation with all that that fact implies. The Zealots held the philosophy of direct and violent action, and they put their philosophy into practice. Jesus chose one of his close followers from among this group, and probably was under suspicion himself from time to time. He was also under pressure to support like tactics.

LEGALISM AND MESSIANISM. Among the issues of Jewish religion that have left a mark in the Christian Gospels, two may be singled out for special comment: legalism and messianism.

Legalism applies to the exaltation of the traditional Law of Moses, the Torah, and the principles underlying this devotion. The line of thinking ran somewhat as follows: Since God has revealed his truth to Moses, it is enshrined in the Law for man's study and obedience. Man can uncover the will of God in the Law, and, when he has found it, can perform the required duties. Therefore, it was concluded, men can by obedience receive God's blessing in the final judgment.

While there were many elaborations and qualifications of this argument, the outline of it is sufficient to explain the seemingly frantic concern on the part of the Pharisees (and certain other Jewish sects) that the Law should be observed to the letter. Jesus seemed to them to be a very bad example, or a very doubtful one, in his attitude of freedom from their traditional interpretation. He must have seemed to them indifferent to the very core of Jewish practical religion.

Jesus and the Pharisees clashed on many matters, but the reader of the Gospels who reflects on the paragraphs about the Sabbath, and sayings about the "clean" and the "unclean," will have sufficient illustrative material with which to describe Jesus' views and those of the Pharisees.

The Sabbath, it will be recalled, was the seventh day of the week (Saturday). The Mosaic Law forbade income-producing work on the Sabbath, and the Pharisees in par-

ticular insisted that this should be observed to the letter.
In Mk. 2:23-24, for example, they protested to Jesus because
his disciples were plucking the heads of grain growing beside the path. This was a form of reaping, and reaping was
forbidden on the Sabbath! In Lk. 6:1-2, the parallel passage,
the further detail is given that the disciples were rubbing
the kernels of wheat out of the spikes. This was threshing
—likewise forbidden on the Sabbath. Worship was not usually required until the Babylonian Exile or later, the day
being, in essence, a day of rest from work. The Pharisees, in
their zeal to obey God's Law, had developed highly elaborate definitions of what was, and was not, work. Jesus had
no patience with this sort of approach to the will of God.
Instead, he asked such questions as: "What is God's will that
is expressed concretely by the Sabbath?" "How can men
live in harmony with that will?" He held that a rigid adherence to the letter of the Law might result in a missing of
God's will entirely in some specific instance. (See, e.g., on
the Sabbath: Mk. 2:23-28; 3:1-6; Lk. 13:10-17; 14:1-6, and
below pp. 202-203.)

Jesus followed the same approach to the problem about
the "clean" and the "unclean." The religious distinction goes
back to the Mosaic Law and to earlier antiquity. In the
Jewish Law it describes a *ritual condition*, rather than a
moral or physical state. That is "clean" which is ritually acceptable; that is "unclean" which is not. Certain animals,
for example, were unclean, and were neither to be eaten nor
sacrificed. Among humans, certain diseases and bodily func-
tions rendered the individual unclean. When this happened,
even though no sense of guilt was attached, the person was
ritually unacceptable. He had become separated for the
time from public worship of God, and was obliged, through
certain fixed rites, to reestablish his privileges.

In the Gospels are applications of this distinction between
clean and unclean. For the Pharisees, Gentile life and all

associated with it (its coins, for example) was unclean; contact was forbidden. When such contact was unavoidable,
there were prescribed rituals of purification. Gentiles were
likewise separated from most phases of Jewish life. They
were forbidden to enter any part of the temple except the
outermost courtyard, and the penalty for trespassing was
death. Jesus, for his part, rejects the principle that any
material thing, in and of itself, can separate men from God.
As in the matter of Sabbath observances, he proceeds to
ask, "What is the will of God underlying the ancient historical principle of the 'unclean'?" He concludes that there
are, indeed, conditions that separate men from God, but
these come from men's moral and spiritual choices contrary
to God's will (see especially Mk. 7:1-23).

In addition to conflict and controversy between Jesus and
his contemporaries about the Law of Moses, the reader will
see in the Gospels a recurring interest in coming events of
history, and in life beyond the scope of history (see Chapter
XVI). This yearning for the Golden Age to come has been
called *messianism* from one of its prominent features—the
expectation of the coming of the Messiah. The word *messiah*
means "anointed," and was used of the Hebrew kings who
(among other Hebrew leaders) were inducted into office
by an act of ceremonial anointing. The application of the
term *the Messiah* to a future ruler came about through the
belief that God would establish his Rule of Righteousness
under a blood descendant of King David. Messianism, however, varied in its content from period to period of Jewish
religion, and always included more than expectations about
the Messiah. Other causes were at work in Jesus' day to
create the keen anticipation recorded in the Gospels. These
are not hard to explain.

In the first century of our era Jewish longing for God's
righteous Kingdom was intensified by the Roman occupation of the homeland. This occupation was oppressive eco-

nomically; it was brutal; it was Gentile. We should find it
hard to say which element in the situation rankled the most.
At any rate, the history of the Roman period of Judaism is
marked, every now and then, by the emergence of a dema-
gogue. This self-styled "messiah" would offer himself as
God's appointed leader, and call upon his countrymen to revolt, to throw out the Romans and to inaugurate the expected Kingdom of God. All such movements failed, of
course, but the hope remained that in God's time he would
establish his Rule with his Anointed One (the Messiah) as
the ruler. As the tension with the Romans worsened, many
were the prayers of the pious that God's final Rule would
come. One of the critical questions about Jesus, accordingly,
was his relation to these messianic expectations. Was he, or
was he not, the Messiah?

What he himself thought about the question we shall
consider in Chapter XXIII—the matter is not a simple one—
but what his followers thought is clear. After some initial
uncertainty early in their friendship with him, they came to
the conviction that he was in very truth God's Promised
One, the Messiah.

We perhaps miss the full import of their thinking because
in most English New Testaments the Hebrew-Aramaic term
messiah has gone through translation into Greek and appears as *Christ*. The Greek word *christos* is a literal translation of *messiah,* and the English reader may discover meanings he had not hitherto noticed, if, in his reading of the
Gospels, he mentally substitutes *the Messiah* wherever the
word *Christ* appears.

Though the concept of the Messiah was important in
messianism, there were other ways of thinking about the
future leadership of God's program. These were only partially identified with the Messiah in Jewish thought, but
represented great religious ideas that Jesus accepted as
valid.

In *Isaiah* 53, for example, the picture of the "suffering servant of Yahweh" displays one who suffers vicariously for the sins of others. This figure seems not to have been important in later messianism. In *Daniel,* as well as in other post-Biblical Jewish literature, a heavenly figure known as the Son of Man acts as God's representative in judgment. This personage appears frequently in Jewish writings about the future, and the name (or designation), "Son of Man," was well known when Jesus chose to apply it to himself (see below, p. 254).

One important difference between Jesus' messianism and that of his contemporaries relates to these three persons. He seems to have been the first to see the three as one, combining in his thought the work of the Messiah–King, the Suffering Servant–Saviour, and the Son of Man–Heavenly Judge. He shocked many of his hearers by applying these categories to himself.

In addition to the sects within Judaism and the important ideas we have been considering, there were other religious groups, each with an individual emphasis. Each made its mark on the religious life of Jesus' day, and the influence of several can sometimes be traced in our Gospels. Although some of this religious sectarianism has been known to modern scholarship for some time, important new discoveries have been made since 1947. These include a considerable number of manuscripts (mostly in fragmentary condition) that were apparently in the library of a Jewish religious group during part of the first Christian century and the century preceding. They were recovered from caves overlooking the Dead Sea and are commonly referred to as the "Dead Sea Scrolls." They represent the greatest discovery of ancient manuscripts in recent years. Although they are of great interest to all readers of the Bible, they have particular importance to scholars at work on the text of the Old Testament, and on the history of Judaism in Palestine.

. . . . for further study and discussion

1. From your reading of this chapter give examples of *all* the parts of Grandmaison's definition of religion as these were found in ancient Judaism.

2. Read *Matthew,* chapter 1, and find at least one example of each of the following subjects, drawn from Judaism: (a) history, (b) social custom and law, (c) sacred books, (d) belief in miracles. Can you see any other influences of Judaism in *Matthew* 1?

V

The modern reader's guide
to the Gospels

*W*HEN modern readers pick up the Gospels, they turn to a way of living and thinking very different from their own. Many readers feel no sense of separation from it. They recognize that the Gospels describe a different era with differing ways of life and thought (some of the latter are described in Chapter XV), but they feel a sense of kinship with Jesus and his times, nonetheless. In most cases, those who feel this kinship center their religious life on Jesus, and participate in the Christian movement.

Many readers of the Gospels, however, do feel a sense of separation from Jesus and his times. Though a general lack of acquaintance with the Gospels and living Christianity may be involved here, the more pressing reason for the separation seems to lie in certain consequences of modern science. People who feel the separation acutely are aware that science looks at life very differently from the point of view in the Gospels. They suppose that the stories told there are very likely open to question when supernatural features are present. For many of these readers, therefore, Christian faith and fellowship require that they ac-

59

cept truths that their modern scientific attitude discredits.
Unless they have a natural curiosity in things of the past,
the details of the Gospels seem irrelevant to modern problems.

What underlies this feeling, of course, is the very modern
confidence in natural science. This often has no room for
God, and in technical terms accepts a "materialistic" view
of nature. Because of this confidence (we shall later see
that it may be called a "faith"), Jesus' assumption that nature
is God's creation, and is subject to his purposes, is deemed
"unscientific."

As the direct result of this confident attitude toward science comes the feeling that stories of miracles are "impossible." These are regarded as the thoughts of men in "unscientific" days.

As another product of this line of thinking it is often
supposed (sometimes with no amount of information on the
subject) that modern research in the Gospels has shown
these accounts of Jesus to be confused and unreliable.

Readers who are affected in these ways do not deny that
the Gospels have meant much to men in previous centuries,
or that they still have meaning for those untroubled by the
implications of modern thought. They do assert that, as a
result of their own environment, Jesus and his doings have
been disconnected from their own world and rendered irrelevant to their problems.

The purpose of this chapter is to show that modern knowledge, instead of cutting us off from the thinking of Jesus,
enables us to come to grips with him. It may guide us to
the Gospels. Whether in our experience there will come a
sense of kinship with the faith and life portrayed there depends at last not on knowledge but on faith.

Let us divide our thinking into a series of topics: (1)
Misreading the Gospels, (2) Seeing faith where it is, (3)
The problem of miracle.

Misreading the Gospels

In the minds of most experts in the study of the Gospels, modern research has not disclosed a basic unreliability in the accounts of Jesus. There are, it is true, scholars with an extremely skeptical attitude toward the texts (I shall describe their position below, pp. 95-98); but the more general view is that, within limits to be described later, a clear picture of what the disciples thought of Jesus has come down to us.

There are a number of reasons why readers may feel that the Gospels are untrustworthy. Some few will be inclined to place a low value on them simply because they are ancient, others because they were written in a pre-scientific age. Other readers have some acquaintance with the ebb and flow of modern research in the Gospels, and know that conclusions of experts have been subject to both conflict and change. The feeling often obtains that when the experts differ, the plain man had better look elsewhere for help than in the Gospels.

Still other readers feel that there must be something fundamentally untrustworthy about the Gospels, because many points of view are supported by appeal to them. "If everyone thinks he is right, who can tell?" expresses a very natural reaction; and the confusion with which the Gospels are used is read back into the Gospels themselves.

This misreading of the Gospels has come about because readers tend to concentrate on matters particularly interesting to themselves. It is easy to neglect other aspects of the Gospels that are equally important and equally present. One specific illustration of this misreading is that many readers in concentrating on literary and historical problems in the Gospels have missed the religious message entirely. This mistake, though it may not always be evident, greatly

affects the quality of books about the Gospels and conclusions about Jesus. Since it is something we must constantly
guard against, let us describe it in a completely different situation in order to see where it takes us.

Suppose one is reading a history of sailing ships from the
days of the first raft to the Yankee clippers. The interest of
this book and its illustrations is centered in the *nautical*
aspects of the story—the use of ropes and masts, shapes of
hulls, and so on. There are, of course, references to trade
routes, migrations of whales, the price of tea in London in
1839, and to other matters economic rather than nautical.
It would not be possible, however, should we use this
nautical history as our basis, to write a complete account
of the *economic* history of shipping before the days of steam.
The references to commercial matters, though suggestive of
many things that went on, would be too fragmentary.

If then, in the context of our illustration, a specialist in
economic history should read the story of the sailing ships,
he would see many points of contact with the history of
trade that the average reader would not see. If, however,
he limited his interest to the scattered references to economic
matters, he would have a very distorted picture of the book
as a whole. If he said that the marine architect who wrote
the book knew very little about economic matters, he might
be right, but the comment might be irrelevant. If, on the
other hand, he tried to argue that because the author was
uninformed in economics, he probably knew very little about
such things as hulls and cordage, then his logic would be
obviously faulty. There is no necessary connection between
the two areas of knowledge. Clearly it would be a misreading of the nautical history to use it for any purpose other
than that for which it was intended, or to question its value
in its own field because of the limits of its subject matter.

If it seems that this illustration has been pressed unduly,
let me say only that the Gospels have been subjected to

such misreading, and more. Modern study can be of great
help to us in showing what the Gospel writers intended to
do in a religious way, and what they did not have in mind
in a literary or historical way. The results of this study in
summary form are the contents of the next two chapters.
With the handicap of misreading removed we can establish
an intellectual contact with Jesus again.

Seeing faith where it is

Our problem, however, may be that even though
we understand the nature and purpose of the Gospels, we
feel that these brief writings rest on a basic faith at variance
with the facts of the real world. Those of us who respond
in this way probably feel confidence in natural science. It
has discovered more about the world of nature than any
single individual can ever learn, and has changed the lives
of all of us. Its methods seem productive, and as far as the
facts with which science deals are concerned, we see no
need of bringing God into the picture. When Jesus intro-
duces God into his thinking about nature, the modern reaction is that he is old-fashioned, far removed from the life
of today.

When we feel this kind of thinking for the first time it
may catch us in a rush. In the confusion that follows we
lose our bearings. It is just here, however, that careful
thinking, looking at Jesus in the light of all we know, may
give some help.

The point is this: Modern understanding of nature indeed
shows that, in contrast, Jesus thought quite differently. But
what is the nature of that difference? When we read the
Gospels we notice that instead of dealing as we do today
with the "laws" of nature, he concerned himself with the
attitudes men should take toward nature. He wanted men
to see that the world is the expression of God's creative will,

exists in some form of dependence on him, and is ultimately
at the service of his redemptive purpose. Not only did he
want men to see this, he wanted them to shape their lives
to it. Thus, Jesus speaks a religious rather than a scientific
language. His thought ranges through the category of interest in the origin, nature, and purpose of life, whereas natural
science deals with the category of measurable facts about
things in the world.

It is because we understand the field of natural science
that we can distinguish between religious and scientific
thought. This is a major attainment that has not usually
been possible in man's religions. Because of it, most of us
will agree that when Jesus said, "Look at the birds of the
air . . . your heavenly Father feeds them" (Mt. 6:27), he
was expressing God's relation to nature (the sphere of
religion), rather than discussing birds' feeding habits (the
sphere of science).

With this distinction in mind we are ready to discuss
the place of faith in human thinking, and see it where it
really is.

It will be rather commonly agreed, I believe, that Jesus is
speaking from the point of view of faith. If some readers
would wish to say that Jesus had special knowledge of God,
and so exclude him from the category of faith, they would
agree that when other people speak of God and God's relation to his world, they, at least, speak in faith. "Faith" in
this setting does not refer to a low grade of factual knowledge. It means man's inevitable effort to interpret the meaning of his world as a whole, and carries with it (either openly
stated or tacitly assumed) acknowledgment of man's dependence on the meaning he has found. It is just this that
Jesus did: he declared meaning and purpose in the world,
and staked his life on it, inviting others to do likewise.

Faith being what it is, it deals with realities that are beyond the reach of knowledge based on experiment. Among

these subjects are to be mentioned the beginning and ending of the world, the purpose of the whole of life, and the act of commitment of the individual in settling how and for what he shall live. In the nature of things, these are realities that reach beyond our observation, or, in the case of personal commitment, involve something more than knowledge.

Most readers, Christian or non-Christian, will be willing to agree that *Christian* faith appears to operate in this way. It reaches beyond our present experiences; it invites men to dedicate themselves to the Unseen.

The fact is, however, that all men show this attitude of faith. Somewhere along the line of living and collecting "facts," all of us turn to the task of interpreting the whole of life. We begin to think about life's meaning, its origin, its end. We wonder what we should do with ourselves in relation to the larger world around us. Some of us arrive at definite convictions we can put into words. Others of us, though making no effort to explain the meaning of our lives rationally, nonetheless make practical decisions as to what is worth our doing. I doubt if there is any man so completely unreflective as to be outside this generalization.

This evaluating and self-dedicating operation is faith rather than science at work, because it deals with a kind of knowledge that may not be open to experimental verification, and because it invites men to do something in their personal lives since they believe that these things are so. It is faith at work when our confidence in natural science becomes the basis for our living. It is faith again when we substitute this trust in science for some traditional religion. Our choice of one instead of the other may be a rational decision; but it is a decision between patterns of faith.

Were it not for the element of personal commitment that is important in religion, we could use the term *philosophy* rather than *faith*. We could say that philosophy (as it does) surveys all the facts of life and then interprets life to us as a whole. That way of speaking would be helpful because it would show us the great difference between Jesus' interpretation of life and modern views.

The word *philosophy*, however, tends to obscure the fact and act of self-commitment which is also involved in our human experience. Men, being men, do not merely decide that such and such apparent facts are facts indeed. They go further. Somewhere in their lives they align themselves with the truth they accept. Some men are very clear about their self-dedication to what they believe to be true; others are confused. Indeed, it is quite possible to profess sincerely one kind of truth and give one's life in practice to another kind, never seeing the division. The seriously-minded person, however, feels intuitively, as Plato put it long ago, that the inward and outward life should be in harmony; and he gives himself to that end. This act of self-direction, or self-dedication, is more clearly included in the meaning of "faith" than of "philosophy," and is, as we have already seen, one of the prime elements in religion.

I suggest, therefore, how fine the line is between science and religion. If men who set out to discuss religious themes sometimes err in trying to be wise in scientific fields, is it not the case that students of science may cross the same line with the same unawareness? I wonder if our new knowledge of the nature of science and religion does not show that every man must be both scientist and person of faith? Is it not impossible to be one and not the other?

The aim of this book is to help us in understanding Jesus so that we may consider our faith more clearly. This study may not bring a sense of kinship with Jesus, but it will put the modern reader into the discussion on the same level as Jesus' contemporaries, who wondered whose faith was more adequate to life as a whole—theirs or his.

The problem of miracle

The other factor we described in a modern man's sense of separation from the story of Jesus in the Gospels is the problem of miracle. This problem includes both matters of fact and matters of faith. We take it up last even though to many readers it comes to mind first.

In the Gospels, to which we are limiting our attention, *faith* enters the discussion when, for example, the Christian writers of the Gospels assume: (1) that God who really exists (2) can act within the world of nature in extraordinary ways, and (3) has so acted through Jesus of Nazareth. Faith, as we have seen, is likewise present when a modern reader affirms for reasons of his own that these Christian assumptions are impossible since they go against the teachings of modern science. We have already seen some of the dimensions of this problem.

The miracle stories also involve problems in connection with the *facts* they report. What shall we say about the truthfulness of the stories as such? What shall we say about the historicity of the details of the stories?

It will be seen at once that different readers may find greater difficulty with one or the other of the problems. Some readers will object to the underlying assumptions about God; they hold a different faith (philosophy). Other readers, though agreeing with the faith of the Gospel writers, will hesitate over the historical truth of certain stories, or about parts of certain stories. Readers of either sort turn to the texts of the Gospels to determine, if they can, the origin of the material that puzzles them and, it may be, runs counter to their own interpretation of life.

At this point the modern study of the Gospels makes a major contribution. It makes the problem of the origins of the miracle stories both clear and difficult.

In a word, the present situation is that although modern scholars usually rate some sources[1] of our Gospels above others in historical quality, *miracles are part of all of them including the oldest ones.* Thus the problem of miracle is involved, in principle, with the origins of the Christian religion.

The problem is made more difficult because experiments have shown that we cannot eliminate the miracle stories from the Gospels by applying principles of *literary analysis.* Some scholars, for example, hold that there can be traced in our Gospels a tendency among the early Christians to dwell upon stories of miracles and heighten the tone of the accounts by adding fictional details. The important point is that even if we grant this tendency as a fact in specific stories, it cannot solve the problem of the presence of miracle as such. It has not been found possible, on any consistent, objective basis, to trace the story of Jesus as a whole back through the sources, show that the element of miracle gradually diminishes, and finally reach the point of origin where Jesus appears freed from the miraculous entirely. It seems clear today that *no literary evidence exists for an original Christian testimony to Jesus which lacked this sign of divine power.*

Experiments seem also to show that there is no literary or historical ground by which we may properly remove materials from the Gospels that conflict with conclusions held in modern science. Such a removal, to be sure, is reasonable to people who are certain in their own minds that miracles just do not happen. When, however, the process is applied to the Gospels, we do them historical violence, since there is no ground within the Gospels that warrants our doing so. Furthermore, the odd result is that in removing everything tinged with the transhuman, we turn the Gospels

---

[1] Scholarship has been able to detect and describe older sources for the present Gospels. The results are summarized in the next two chapters.

into shreds and Jesus disappears as a distinct and recognizable personality. When one considers the influence Jesus has had, there seems something wrong with a method of study that destroys our knowledge of him.

Modern research, therefore, heightens the problem of miracles by insisting that they "are there," and that we may not act as if they were not. How, then, did these stories originate, in a few known cases as early as twenty years after Jesus' death?

The general Christian answer, resting on faith in God, has been that essentially the Gospels are correct and Jesus did in fact do miracles. They are reported because they took place. This understanding does not necessarily account for all the reported details, but it accounts for the element of the miraculous in the stories generally. It is felt that in some way these miraculous acts show the power of God in action. The stories have become testimonies to Jesus' character and his message about God's Kingly Rule (see further, below, pp. 125-28).

Readers who have held the faith that the Unseen is not likely involved in Jesus' activities have proposed a number of different explanations of the origin of the miracle stories. The keynote of these explanations is that the stories may be *rationalized*. That is, they may be explained in terms that fit all other human phenomena as well, and we must remove from them all that is in conflict with the apparent results of natural science. The explanations are of various sorts, and in some cases overlap. Each has difficulty hidden in it; some recognize important problems in the study of the Gospels. Whether these and the approach they represent yield the best understanding of Jesus is one of the questions we are examining throughout this book. I list here a few typical suggestions with a brief note on problems raised.

(1) It has been proposed that the first followers of Jesus deliberately falsified the reports about him. They were re-

ligious enthusiasts, it is suggested, and wanted to spread a
point of view by falsely citing examples of Jesus' power.

Although evidence for this sort of thing can no doubt be
found within the story of men's religions, what this proposal
strangely says is that the followers of Jesus taught (as we
know they did) a religion of piety, purity, and proper human
relations, *reinforcing their teaching with false stories about
Jesus as evidence*. When we consider the story of Christian
beginnings taken as a whole, it seems unlikely that the followers of Jesus created his miracles out of thin air.

(2) It has been suggested that the disciples were *mistaken*
about Jesus. They credited him with miraculous powers
because, being men of the first century, they took miracles
to be the sign of spiritual leadership. Thus they were inclined to see miracles where none existed, and to report as
miracles events that had once had natural causes.

If this proposal accounts for the origin of any of the stories
in the Gospels, it must be said that the followers of Jesus
were consistent in their error. We must assume that nothing
ever happened to open their eyes.

(3) It has been suggested that the disciples were only
partially mistaken about Jesus' powers. It might be, for
example, that Jesus, through an intuitive understanding of
human beings, was able to release spiritual energy within
another human personality. Perhaps he did effectively en-
gage in what is called in our day "faith healing." His followers observed this kind of activity many times, and naturally they could not understand its "natural" causes. Hence
the belief grew that Jesus had miraculous powers and did
other types of manipulation of reality.

This line of solution has attracted the attention of many
modern readers, just as the healing activity of Jesus attracted many Jews in ancient Palestine. Obviously it has
significance in relation to the miracles of healing. In connection with other types of miracle story it begs the ques-

tion, asking us to believe that the disciples made a mistake and never noticed the error.

(4) Another important interpretation puts the contribution of the disciples a little differently. It is suggested that the disciples, in trying to continue the religious movement Jesus had begun, retold stories of their experiences with him. In many cases these were reminiscences of a real event which they adapted for Christian religious purposes. In the process of retelling, the original event became miraculous, and the story became a "legend."

I shall examine the background of this important suggestion in detail in Chapter VII. To the extent that it is correct, the problem of the careful reader is to take each miracle story, peel off the layers that the story-tellers may have added, and disclose the original event. But how shall we do the peeling? What kind of "event" do we expect to find? Here again is a process of studying history in which the historical memories of Jesus may be dissolved. It is possible that in this approach the significant results may be largely determined by the philosophical views of the student. In any case, not all the stories show layers of accretion, and with respect to those that do, the results of different scholars have varied greatly.

What to do about miracles

Modern study, then, gives us the problem of deciding what to do about miracles, and makes every answer difficult. In the face of such diverse problems and proposals I prefer to speak only with caution.

As for the problems raised that involve a man's basic *faith,* I believe it important to recognize as clearly as we may the faith we actually hold. I also feel that this should be distinguished from practical results in science, whether natural science or Biblical studies. Faith is a long-term business, but the conclusions of man's intellectual activity change with the passing years.

Regarding the quality of the *facts* related in the miracle stories, the point now is to examine the materials in the hope of forming our own conclusions. From the Gospels the reader will get impressions of the character of Jesus' disciples. Some of the ways of accounting for the origins of miracle stories raise very serious questions about the intelligence, the intentions, the integrity, and the truthfulness of Jesus' friends. What impression do we get as we read?

In Chapter VII we shall take up the Christian setting in which the Gospels originated, and, in connection with the stories about Jesus, consider *what probably happened* in the years A.D. 30-90, *or probably did not happen.*

In Chapter X, in treating the public life of Jesus, I shall mention special characteristics of the miracles of Jesus in *Mark* and raise questions about the meaning of this evidence.

In the long run, however, the problem of the facts in the miracle stories merges with another, the nature and purpose of Jesus himself. This is *the* issue with which we are concerned throughout, and which I propose to bring to focus in the last chapter.

The point of summary that we have now reached is something like this:

(1) There is associated with Jesus a consistent tradition of miracles.

(2) The Christian understanding is that actions of many sorts, contravening the usual processes of nature, were both tokens of and expressions of Jesus' spiritual message about God's Rule.

Christian views about the truthfulness of the stories of miracles in the Gospels vary somewhat. Some Christian groups accept all the stories as a matter of faith since they are in the Bible. Other Christians begin their thinking about the separate stories with the willingness to grant the *possibility of miracles in principle*. They rest this attitude on their faith in God. They then consider the reliability of each story in the light of such evidence as there is, drawn from literary and historical studies. In this way of thinking conclusions vary widely. There is no general agreement as to which stories of miracles are directly factual, which may be Christian efforts to describe Jesus by the use of stories that are partially fictional in character, and which may simply be fiction told to enhance Jesus' reputation.

(3) Of course, readers in the West outside the Christian faith tend to hold views of the world that rule out miracle anyway. If a man's faith does not rest in a redemptive God, he will explain the miracles with reference only to human life and activities (an attitude that involves faith).

(4) Thus all readers who seek to study the Gospels by rational methods find that faith as well as reason is involved. We judge stories from the past not only by historical evidence but by our faith in what life is really like.

Postscript

It is Christian testimony that even in this modern world the Gospel story of Jesus may have meaning in human lives and create a sense of fellowship with God. This result, Christians affirm, is possible even when the individual, within the framework of his faith in God, recognizes intellectual difficulties and questions that he is obliged to hold in suspense.

. . . . for further study and discussion

1. In the discussion of this chapter is *faith* a "belief," "sentiment," or "practice"? (See the dictionary for a possible distinction between *belief* and *faith*.)

2. It is sometimes said, "I never saw a miracle, therefore I don't believe in miracles." What might a person be thinking when he says this? Does the speaker mean that he will believe in miracles *if* he sees one?

3. What would you say is the most important *religious* idea in *Matthew* 1?

4. By way of contrast with this religious idea, what are some interesting or important facts of any person's biography that are not mentioned in *Matthew* 1? Do your observations lead you to any conclusion about the *purpose* of the writer of *Matthew* 1?

VI

The Gospels as written testimonies

$\mathcal{T}$HE only factual information about Jesus that has survived is contained in four short writings now called "Gospels." The term comes from the Christian view of the contents and means "good news." These writings are referred to by the names of the Christians who were believed to have written them, Matthew, Mark, Luke, and John. They are printed in that order at the beginning of the New Testament, and were probably written (not in that order) during the final third of the first century.

These are the memoirs of Christian partisans, and they stand alone in the field. Other writings of the New Testament show the same Christian attitude toward Jesus and testify, therefore, to its currency in the first century. They do nothing to weaken the evidence of the four Gospels, but they give only general evidence in support of most of the detailed facts in the Gospels. At one time there was a large amount of additional information about Jesus in Christian circulation. This never became part of the sacred collection, later known as the New Testament, and has disappeared save for tiny fragments quoted in later Christian authors. The surviving scraps have nothing to increase our knowledge of Jesus.

The first non-Christian references to Jesus, dating from the early second century, are more interesting in the support

75

they give to Christian claims about the spread of the new
movement to Rome than in testimony to Jesus.

The result is that modern Christian believers, with their
faith in Jesus as Saviour and Lord, and modern unbelievers,
curious but with faith in other things, all are limited to
Christian sources for whatever knowledge is to be had of
the factual life of Jesus.

This necessary restriction has led to questions about the
bias of the Christian authors, and to the most exhaustive
literary study ever made of such a limited number of pages.
The results of the literary analysis, as far as they bear on
our study of the life and words of Jesus, are sketched here,
but this must be added at once: the most intensive *literary*
scrutiny of the Gospels does not answer all the questions
about the reliability of the texts. It shows that the problem
must be followed back hand over hand into the half-hidden
Christian movement during the first century. This we shall
do, as far as it concerns an understanding of Jesus, in the
next chapter.

Literary relations of the Gospels

There are several places where one may start a
study of the Gospels. The oldest texts are in handwritten
books (manuscripts) in the Greek language, and an exact-
ing science known as textual criticism is devoted to them.
The results of this work are seen in recent translations such
as the Revised Standard Version of the Bible (1952). The
fact seems to be that very little has happened to the texts
of the Gospels since these were written that cannot be de-
tected and, in most instances, corrected.

One could start serious study simply by reading the Gospels. In doing so, and with an eye to their interrelationships,
one would soon notice that *Matthew, Mark,* and *Luke* have
many paragraphs strikingly similar across all three, while

Matthew and *Luke* have paragraphs in common that are without parallel in *Mark;* and *Matthew* and *Mark* have material not found in *Luke.* The student would also read in Lk. 1:1-4 that when that Gospel was written (perhaps around A.D. 80), there were numerous accounts of Jesus' life available, and that the author had engaged in scholarly research. Just how extended was his research has gone unrecognized until recent times.

During the last century scholars have framed a number of different hypotheses[1] to account for the facts mentioned above: (1) the testimony of Luke; (2) the parallels in three Gospels; (3) the parallels in *Matthew* and *Luke;* (4) the fact that these parallels may be of blocks of sentences, of single sentences, or of smaller groups of words; (5) the fact that *John* is almost entirely different, and that *Matthew* and *Luke* have materials peculiar to themselves only.[2] The hypothesis commonly accepted by Protestant scholars today as best accounting for these *literary* facts is the "documentary hypothesis," which is described as follows, omitting the supporting evidence.

Our Gospel *Mark* is the oldest of the three (*John* does not have a place in the documentary hypothesis) and was known and used by Matthew and Luke. *Matthew,* in fact, is sometimes spoken of as a "revised edition of *Mark.*" Luke copied less of *Mark* than did Matthew, but his borrowings are extensive. *Mark* appears to have been written in the A.D.

---

[1] Not just a long word for "guesswork." According to *Webster's New Collegiate Dictionary* (Springfield, Mass.: G. & C. Merriam Co., copyright, 1949, 1951, 1953) a hypothesis is "a tentative theory or supposition provisionally adopted to explain certain facts and to guide in the investigation of others." (Reprinted by permission.)

[2] As a matter of convenience the traditional names are used. The Gospels themselves are anonymous, the names of the supposed authors having been added later. The reader will keep in mind that the italicized forms *Matthew, Mark, Luke, John* refer to the *texts of the Gospels;* the forms in ordinary type are the names of the writers. *Matthew, Mark,* and *Luke* are called the *Synoptic* Gospels because they view the life of Jesus from the same general viewpoint. (*Synoptic* in this usage means "having a common view.")

60's or 70's, and the high regard in which it was held is attested by the use to which it was put. This relation of dependence on *Mark*, then, accounts for the presence of extended parallels in *three* Gospels.

With this relationship as a clue, investigators were quick to explain by a second common source the remaining parallels between *Matthew* and *Luke*. The matter is not quite so simple as in the parallels with *Mark*, for the evidence is that this source existed in more than one form. It was some type of Christian gathering of Gospel materials that has disappeared except for the portions preserved in *Matthew* and *Luke*. These surviving sentences (about 250 verses) are mainly concerned with the *teachings* of Jesus, though they may once have been part of a story of his life. Whatever the details are, these parallels are additional evidence of early Christian literary activity. This source is thought to have been compiled around A.D. 50, and thus may be slightly older than *Mark*. In scholarly books this is referred to by the symbol "Q."

In addition to this Gospel material in *Matthew* and *Luke* for which we can assign earlier sources, there are additional details and paragraphs peculiar to each Gospel. In the case of *Luke* this is an extensive body of material, some of it well known, representing approximately half of our present text of that Gospel.

There is evidence that some of this material was in writing when used by Matthew or Luke, but it is likely that part of it passed from one Christian to another by word of mouth. The things found only in *Matthew* have been designated by "M," and those only in *Luke* by "L." Thus, for convenience, it may be said that *Matthew* consists of *Mark* plus "Q" plus "M," and *Luke* consists of *Mark* plus "Q" plus "L."

The Christian sources lying back of the oldest texts, *Mark* and "Q," are beyond certain identification. All we are sure of is that Jesus did not write about his own life and teachings, and that his first followers spread his story by word of mouth. This period of time in the first century (A.D. 30-60?) may be referred to as the "period of the oral Gospel," because during it the scattered Christian churches depended upon memorized and recited stories about Jesus, rather than upon written records. This period lies behind our present texts, which did not entirely supplant the use of the memorized Gospel until some time in the early second century. We shall return to this matter in the next chapter.[3]

The value of source analysis

The process we have been describing is called "source analysis" or "source critical analysis." It has many values for the historian of early Christianity, but quite apart from these it has become a guide for many readers in evaluating the trustworthiness of the evidence for the life and teachings of Jesus. This contribution of modern research works out somewhat as follows.

"Q" and *Mark* are commonly regarded most highly. There are two general reasons for this evaluation. There are evidences in the material itself that point directly to the presence of reliable memories about Jesus. There is the fact that these two sources are the oldest compilations of Gospel material that have survived, thus being the evidence most nearly contemporary to the events that we have. Of course, neither line of reasoning guarantees the accuracy of *Mark* and "Q," but each creates a presumption in favor of them.

The materials found in *Luke* alone ("L") are rated about as highly as *Mark*. The most serious negative criticisms are reserved for portions of Matthew's peculiar material "M." It will be understood that, in evaluating either "L" or "M,"

---

[3] Reconstructed texts of "Q," "M," and "L" are printed (or summarized) in the appendices of Archibald M. Hunter's *The Work and Words of Jesus* (Philadelphia: The Westminster Press, 1950), pp. 131-192.

Mark and "Q" are used as standards. It will also be kept
in mind that in these comparisons the historian makes judgments where conclusions are difficult, and where, in some
cases, he must be guided by his own prejudices.

On this foundation of source criticism most modern discussions of Jesus have been written, depending most on
Mark and "Q." Materials from "M" and "L" have been used
to the extent that, as it seems to the individual scholar,
historical and literary research have justified the employ-
ment of them.

As far as it goes, this method is valid and is followed here
for practical purposes. It does not, however, satisfy the questions of modern people about the *reliability* of the Gospels
because transhuman qualities are attributed to Jesus in "Q"
as well as in *Mark* and the other (later) Gospels. The questions still remain concerning the origins of this evidence.

Another limitation in the *method* of source analysis is
that it becomes, when used to the exclusion of other evidence, too mechanical in its approach to the story of Jesus.
The literary evidence is too complex to fit a neat diagram;
neither can a reconstructed gospel be formed with scissors
and paste. Modern scholars are increasingly studying these
sources for our knowledge of Jesus *in the light of the activities of his first followers.* When we see clearly what the
Christians *did,* how they preached, where they went, what
was the scope of their theological faith, then we are better
able to understand what they said about Jesus and why they
said it.

Perhaps we may compare the process of study to that of
the archaeologist digging up an Indian village. He will be
able to fit many of his clay and stone pieces together and
make sense from them; but when, from other sources, he
understands the agricultural and economic life of the village, the clay and stone remains will become far more significant, being now parts of a living picture.

Does source analysis destroy the Gospels?

This question is frequently asked by students who are meeting source criticism for the first time and feel that somehow the fragmentizing processes it follows threaten the real meaning of the Gospels. The feeling seems to assume that, to try an analogy, if we should reduce a bicycle to its smallest parts with our tools, we should lose our bicycle. Because we had found its component parts and laid them out on the floor, we should never ride again! It is in this spirit that the question often is asked, "What happens to the Gospels under source analysis? Where do they go?"

An answer may be framed two ways. In terms of the analogy of the parts of the bicycle, we might say that the bicycle consisted of parts while it was being used, and we have not damaged its usableness by separating them from each other, except momentarily. We could even insist that what we say is true even though many small boys have needed help with their bicycles in order to ride again after a "repair" job!

The more serious way of answering the question is to say that nothing destructive happens. The Gospels have had their influence as integrated writings showing unity, purpose, and the impress of a creative intelligence. These facts, and the message that the Gospels have for readers, are not destroyed by our recognition that they are impressed in, or expressed through, collected materials. Certain of the plays of Shakespeare are effective and dramatic masterpieces, notwithstanding the fact that the author borrowed from the past.

However, the intuition may be right that study of the sources of the Gospels has adversely affected *something*. This "something" may be our preconceptions about the Gospels, with which we come to a study of the texts. Some

of these preconceptions may have quite a legitimate origin
in the worship of Christian churches. The religious use of
the Gospels in worship is usually such as to lead the unre-
flecting person to conclude that the texts were written spon-
taneously by individuals, or indeed that they were delivered
from heaven through a chute. Neither conclusion is justified in the minds of most of those who have studied the
evidence; nor is either one necessary to the fullest religious
usefulness of the Gospels in Christian life, as far as the
present writer is aware. Possibly this is one of those intellectual problems in which we gain clarity as much by understanding ourselves as by resolving the historical problem.

There exist, however, Christian teachings about the Gospels that run counter to the methods and apparent results of
source criticism. It is a matter of record that some Christian
groups have dogmatic objection to source criticism, and
some appear to hold certain "official" conclusions. This is
done in the guise of "defending the faith," and it is not
intended here to debate the matter. In a spirit of friendli-
ness it may be said that, to many concerned with this portion of Biblical history and its meaning, these dogmatisms
seem to be an expression of unnecessary fear for the Gospel
text rather than of vital faith in the Gospel message.

The original language of the Gospel

The story of Jesus was first told in the Aramaic
language of Palestine which Jesus himself spoke. Save for
a few chance quotations in the Greek Gospels which have
been kept in the English translations, such as *"Talitha cumi"*
(Mk. 5:41), the original words of Jesus have all disappeared.
Evidences of the translation from Aramaic to Greek are
clear in many additional sentences to readers who know
both languages, and linguistic researches of this sort are

one of the important activities of modern Biblical scholarship.

The process of translation into the Greek language began
almost at the start of the Christian movement in Palestine,
and probably during the first decades there were bilingual
Christians who told the story of Jesus in either language.
By the end of the first century, the number of Christians
using Aramaic was insignificant in comparison with the
number using Greek; and when around the year A.D. 200 a
group of Aramaic-speaking Christians wanted the Gospels
in their own language, they were obliged to make a translation from Greek into Aramaic.

The significance of the Aramaic origin of the story of
Jesus, and its subsequent translation into Greek, is this: (1)
To "feel" the thrust of Jesus' words, it is sometimes necessary to appeal to scholars who know Aramaic. (2) Since the
literally exact form of Jesus' words has been lost, the student will have special concern to get the *central meaning* of
each saying. (3) Traces of the original Aramaic belong
historically to the oldest literary witness to Christianity we
have. We can get no closer to the original words of Jesus
than when we see the form of the Aramaic language, veiled
but discernible, in the translation.

The Gospel of John

It is usually felt that in moving from *Matthew,
Mark,* and *Luke* to the Gospel of John one enters a different
realm. Certainly it is true that the atmosphere changes. It
is also true that very few parallels to the material of *John*
have survived, and we look, as it were, with but a single
eye, deprived of the depth of vision that two eyes bring.

The usual conclusion about this Gospel is that it may represent the teachings of the Christian circle formed around

the disciple John. It appeared in its present form at the end
of the first century, but nonetheless has in it evidences of
direct translation from Aramaic texts which point to days
when Aramaic-speaking Christianity was strong. It shows
concern for dealing with certain problems in current philosophy. It concerns itself with Jesus as he was in his own person
rather than as he was in his mission as the Messiah. It is
reflective, meditative, mystical. Probably it presupposes a
knowledge of the stories about Jesus such as are found in
Matthew, Mark, and *Luke.* It tells practically nothing that
is reported in the others, it stresses different moments in the
life of Jesus, and toward the close of the book presents long
conversations between Jesus and his disciples.

Clearly, then, this Gospel was prepared on a highly selective principle. Its motive, however, is similar to that of
Luke and is expressed in chapter 20, verses 30-31: "Now
Jesus did many other signs in the presence of the disciples,
which are not written in this book; but these are written
that you may believe that Jesus is the Christ, the Son of
God, and that believing you may have life in his name."

The present position in scholarship is such that there are
many different opinions about *John* and fewer certain conclusions. As working observations we may note the following:

(1) The story of Jesus in the first three Gospels is easier
to grasp, but it is enlarged *qualitatively* in the Fourth Gospel.

(2) John's Gospel was published late in the first century,
but includes testimony to Jesus that took form in Aramaic,
probably much earlier in the century. There is no agreement yet about the source analysis of *John.*

(3) This Gospel shows an interest in chronology in its
presentation of Jesus, yet its real concern is with the inner
life and spiritual significance of Jesus.

(4) John's Gospel blends words of Jesus with meditations about Jesus which are cast in the form of a monologue in the first person singular. Obviously the writer feels no need to distinguish between the words of Jesus and his own words, for there are often no divisions apparent and the grammatical style is homogeneous. It is apparent, therefore, that the quotations are to be taken as approximate; and, at any rate, they usually (although not always) sound quite different from the quotations in the other Gospels.

Therefore, I feel that it is best to begin the study of Jesus with *Matthew, Mark,* and *Luke,* even though *John* seems to contain added information of biographical value. The existence of *John* is clear-cut evidence that the first Christians knew more about Jesus and said more about him than a reading of the other Gospels might lead us to suppose. The historical management of the material in *John* is admittedly difficult, but we are hardly by that fact justified in leaving it out of our search for the proper understanding of Jesus.

Thus we come again to the problem of the Christian faith and life in the first century in its bearing on the written Gospels. Men may indeed act before they think; they live, however, before they do either. In the language of the Christian Gospel, they *believe* before they bear witness (e.g. *2 Corinthians* 4:13).

. . . . for further study and discussion

1. From Lk. 1:1-4 what answers can you give to the following?
   (a) Name of writer? Name of man for whom this Gospel was written?
   (b) Exact source of the writer's information about Jesus (vv. 2,3)? (You should be able to name one or two of these!)
   (c) What is the purpose of the writer of *Luke?*
2. Read the opening sections of the Gospels (Mt. 1:18-2:23;

Mk. 1:1; Lk. 1:5-2:40; Jn. 1:1-18) with particular interest in the story of Jesus' birth.

(a) What pieces of factual information are found in more than one Gospel?

(b) In which Gospels do we learn the most about Joseph? about Mary? about John (the Baptist)?

3. Compare Mt. 13:1-9 with Mk. 4:1-9 word by word.

(a) If we take *Mark* as the source of the text of *Matthew*, what can you say about the similarity between the *words* of *Matthew* and *Mark?*

(b) What can you say about *difference in meaning* in this passage between *Matthew* and *Mark?*

4. Compare Mt. 4:1-11 with Lk. 4:1-13.

(a) How much agreement is there *in words* between *Matthew* and *Luke?*

(b) What bearing do differences in words seem to have on possible difference of meaning?

VII

The religious setting
for the Gospels

*T*HE Christian accounts of the life of Jesus are
the written forms of the talk of Christians
about him. Like many other books they preserve talk that
would have been lost had it not been transferred to writing.
This talk was about the amazing quality of Jesus' personal
living, his acts and attitudes, his words, his death and resurrection. It was vital talk, too. It was the conversation of
men who had made a religious decision to follow Jesus,
and were seeking to mold their lives according to their
decision. It was the talk of convinced followers of Jesus as
they sought to persuade the minds and win the hearts of inquirers.

Thus it is that the best clues to understanding the Gospels
are found in studying the activities and kinds of talk that
produced them. When we are clear about the nature of the
first Christian talk we are ready to use it in the task of understanding Jesus. What is meant here by the phrase "the
religious setting for the Gospels" is the activity in which the
stories about Jesus were used in Christian conversation, and
so preserved. At the close of this historical description we
shall consider the matter of the reliability of the Gospels.

Telling the story

The Christian movement after Jesus' death grew through the medium of public declaration. In religious assemblies and in less formal groups, the friends of Jesus zealously talked about him. Out of this talking little groups of men and women were formed which held to the points of view of the followers of Jesus. These groups became known by the middle of the century as "gatherings" ("churches"). Sometimes this activity of talking was called "preaching good news," because the content of the story of Jesus was regarded by his followers as good news for men. Another way of speaking of this same activity was as a "proclaiming" or an "announcing." This involved the concept of a herald who proclaims or announces on behalf of his master. It implied that the followers of Jesus thought of themselves as his representatives to the world of men. It was a bold conception, when we consider the ignominious death of the proclaimed master and the humble social status of his followers.

The content of the Christian "proclamation" was equally bold. Modern scholarship, as a matter of convenience, has come to use the Greek noun *kerygma* instead of the English noun *proclamation* to denote this material. Although the latter would serve, it is ambiguous, since it may refer to the act of proclaiming as well as to what is proclaimed. The factual content alone is in view in the term *kerygma*.

Put briefly and in a general way the gist of the *kerygma* is as follows:

(1) Its central affirmation was that the New Age of God's Messiah, foretold in the Old Testament, had arrived. Jesus had affirmed this; his followers repeated it. This declaration was the crux of the message.

(2) The Christians supported this declaration with a re-

cital of the story of Jesus, beginning with his baptism and continuing through certain of the aspects of his public life. They stressed his miracles of healing, to which he also appealed (Mt. 11:2-5), and told the story of his death in detail. Herein lies the evidence for the message about the New Age.

(3) Then, in an appeal based on the coming of the New Age, the Christian preacher warned that God's judgment on the wicked was just ahead, and pleaded with his hearers to repent. Men should confess their sins, and accept the "way" [1] of God's Messiah. This was the decisive issue.

Thus the first Christians talked about actions. They said that God was acting in establishing the New Age; that Jesus had acted in Jerusalem in dying and rising; and that Jesus was now acting through his followers in order that men should act in repentance. The aim was so to inform men about these divine acts as to win their adherence to Jesus. It was an "evangelistic" aim, a telling of the "good news" primarily to gain assent and conviction.

The story of Jesus

Within the body of the *kerygma* the main weight fell on the story of Jesus. One specimen of this Christian talk has been preserved in *Acts* 10:36-43 where the Aramaic coloring gives clear evidence that this particular specimen received its form very early in the first century. (We may neglect the setting in *Acts* in order to concentrate on the details of the paragraph. The reader should have his New Testament open before him at this point in order to see the relevance of the following notes.)

---

[1] "The Way" was the oldest name of the Christian religion. The term *Christian* arose in the middle of the first century among outsiders. Spoken with a sneer, it meant "messiah-men" with the original sense of "messiah," i.e., "anointed," "smeared with oil." The "messiah-men" were the "smeared ones."

The passage opens with a reference to what the hearers
know already, that God has sent a "word" of "peace" by
Jesus (v. 36). This is not further expanded, but refers to
the "peace" which, according to the Old Testament, God's
Messiah will inaugurate.

The story of Jesus begins with a Jew named John (i.e.,
"the Baptist") and Jesus' baptism. It specifies Jesus' divine
power, his good works, his healings, and his intimate association with God (v. 38). This, the speaker asserts, is activity for which there are witnesses (v. 39). Next comes
the crucifixion and resurrection (v. 40), and again the fact
of witnesses is asserted (v. 41). The message as a whole
closes with three brief references: Jesus' command to tell
his story; the conviction that he is the coming Judge (v. 42);
and an appeal to repent (v. 43).

Of course, this sample of Christian talk is too brief and
too compressed in its present form to be more than the outline of a public address. It is, if anything, more impressive
on that account. It is similar to other instances of the
kerygma, and except for differences in detail *it parallels
Mark's Gospel.* This similarity suggests that our oldest
Gospel is a written form of the early preaching, and as far
as it goes supports the tradition that Mark wrote his Gospel
from what he had heard Peter say.

This all points to the fact that the *story* of Jesus was of
prime importance to the first Christians. In the context of
the book of *Acts* it is clear that the motive in telling the story
was to give evidence that in Jesus God's New Age had begun. Beyond this, the aim of the proclamation was not to
inform men, but to call them to repentance and faith. The
biography, that is, served the needs of Christian evangelism.
The details specified in *Acts* and elaborated in *Mark* probably represent, as far as evangelism was concerned, the chief
evidential aspects of Jesus' life.

In this evangelistic use of the story of Jesus we notice the

absence of certain things that appear in the present Gospels
in different ways. There is nothing here on the teachings of
Jesus. This omission was because Jesus' teachings appeared
in Christian instruction rather than in evangelism. There
is nothing here on the divine nature of Jesus as distinguished
from his God-given task as the Messiah. This topic too was
an aspect of Christian instruction. Nor is there any attempt
at biographical completeness. The "kerygmatic" presentation of Jesus frankly told a partial story, being guided by the
aim of converting the hearer.

The last point suggests a further conclusion, for which
there is other evidence, that within the general bounds of
the biographical outline seen in *Acts* 10:36-43, different
Christians told the story of Jesus with varying emphases
and details, the aim being evangelistic. Probably our Gospels, through their sources, preserve some of these variations. Probably, also, they exhibit in written form the same
Christian freedom to make a selection out of the common
store of material about Jesus as seemed most pertinent in
some specific time and place. The Gospels, however, were
not so strictly evangelistic in aim as was the *kerygma*.

Teaching the new believers

A second sort of Christian talk was concerned with
the instruction of Christians rather than the converting of
those outside the church. In fact, the whole of the New
Testament as it stands now was composed for this purpose,
though, as we have seen, the *kerygma* was originally put
together with an evangelistic aim in view. In this work of
Christian instruction the teachings of Jesus held a prominent
place.[2]

---

2 It is significant that the verb *preach* is not used in connection with this
Christian instruction. Most Christian "preaching" today would be termed
"teaching" according to the viewpoint of the *kerygma*.

Source criticism has shown that in addition to the *kerygma* materials, there is in *Matthew* and *Luke* a collection of words of Jesus labeled "Q" which existed as early as *Mark*. "Q" seems to have been the major gathering of Jesus' teachings; but there were others, traces of which may be seen in *Mark* and in the materials preserved separately by Matthew and Luke. These numerous quotations from the teachings of Jesus circulated orally. They made no appeal to the hearer to accept personally Jesus' claims as a fact in his life. They rather presume that acceptance, and are for the instruction of those who have already accepted.

Illustrative of this is the way the famous Sermon on the Mount is introduced in Mt. 5:1-2 where the teaching of chapters 5-7, contrary to some later uses, was meant, it is said, for "disciples." The same teaching point appears in Lk. 11:1 where the less familiar form of the Lord's Prayer is given in response to the disciples' request for instruction.

In these two cases the teachings of Jesus are related to specific circumstances in his career, and this intimate association with life is generally true of the surviving teachings. Jesus was not one to sit on a grassy bank and discourse at length. His was the conversational method, and probably also the conversational style, even when his remarks were extended. Unfortunately, in many cases the original occasion of specific teachings has been lost from the record. Scholars differ on the extent of this loss and on the importance of it in understanding Jesus.

In principle, however, Jesus' teachings were of immediate application, and those that have survived were used in Christian talk about the various problems of Christian living. What Jesus said about the Old Testament, or personal life, or the duty of man to God was recalled by his followers, and used pretty much to the extent that these matters were vital issues among themselves. Since different problems might arise in different communities, the crystallizing of the sayings of Jesus might be different in different places. Furthermore, different quotations could be used in dealing with the same problem; and the same quotations could be applied to different problems! Evidences of this are to be seen in *Mark*, "Q," "M," and "L."

Yet, throughout the religious talk of the first Christians about the problems of living, the practical characteristic stands forth: materials out of the life of Jesus were used because they suited the needs of men at the time. It was not at all that these were more "true" and others less so. Rather, this or that was usable and proven in practice. Before the later first century, that is, prior to the writing of the Gospels, there is little evidence of desire to preserve sentences merely because Jesus had uttered them. His teachings were a treasury to which men turned as if they never dreamed that it would disappear apart from use in Christian talk (see Jn. 21:25).

Recollection and reminiscence

The Gospels, as now constituted, consist largely of stories of the life of Jesus used in evangelism or in instruction in Christian living, together with summaries and collections of his teachings. This is not said, however, to deny the lingering in primitive Christian memories of any details of Jesus' life that lacked effective use. It is only asserted that in the main the Gospels show that the test of practical, public usefulness was applied. This may have been done unreflectively, simply under the stresses of life. The result, nonetheless, was to eliminate many biographical details from the public record. Evidence of this may be seen negatively in the absence from the Gospels of references to the color of Jesus' hair, the shape of his face and figure, the sound of his voice, and so on. One will search in vain for comments by Jesus about strictly secular matters, the qualities of building materials, political ideals, or the value of domestic animals—just to pull illustrative possibilities out of the air. Certainly such comments as these were remembered for a time; but memories of them have not continued.

It appears, likewise, that strictly private and individual recollections disappeared. One of the surprising things is that the first followers of Jesus did not communicate any "private" biography or description to the Christians. The Gospels represent the talk of the whole community about its Lord rather than the talk of individuals who reminisce. Beyond doubt the individuals in question had such reminiscences. Only here and there in the Gospels, however, does the light of individual memory seem to shine through.

In addition to the texts of our present Gospels, we know that there existed into the second century a considerable amount of oral material about Jesus, of which only bits and fragments have survived. One such is preserved in a quotation in *Acts* 20:35, and others appear in ancient Christian books and Bible manuscripts. To the extent that these quotations are genuine they represent Christian recollections of various sorts, which may have had less general currency than the things in *Mark* and "Q." Among these floating sayings the Gospel writers made selections with their own literary and religious aims in mind. The results of this process may be examined in "M," "L," and the Gospel of John.[3] Some readers of these words will feel considerable surprise to learn that the Christmas story in *Matthew*, chapters 1 and 2, belongs to this supplementary category. It seems not to have been widely known in the first decades.

---

[3] For "M" and "L" see Hunter, *The Work and Words of Jesus*, pp. 147-192. A quotation of a saying of Jesus that may be genuine, though not Biblical, is given below, p. 205.

The stance of the Gospels

We have seen in our discussion that as the Christians talked to one another and to outsiders about Jesus and his claims, the Gospel materials took shape. The following points summarize our discussion:

(1) The Gospels are compilations largely of materials used in Christian preaching and teaching. They are not the creative literary works of individuals, the authors being more strictly speaking "editors."

(2) The Gospels were written to report those events which, on some earlier hearing, had convinced both author and reader, and led them to faith in the risen Jesus. They were not written to record events for the sake of preserving a record.

(3) The Gospels were circulated as compilations of effective texts rather than as "official" texts. They faced comparison with Christian memories and other written reports.

(4) The Gospels were part of the Christian missionary movement of the first century. It seems assumed in each case that the readers are Christians. The books, then, were aids to faith.

(5) Each Gospel was prepared with the specific needs or interests of some Christian group in view. Each has its own individuality, unity and purpose. It is Christian talk built up from earlier sources that were in turn the remains of still earlier talk.

Form criticism

In our discussion up to this point I have described how the stories and sayings of Jesus were preserved through vital use in Christian groups. We have considered certain obvious cases of this use-and-preservation that led to the

forming of sources from which the Gospels were written.
Our study leads to two concrete questions and one question
of a general nature.

First, how has the historical value of this source material
been affected by the process of transmitting information
orally?

Second, what has happened to historical facts under the
pressure of organizational needs?

The more inclusive question is, "How reliable are the Gospels?"

I shall discuss in the next section of this chapter reasons
for believing that the Gospel reports are essentially reliable
in their picture of Jesus. (In what I have written this far
in our study I have followed what the Christians themselves
said, and what seems to me to be a natural understanding
of their words.) This belief in the reliability of the Gospels
should be examined carefully because, if for no other
reason, we know that the process of oral transmission of
any material is open to many opportunities for change.
When we also stipulate that the Gospel narratives were
preserved *for a purpose,* then we introduce reasons for
shaping original words and events to suit the purpose in
view. The factual question is: How did these general and
specific causes of change affect the reports about Jesus?

The prominent modern approach to the Gospels known
as "form criticism" takes quite an extreme stand. It concludes that the Gospels give us very little knowledge of
Jesus, as a result of changes that took place before the writing of our Gospels. These texts now show us, it is held, *how*
the Christians told their stories, and *what* they felt they
needed to tell; *but both the kind of story told (its "form")
and the content of the story arose more within the Christian movement than within the life of Jesus.*

Although I believe that this radical revaluation of the
Gospels together with its skepticism about the knowledge of

Jesus is unnecessary, a brief description of the method of form criticism will aid us in seeing the problem of studying our sources and the Christian activities that underlie them.

Form criticism starts with the twofold observation that when historical information is transmitted orally, it is exposed to two contrary forces. One tendency is that it becomes polished in use, sharpened, as it were, to convey its main point. On the other hand, narrative may become elaborated with details that satisfy desires for further information about the event reported. In either case, the historical matter is shaped into recognizable forms (that is, different kinds of paragraphs), depending on the use to which the material is being put.

A number of competent scholars feel that they can detect various forms in the Gospels. Some paragraphs, they hold, were used in Christian controversy. Some were told to illustrate the power of Jesus, or his claims, or teaching on some specific point. There is no complete agreement in identifying these "forms."

A second point of observation which form criticism has developed is the fact that our Gospels are made up of many short paragraphs strung together quite like beads on a thread. These paragraphs themselves, it is held, represent differing "forms" collected together according to various principles of arrangement; but since they are fragments, we cannot assume any line of *historical* connection. Thus a detailed outline, or any outline at all, of the life of Jesus becomes impossible. We must assume that the connections now appearing in the Gospels are unauthentic, or at best, guesses from the contents of the paragraphs.

With this very "practical" approach to the use-and-preservation of the stories in view, form criticism has argued that in many cases (perhaps we cannot be sure in many paragraphs) the stories of Jesus together with his quoted words have been freely reworked. Not only have sayings of

Jesus been detached from the original setting in which Jesus
spoke the words, but probably new settings and new sayings have been created by the Christians to meet the needs
of the church. Indeed, it is held that some, if not most, of
the "forms" are the creation of the Christian movement. As
a result, form criticism is not merely an analysis of our
Gospels; it is a theory about the early growth of Christianity.
It disputes the claim of the first Christians that the content
of the Gospel message was the force that built the community after its origin in personal association with Jesus. Instead, it believes that the church originated "forms" and,
around an uncertain nucleus of truth concerning Jesus, created the Gospels.

Thus the technique of form criticism combines literary
study with historical reconstruction. This, I believe, is a
serious difficulty. For the purposes of this book we shall
see the Gospels more clearly, in my opinion, if we try to let
them speak for themselves. Form criticism is certainly right
when it tells us that in these Gospels are the things the
Christians found most significant to themselves and the
growing religious community. It is likewise right in raising
caution signals along the outline of Jesus' biography. We
need not, however, conclude that all knowledge of Jesus
has been lost. Whatever our views about early Christianity
may be, it is a fact that eyewitnesses continued in the Christian group through most of the first century, and would
tend to keep the stories of the doings of Jesus in accord
with the facts. Furthermore, the enemies of Jesus also were
important eyewitnesses and vigorous opponents of the new
movement in Palestine. Their memories would also serve
as a restraint on the Christian reports.

In addition to the influence of eyewitnesses there were
other forces in Christianity that tended to preserve the essential truthfulness of the story of Jesus. Let us look at these

in relation to the general problem of the reliability of the Gospels.

The reliability of the Gospels

The reader whose interest is in understanding Jesus as a person of history is now in a position to discuss the question, "Are the Gospels reliable sources of information about him?"

This question had to be postponed from the beginning of the preceding chapter because, in order to answer it, we needed to describe the historical background of the Gospels. The theoretical answer to the question may be "Yes," although it interlocks in practical thinking with two other questions, "How shall one learn to know Jesus?" and "What kind of person was Jesus?" As a result, our answer, even a partial one, to any one of these questions affects our answers to the others.

Apart from the reaction of some readers that since miracles are impossible, the Gospels, reporting such, must be unreliable, there are three facts about the writing of the Gospels that raise questions about the reliability of the accounts. These are implicit in what we considered earlier in the chapter, but may be restated here from another point of view:

(1) The Gospels were written thirty to sixty years after Jesus' death. Though this distance is not so great as scholars once supposed it was (and uninformed modern readers still believe it to have been), it is nonetheless sufficient for vagaries of memory to appear.

(2) The Gospels were written not primarily as matters of record, but to influence men's beliefs and lives. This motivation, we might suppose, could lead authors to modify stories

for the sake of supporting the Christian point of view.

(3) The writers were untrained in dealing with historical evidence. Luke, the most highly educated as far as we know, was said to have been a medical doctor, not a historian; but most of the Christian believers who passed on the materials about Jesus were plain folk. One does not speak disparagingly of them when one questions their discrimination and judgment in historical reporting.

These facts did indeed surround the rise of the Gospels. What may we then say about the reliability of the Gospels in view of such circumstances?

We may say that from the historical standpoint the Gospels are reliable sources of knowledge about Jesus. We need to be clear, however, as to what we mean when we speak of reliability.

We do not mean, for example, that we can know past history in the way we know facts of natural science. In a laboratory we can test the chemical formula that ordinary water is composed of two parts of hydrogen and one part of oxygen. We know, therefore, that the chemical formula H_2O is correct. In historical studies, on the other hand, we have no access to a laboratory for the past. We are unable to repeat the events of history under controlled conditions. We are obliged to judge the evidence available in each case, and describe the factuality of the alleged events as certain, or as probable, or as possible, or, for that matter, unlikely. In addition, we may qualify these degrees of certainty if we feel the evidence requires it.

Thus, within the sphere of historical knowledge there is room for differences of opinion, for reservations, and for honest doubts. Furthermore, it is likely that the attitude and character of the historian, in addition to his faith or particular philosophical presuppositions, are involved in his judgments. If his spirit is censorious and cynical, things will look different to him than they appear to one who is by nature generous and optimistic.

For a second thing, when we hold the Gospels to be reliable, we do not mean that we have as good a biographical knowledge of Jesus as we might wish. The Gospels, not being written to provide a documentary account of his life, present their materials in different ways and with religious aims in view. The modern historian, therefore, is obliged to piece together out of the Gospels what he wants for his historical purposes. This can be done, though the task requires a high degree of technical knowledge. It may result, and probably does, in a sense of greater certainty about some parts and facts of the Gospels than about others. It yields, however, rather limited factual information, and gives, of course, *historical* knowledge rather than knowledge established by experiment. Though this is not the quantity of knowledge we might wish for, there is no reason to suppose that what we have is out of line with what actually took place. It gives us evidence that we may use, as in this book, on the ground that it is the best we have.

However, when we say the Gospels are reliable, we refer primarily to the *purpose of the Gospels to describe Jesus and show us what kind of person he was.* The reliability of the presentation of Jesus rests, of course, on the reliability of the facts told about him, but the two matters are not identical. One concerns the Gospels taken as wholes, the other is limited to the correctness of details out of which the whole is made. It is quite possible to hold that the Gospels are reliable as a whole, even when one questions the genuineness of some reported event or saying, just as it is possible to cross safely a wooden bridge that has a bad plank in the flooring. Once we recognize, as I believe we must, that the Gospels were not written with intent to deceive, and that the materials about Jesus are not false testimony, we face the problem of the *whole* of the account in distinction from its parts.

Let us consider briefly the various lines of evidence that show, I believe, *the reliability of the Gospel accounts taken as a whole.*

THERE IS THE IMPRESS OF A FORCEFUL AND CONSISTENT PERSONALITY. We have noted already the purpose of the Gospels to bear witness to Jesus, in whom both writers and readers already believed. The Gospels show what these people considered important. We may consider the accounts as collections of "biographical impressions" that Jesus made on his followers. We study, when we read them, not Jesus directly, but the impression that he made, just as if we were examining the imprint of a stamp in order to learn from it the form and design of the stamping device. So we read the stories in the Gospels and ask ourselves, "What sort of person was Jesus that the memories of him are as they are?" "What did he do that led his hearers to report these events concerning him?" "What did he say that led his hearers to quote him as they did?"

These questions are not always easy to answer, but when we approach the Gospels in this way there appears, I believe, regardless of factual correctness or error in the details, the impress of a forceful and consistent personality. The Gospels make biographical sense. Jesus was a vital person; he was not imagined. He made a tremendous impression on his followers, and they have conveyed to us a convincing and real person. To this extent the study of the impress leads to a feeling of certainty about the impressing agent. It raises, of course, questions about the kind of person Jesus was, and to these we shall turn shortly.

It may be pointed out in passing that in this way every reader has in his hands a means of judging the separate episodes in the Gospels, as far as Jesus is involved. His question will be, "Does this quotation or that fit what else Jesus said?" "Is this or that the sort of thing he would have done?" The critical weakness in this way of reading the Gospels is that probably few of us know Jesus very well, and probably we can never eliminate our own prejudices and character from our judgments.

THERE IS THE INTENTION TO PORTRAY A RELIABLE FIGURE OF JESUS. It was important to the first Christians to show what Jesus was like because their faith found its basis in him and what he had done. Two important principles operated to keep their reports about him within the bounds of events as they were. One is the principle of *sincerity*. This held a place of high importance in the religion of the disciples of Jesus. Falsehood and falsification were alien in spirit. If we omit, for the sake of the discussion for the moment, the problem of the supernatural, it is hard to see why these friends of Jesus should falsify references to his day-to-day living, his friends, his prayers, or his teachings. They used these bits of fact in support of a religion teaching a righteous God who willed men to be righteous; they were under both religious and psychological impulses to stick by the facts.

The second operating principle is the fact that the Christian religion of Jesus' followers was a *historical faith*. Jesus was important, so the Christians said, not in his teachings or leadership, but in his history—his example of life, his miracles, his tragic death, and the climactic miracle of his resurrection. Whether they were right or wrong about the facts, they based their faith in what they understood to be historical events. They stood in the certainty that specific things had happened. Back of this faith in historical events lay, of course, the conviction that it was the unseen God who was at work in and through Jesus of Nazareth in the real life of Palestine.

In this historically directed faith, therefore, any deliberate

fictionalizing of the life of Jesus would undercut faith rather
than serve it, because it would tend to draw faith away
from the support of God's historical actions. It cannot be
said too often that the tremendous message of the Gospels
is that God is acting in and through Jesus of Nazareth.
While this historically based faith is no guarantee that indeed all fiction has been kept out of the accounts, it seems
to have been a guard turned in that direction.

THERE IS RELIGIOUS USEFULNESS AND A CONSISTENT
IMPRESSION OF JESUS WITHIN THE VARIATIONS OF THE GOSPELS.
This is an important principle, and difficult to discuss briefly;
but it may be illustrated by the two forms of the prayer
Jesus taught his disciples (Mt. 6:9-13 and Lk. 11:2-4).
Either form is compatible with the general impression of
Jesus in the Gospels. Each survived because, once it had
been created, it commended itself to men in practical usefulness, the form in *Matthew* being more useful in the long
run. Were it not for our desire to know all we can know,
there would be no need of asking which is authentic, since
each is marked, it seems to me, with the impress of Jesus'
mind and teaching. Each is trustworthy as an imprint of
Jesus' attitude. At the same time there is definite variation
here. The two forms are not the same, and we know very
little about the origins of either. The usefulness, the consistency of impress, and the variations go together. This
principle probably applies in general across all the variations in the presentation of Jesus; but it obviously requires
testing at the particular points where the differences occur.

THERE IS THE INFLUENCE OF THE STRUGGLE AND PER-
SECUTION WITHIN WHICH THE GOSPELS WERE WRITTEN. The
stories came from the friends of Jesus, who were dedicating
their lives and hopes to the reliability of their words about
him. These were received and held by men who, in receiv-
ing and holding them, put their lives in danger. In the testing of daily existence the written forms made their way to

acceptance beside the memorized Gospel materials, which they gradually supplanted. The realities of life in the Jewish communities of the first century, whether in Palestine or the Gentile cities, were too pressing to make it likely that men of the sort the Gospels describe as disciples of Jesus would wish to present a fraudulent report about him, or be able to succeed in presenting one, had they tried.

I conclude, therefore, that there are good historical reasons for believing the Gospels to be reliable reports about Jesus. It is true that these reports emphasize limited aspects of his life and teaching, but they do convey to us an impression of the impressions that he made on his followers. These reports are consistent; he was somehow like this.

It is at just this point that the problem of the miracles, which we have been holding to the side momentarily, comes back into the discussion and creates the chief issue in reading the Gospels. Was Jesus a reliable interpreter of God and human life?

The final issue:
The reliability of Jesus

Our discussion has shown that the origin of the supernatural orientation of the Gospels may be traced back to Jesus himself. In all our sources, forceful though his figure is, there appears in the delineation of him transhuman elements which some modern science discredits. Miracles in the specific sense are only part of this picture. Jesus seems to have assumed for himself divine authority and prerogatives. He assumed that he in himself was more than men are in themselves; and that he could do more for them than they can do. (What Jesus specifically taught about himself, and what he seems to have assumed about himself, we shall treat in detail in Chapter XXIII.)

Modern readers, considering the reasonableness of the

claims of Jesus to interpret the ultimate nature and meaning of life, are caught between the faith of the Gospels and
the attitude that many people take toward modern science.
Either commitment is regarded by those who hold it as reliable, that is, as offering a trustworthy pattern of life, and
thought about life. Either point of view interprets the material in the Gospels to give a distinct portrait of Jesus. We
shall see these in detail in Chapter XXV.

Our question at this point is this: What is the problem we
face when we ask whether Jesus is a reliable interpreter of
life? I believe we may put the matter somewhat as follows:

(1) Jesus dealt with issues of life and life's meaning. Decision in this sphere involves matters of religious faith as
well as matters of fact. Though we grant that Jesus' knowledge of the natural world was limited and ours is extended,
that is not quite the point. The discussion about his reliability is concerned with the value of his views in religion,
not in science.

(2) Two lines of thinking regarding Jesus' reliability present themselves. It can be asserted that Jesus is *unreliable*.
We must say this if we believe that the world, contrary to
Jesus' view, has no place in it for God. This means that if
we believe that his supernaturalistic orientation is contrary
to things as they are, we must make the decision of faith
against him. On the other hand we may assert the possibility that Jesus is *reliable*. We can do this if we believe
that the world has two sides to it, the natural and the supernatural. In relation to a world of this sort, it is commonly
recognized that Jesus lived and taught consistently. His example of life, therefore, has convinced many readers, from
the first century on, that his view of life is trustworthy. These
people have chosen to live *as if he were reliable*. Their united
testimony is that *what is in logic only a possibility* becomes

in men's living the actuality: Jesus can be relied on as the interpreter of God and human life.

(3) Whichever line of reasoning (and its associated faith-decisions) we follow, we come upon difficulties. If we accept Jesus' reliability, we have intellectual problems of various sorts. If we deny his reliability, we create unanswerable questions about Jesus, and have the problem of establishing an alternate faith.

(4) We probably should not say that we "understand" Jesus until we come down conclusively on one side or the other of a decision about his reliability. This is an individual matter. We cannot suppose that we understand him merely by repeating what others say about him, for this means that we are phrasing other men's decisions or faith rather than our own. Our understanding of Jesus, therefore, will reflect our own thought about life, and our own act of self-commitment called faith. If it is somehow through faith that men decide *for* Jesus, is it not also through faith that they decide against him?

. . . . for further study and discussion

1. Collect ten words that are basic to the discussion in this chapter. Write an explanation of the meaning of each, using the dictionary and the suggestions here.

2. What *qualities* would you expect to find in the Gospels if it is a fact that they resulted largely from the activities of the Christians as a group. (Include qualities that may seem to you undesirable, as well as ones that are desirable.)

3. How do the statements in Lk. 1:1-4 fit into the discussion in this chapter?

4. Explain how the religious attitudes of an observer are involved in his decisions about Jesus' reliability.

SECTION TWO

The story of Jesus

VIII
The outline of Jesus' life

*A*NY proffered outline of the life of Jesus is in fact a summary of conclusions about the biographical value of the Gospels. There are a number of outlines. "Lives" of Jesus have been based on all four Gospels, on *Mark* alone, or on some combination of Gospels and Gospel sources. The point of major agreement in all these outlines is that Jesus, after his baptism, spent a period of time in Galilee. Then he went to Jerusalem where he was crucified.

There is great diversity of opinion when the attempt is made to fill in this outline from materials surviving in our Gospels. Indeed the technique of form criticism, as we saw earlier, denies any validity to such meager indications of time and place as do appear. Scholars of the form critical school hold that we can say practically nothing about the course of Jesus' life.

Although I believe that this skepticism goes too far, it is at least valuable warning that the details of Jesus' life are obscure at many points, and that brevity in this case is a virtue. For our purpose let us lay out the description of Jesus' life that the first Christians seem to have had in mind. It will furnish a useful key to the story in the four Gospels.

111

Biography

The following outline makes room for all the phases of Jesus' life reported in the canonical Gospels. It depends especially on the historical trustworthiness of the outline of *Mark* and *John*.

(1) About 30 years of preparation (Mt. and Lk. on his birth; one story at age twelve in Lk.)
(2) The opening events of Jesus' public life (all four Gospels)
(3) Early activity in Judea (Jn., with possible indirect references in the Synoptics)
(4) The ministry in Galilee (the content of Mk. 1:14-9:50 and its parallels in Mt. and Lk. Not in Jn.)
(5) Later activity in Judea and Perea (Jn.)
(6) The last week (all four Gospels)
(7) The resurrection and afterward (all four Gospels)

The body of the outline uses the names of the geographical areas where Jesus centered his activities during the several periods. This has a mnemonic value. He began religious discussions in Judea near the center of Jewish religion. He became an active preacher of a new message in his home province of Galilee. He returned to Judea briefly from time to time, and finally died there.

One weakness within the outline itself is that it fails to show the relative amounts of material surviving from the different periods of Jesus' life. Best described is the last week, to which *Mark* devotes about a third of its space. Next best known is the period in Galilee, to which the other two thirds of *Mark* are given, including chapter 10 which describes Jesus' trip from Galilee to Jerusalem. The other Synoptic Gospels follow this distribution of materials, though not mechanically. They include numerous episodes which it is impossible to locate exactly in a detailed outline of Jesus' life.

A second weakness in an outline that deals with the surface events of Jesus' career is that it takes no account of the forces at work about him, either those that led him to begin his public activity, or those that developed after he began and brought his life to its grim ending on the cross. Of course, to outline the career of Jesus in such a way as to describe these forces calls for a thorough understanding of Jesus himself.

Chronology

Within the framework of this outline it is difficult to establish dates for the various divisions of Jesus' life. The writers of the Gospels were little interested in calendar dates in connection with Jesus, and give no references of time which we can date beyond dispute. The stress in the story was on the *meaning* of Jesus' life as evidenced by selected events; the writers (and their sources) were satisfied with such general indications as "immediately," or "after a few days," or the language of Lk. 3:23. The seemingly specific dating in Lk. 3:1 may point to A.D. 26, or A.D. 28-29.

The dates on which, apart from an attitude of historical skepticism, there has been considerable agreement may be stated thus:

(1) Birth: between 8 B.C. and 4 B.C.
(2) Baptism: between A.D. 27 and 29
(3) Crucifixion: about A.D. 30

These dates, however, should be regarded as no more than convenient. In the case of Jesus' birth all we really know is that Jesus was born, according to Matthew and Luke, before the death of Herod the Great. We now know that Herod died in 4 B.C. The Christian monk who worked out the Christian calendar in the sixth century made a mistake of about four years at this point, so that in our modern system of dating, Jesus was born several years before the beginning of the Christian era! There is no hint as to how long before Herod's death the birth of Jesus took place. Both the month and the day of the month of his birth are unknown.

The dates for the baptism and crucifixion are similarly uncertain. The reference in Lk. 3:1 may mean that John the Baptist began his activities as early as A.D. 26, or as late as A.D. 29; in any case we cannot relate the baptism of Jesus to any special time in the work of John.

The Synoptic Gospels give no certain indications of the length of Jesus' public life. The Fourth Gospel may mean a period of two years, or it may mean three if the unnamed feast in Jn. 5:1 was a Passover. The crucifixion occurred at the time of the Jewish Passover, but whether on the day of the Passover meal or the day before is obscure (compare Mk. 14:12 with Jn. 19:14, 31). Many scholars now prefer John's date of the day before the Passover.

The reason for this uncertainty about the dates is largely that the Christians who told the story were not interested in details of chronology. In part this represents the imprecise way in which history was recorded in those days. In part it shows where the Christian emphasis lay. The important thing for the Christians was not the dates of Jesus' experiences, but the tremendous fact that in God's good time the Saviour of the world and Lord of the Christian Church had been born, had lived, had suffered, and having died was alive after death.

. . . . for further study and discussion

George Washington was born on February 11, 1732, according to the Julian calendar in use at that time. According to our present calendar Washington's birthday is February 22. Is this change of date important in commemorating Washington's contributions to his country? Does the principle underlying your answer to this question have any application to the modern commemoration of the birth of Jesus? Explain your answer.

IX

"The beginning of the Gospel
of Jesus Christ"

*T*HE oldest connected presentation of Jesus is in
Mark. If this was written, as it may well have
been, by John Mark, the friend and companion of both Paul
and Peter, it probably represents the substance of the Gospel
story as these and other Christian evangelists retold it. In
this chapter we shall discuss the beginning of Jesus' public
life as Mark gives it to his readers. In the next two chapters
we shall take up Jesus' activities in Galilee and the culmination of it all in Jerusalem.

Since the story of Jesus' public activities begins in Mk.
1:14, it is proper to regard verses 1-13 as introductory. They
set the scene, as it were, giving those bits of information or
background that Mark probably views as basic to an understanding. At the very least, these verses form the front porch
to the main structure, which the reader enters in verse 14.
In these opening lines Mark sets down one historical-re-
ligious principle and three events of history:

(1) The testimony of Old Testament prophecy (vv. 2-3);
(2) The person and message of John "the baptizer" (vv.
4-8);
(3) The baptism of Jesus (vv. 9-11);
(4) The temptation of Jesus (vv. 12-13).

116

Old Testament prophecy

It is significant that the story of Jesus begins with Old Testament quotations. The specific words are less important than the underlying principle: *that the divine purpose at work in previous generations is moving again in the events associated with Jesus of Nazareth; that the Holy Scriptures of the Jewish religion describe these earlier events.* This represents a clear view about God and the nature of his providence, as well as about Jesus. The reader, finding this at the very beginning of the presentation, would naturally expect the following pages to illustrate it in detail.

The Biblical quotations give substance to Mark's description of Jesus. They deal with the coming of God to his people, describing especially the voices of human messengers who call men to prepare for the coming of the Lord. Mark takes the Scriptures a step further to realization. It is a Jew named John, he says, a stormy and popular preacher of the later A.D. 20's, whose activities satisfy the prophetic vision about a special messenger.

Mark presents Jesus of Nazareth as the one whom John announced, though the fact is interesting that he gives no direct statement on John's attitude toward Jesus. From the titles given Jesus in 1:1,11, and implied in 1:7,8, it is clear that Mark intended to equate Jesus through these titles with the divine Lord of the Old Testament prophecies. One notes that the terms in *Mark* and in the prophets cited are not identical. The differences would not be a point of difficulty to Mark or to his original readers.

John

John was cast in the same mold as the Hebrew prophets. Though by virtue of his birth he was a member of a lesser order of priests in Judaism, his importance to Mark and to religious history lies in his independent religious activities. Though we do not know the story of his own personal religious development, it is clear that John was, for a few years, the voice of protest against the worldliness and insincerity of his people's life. His social and religious message created great popular interest; and while we are chiefly acquainted with him through the New Testament, he is also mentioned with sympathy by the Jewish historian Josephus, who wrote toward the close of the first century. There appears to be no question about the influence of John. In some cases men who became followers of Jesus had initially been awakened to the claims of God on his people by the activity of John. In other instances we know of the continuing existence of groups of followers of John for a number of decades at least after his death. Traces of his influence can be clearly seen in non-Christian literature of later centuries.

Mark, as has been said, presents John as one through whom God's purpose is at work. In his description, apart from personal matters, three things about John's activity seem to stand out:

(1) his water baptism based on repentance;

(2) his message about sin and righteousness;

(3) his assertion about a greater one to come who would baptize with the Holy Spirit.

Any reader finding points such as these stressed in the opening lines of a book would expect to see them recur, as indeed they do, later on. To the ancient reader, however, these lines had more than literary value. They stated a common emphasis and faith which bound the work of John and Jesus together, the Christian movement being the continuation and fulfillment of John's activity.

The baptism of Jesus (vv. 9-11)

Mark records neither the reason for Jesus' baptism nor the particular form it took. Either these were matters clearly known at the time he wrote or were considered of secondary importance. We suppose that Jesus dipped himself, at least in a symbolic way, in the Jordan River. Presumably this was like the baptisms of many of his countrymen. We may understand further that people received baptism in specific response to John's call to repentance. Thus, the intent of the action was to recognize John as a true prophet and to express an attitude of obedience to God.

The rite itself has further implications. Mark connects it with forgiveness of sins (v. 4), and places this in a setting that anticipates the coming of God to his people. We have, therefore, a cluster of ideas: the coming of the Lord in justice and judgment; man's acceptance of the coming; man's repentance and active participation in preparation for the coming.

Water baptism clearly fits into this setting as a visible expression of a man's renewed relation with God. Mark, however, leaves the inner meaning of the rite unspecified, and there are varied views as to what John (and Mark) had in mind. The act has been taken as a ritual of purification, or of public initiation into the community of God's people. It has been understood to go more profoundly into man's religious problem than these suggest, and to be efficacious in gaining the rebirth of the human soul into heavenly life. Along a still different line of reasoning it has been proposed that to John, at any rate, submission to baptism displayed a humble acceptance of God's coming judgment.

Although this discussion is interesting of itself and important because of its relation to the rise of Christian baptism, there is no general agreement among Biblical scholars.

Mark also passes over another difficulty which later Christian readers found in his account, namely, *the reason why Jesus accepted water baptism.* The Christian problem originally was: How could Jesus, in view of his sinless character, share in a baptism of repentance for sins? Mark apparently saw no problem such, for example, as the one Matthew records in Mt. 3:13-15. It may be that Mark is deliberately posing another matter which he means to interpret: the *fulfiller of the divine coming foretold in the Old Testament accepts baptism,* that is, *accepts a place within the people to whom he is coming.*

This identification of Person and People is associated, in verses 10 and 11, with Jesus' religious experience which stresses his sense of unique mission. To what degree the language of these two verses is meant to be symbolic, it is hard to say, though the general sense is clear. Mark would have the reader understand that out of Jesus' obedience in baptism came an endowment with spiritual power (v. 10), and a sense of unique acceptability to God (v. 11).

The temptation of Jesus (vv. 12-13)

In common New Testament usage *temptation* means not so much an enticement to evil as an inward probing of character, through events or reflection, which tests and discloses one's inner strength. The famous temptation of Jesus is described as just such a testing. *Matthew* and *Luke* give the only detailed account of it (see below, Chapter XIII). Mark limits himself to a brief word about the meaning of Jesus' reflections during the period of solitude before his public career got under way. He sees struggle reflected here. Jesus, baptized and with a sense of unique relationship to God, is now pinned in the center of the tension between God's purposes in the world and all that is in opposition.

The sense of loneliness which Mark breathes into the account heightens his picture of Jesus' unique qualities. It is probable, however, that here too we are in the presence of symbolic language.

Let us recapitulate. Mark proposes to tell a story, the outcome of which is clear, as he indicates in his title, "The Gospel of Jesus Christ, the Son of God."

His first point is that Old Testament prophecy was fulfilled in a prophet named John, whose message called men to repentance and warned of coming judgment.

His second point is that Jesus, the Son of God, was part of his people in obedience, and after confession of that obedience, was given some special gift of power and a sense of divine recognition.

Third, Mark sees significance in the fact that Jesus in his own inner struggle with evil persisted in his devotion to God.

. . . . for further study and discussion

1. To what possible events or things does Mark apply the word *beginning* (1:1)?

2. Compare the accounts of John the Baptist in Mt. 3:1-17; Mk. 1:1-11; Lk. 3:1-22; Jn. 1:19-34.

   (a) Describe in your own words John's activities.

   (b) Summarize his *religious* ideas.

   (c) Summarize his *social* ideas.

3. Point out differences between the *texts* of the four Gospels in the references given in the second question. Which of these differences may involve differences of *meaning?*

4. How does Mark describe Jesus' temptation?

X

The Galilean phase

*A*s THE reader works his way through Mark's description of the main period of Jesus' public life, he should bear in mind that he is looking for understanding through a relating of two distinct sorts of information.

He is looking for a knowledge of the structure or form of the writing. He keeps asking himself about the progress of thought, the logical development, in the written word. This is important because it provides a context within which we may study Jesus.

He also seeks details of content. He will wish to learn the facts recorded about Jesus. While it is through a study of the *contents* of *Mark* that we can see its literary pattern, it is also true that the *force of the details* in *Mark* is clearly understood only when related to the whole presentation. This principle of analysis applies to the other Gospels as well.

To be most helpful to the reader, this chapter treats separately the study of the literary structure of *Mark,* and the contents, from 1:14 through 9:50.

Literary structure

The story of what we call the Galilean phase reflects a beginning, an early stage, a period of development, a climax (or better, a series of climactic moments), and a close as Jesus apparently changed his method of dealing with his contemporaries.

The following, though not a full outline, may suggest the progress of thought the reader will wish to trace through the story:

(1) 1:14-45   The beginnings in Galilee; favorable responses.

(2) 2:1-3:6   Unfavorable responses; hostile plot.

(3) 3:7-6:13   Appeal to the nation as a whole. The message is illustrated by parables (4:1-34), and related to the principle of faith through miracles (4:35-6:6).

(4) 6:30-44   Tremendous popular enthusiasm of the wrong sort which Jesus rejects.

(5) 6:45-7:23 Jesus' renewed dedication; his refusal to change his message notwithstanding the inability of the crowds, the disciples, or the religious leaders to understand.

(6) 7:24-8:26 Jesus avoids false popularity; the importance of faith underlies the narrative.

(7) 8:27-38   The disciples' faith established (the turning point in the story in *Mark*).

(8) 9:1-8   Jesus finds mystical confirmation of his spiritual obedience to God.

(9) 9:9-50   Necessity of faith; secret travels; instruction of the disciples.

Content

To study the contents of this section of *Mark* effectively (not merely to "read them over"), the following questions will serve as clues. These do not cover all aspects of *Mark* by any means, and some have more apparent answers than others. They lead, however, to the significant matters in *Mark*, and the study of them will be valuable later in providing points of comparison and contrast with the other Gospels.

(1) What is Mark's way of *beginning*? When, in Jesus' life? Where?

(2) What is the climax or turning point? The ending?

(3) In what specific activities did Jesus spend his time?

(4) Give specific consequences of Jesus' words and actions.

(5) What may be said about Jesus' motives?

(6) Why was there outspoken opposition to Jesus?

(7) What was Jesus' message, giving several references?

(8) Who are the characters in Mark's story? Do their relations with Jesus give any knowledge about Jesus?

(9) What does Mark emphasize in telling the story? By direct words regarding import? By repetition?

(10) As an illustration of the preceding question, what does Mark seem to point out about the following: Jesus' desire for secrecy? The disciples' lack of understanding? The relation of faith to miracles?

(11) What is the place which the Old Testament has in the story?

(12) Give specific instances in which the story is affected by some aspect of Jewish religion other than text of the Old Testament.

Portrait of Jesus

In our study of the content of the Galilean phase of Jesus' life, we have as one particular end in view a better understanding of Jesus. Mark's biographical sketch is quite strongly drawn, and though it has subtle points, is clear. The following is a suggested summary of Mark's point of view about Jesus:

(1) Jesus approaches men actively with a message about the Kingdom of God. He calls for repentance and acceptance.

(2) Some heed, some object to the way he disregards convention and interprets the sacred laws. Tremendous popular interest hinders his activities, as the crowds largely miss the spiritual meaning of his words.

(3) Jesus refuses cheap popularity, refuses in any way to modify his message. He insists on faith as the necessary response to God's message.

(4) Jesus devotes increased attention to his followers as it becomes evident there will be no nation-wide acceptance. He avoids further acts that will breed only wrong sorts of enthusiasm.

The reader can easily find a reference or two that clearly fits each case mentioned above. It will be even more helpful to trace these principles in paragraphs where they are obscured by the factual details. In *Mark* 9, for example, there are a number of different matters, but it may be suggested for study that underlying the whole is Jesus' insistence on a basic attitude of faith in God. It is faith that sees the vision of the Kingdom, or understands that in John the Baptist the prophecy regarding Elijah is fulfilled. Only faith is adequate to deal with the epileptic boy or to understand God's purpose in the Messiah. By faith one has the humility of a child, one serves the Messiah and honors his followers, or one properly elevates the value of the spiritual life above that of the material.

Miracle stories

Mark describes Jesus as engaging in activities that are commonly referred to as miraculous. These include acts of healing (usually instantaneous), evidences of control over a non-material world of beings (demons), and various expressions of power over the world of nature, including physical mortality.

As supplement to what we saw earlier (pp. 67-73) about the problems raised by these miracles in general, there is value at this point in studying in more detail the place that miracle stories occupy in Mark's account. His point of emphasis is somewhat different from what the modern reader may suppose.

(1) Mark's name for miracles is "mighty deeds." The miracle for him is not something that rouses awe and is to be wondered at (the sense of the English word *miracle*), but rather something effective in life that represents the application of power, God's power, to man's problems or his world.

(2) The reason for miracles was to express the message about God's Kingdom through *actions*. In most cases these acts (of healing or otherwise) restored normal human living, or made it possible.

(3) The miracles are based on an attitude of receptivity and response that may be termed *faith*. This is the rational interpretation given, when one is given at all. There certainly is a ring of genuineness in the statement in Mk. 6:5-6 about the inability of Jesus to do any "mighty work" in Nazareth because of a lack of response on the part of those in need. In fact, a considerable number of the sayings in *Mark* turn on the need for an active response to Jesus. It is clearly suggested that Jesus is an agent of spiritual power moving in a realm of life larger than the physical, a realm in which the flow of energy is controlled by one's voluntary response to it. Mark does not describe Jesus as an arbitrary wonderworker. In 9:29 the source of spiritual power is "prayer," without which the disciples (and Jesus, too) are impotent.

(4) The miracle events do not become a substitute for the ordinary means of life. They do not serve Jesus' private interests. They do not make life easier, but in some specific way they make it possible or increase its scope.

These observations fit naturally into a discussion of miracles of healing, whether of the mind or the body. In the case of miracles that exhibit power over inanimate natural forces (the "nature miracles"), the point of view is still that faith is essential, though in this case it is Jesus' faith (4:40), or the similar faith of a disciple (11:23). The same idea appears also in "Q," e.g., Lk. 17:5-6.

In studying the relation of faith and miracle, the reader will be struck by Jesus' constant refusal to do miracles in order to *prove* his message. To the modern reader, as to the ancient questioner, there seems something reasonable in the challenge that Jesus should exhibit the resources of spiritual force of which rumor made so much. Jesus, however, held that the attitude of mind which says, "I'll believe *if* you prove yourself" is an attitude of rejection or "unbelief" already, and negates any efficacious activity of a spiritual sort (6:4-6 and 8:11-13).

Jesus, however, showed himself sympathetic toward the sincere questioner. In 8:14-21 he refers to miraculous events as a ground for a stronger faith than that which the disciples were showing. This way of referring to the miracles is cast in even more general terms in "Q" (Lk. 7:18-23). Though the logical connection is not made in so many words, it underlies other episodes in Mark such as 8:27-29 or 10:17-22.

I believe a natural solution to the problems raised by the Gospels and the sources is to conclude that, in fact, unusual phenomena were associated with Jesus of Nazareth, and that he accomplished things called "mighty works" by Mark, and "miracles" by later followers. There is good evidence that he regarded these events as effected by spiritual energy released, in individual lives and specific situations, by an attitude of receptivity and response called "faith." He associated his activities of healing, and so on, strictly with his religious message about God's Kingdom.

I do not suppose, especially at this distance, that we can penetrate the workings of miracles, or feel equally confident, on an intellectual basis, about all the reports. There is nothing particularly difficult, of course, in holding that Jesus had some intuitive sense of the functioning of human personality, and that this resulted in healing episodes of the type accomplished in psychiatric practice today. Faith in God, however, refuses to limit God's work by the limits of human understanding or hypotheses. It is possible to hold that Jesus was responsible for events of an unprecedented sort in the world of nature without being able to describe his connection with them.

I firmly believe that the early Christians concocted no significant number of the miracle stories. There were, it is true, tendencies operating in that direction. As the Gospels tell us, the disciples tended to miss the essential connection between Jesus' miracles and his message about God's Kingdom. They were amazed by surface events, and probably retold among themselves stories of things they had seen. There may have been a considerable pressure, born of the superstition of the times, to exaggerate the details of the miracle stories. Some of this expansion may appear in our Gospels. If this is so, such principles as we considered in Chapter VII (see pp. 101-105) worked to restrain it. It does not determine the character of the surviving accounts of miracles to any important degree.

I believe that it is reasonable to argue that if these stories of miracles had been the product of Christian piety and superstition, they would be more numerous now, and more trivial in quality. They would also show a greater kinship with the thinking of the disciples. As it is, the stories on the whole reflect Jesus' spiritual position rather than that of his followers.

. . . . for further study and discussion

1. Study the questions on pp. 123-24.
2. Give references from *Mark* which you feel illustrate the points of the "portrait" on pp. 124-25.

3. Imagining yourself a disinterested reporter of Jesus' own time:
   (a) Summarize the apparent results of Jesus' efforts in Galilee.
   (b) How would your summary differ if you were to put yourself in the place of a sympathetic friend of Jesus?
   (c) What would you say if you were an enemy?

XI

Jerusalem and Calvary

*J*N Mk. 10:1 through 16:8 there is a steady line of progress from the point of Jesus' departure from Galilee to the resurrection. Indications of time are lacking for the period as a whole (which may have lasted as long as six months), but the account of the last week is more definite.

The division over the days of the week seems intended to have been as follows:

11: 1-11	Sunday
11: 12-19	Monday
11: 20-13:37	Tuesday
14: 1-2, 10-11	Wednesday (?)
14: 3-9	?
14: 12-31?	Thursday
14: 32?-15:47	Friday
16: 1-8	Sunday

Mark gives 37% of his space to the description of the last week and 15% to the last twenty-four hours. Since no other periods of time in the life of Jesus are described in a comparable way, we have a clue to the importance of the crucifixion in the first Christian preaching. In Mark's story the climactic movement begins to gather strength at the beginning of chapter 10. At this point, Jesus, leaving Galilee, came southward in a course of action that closed only with his death and the awe-struck words of a nameless centurion, "Truly this man was a son of God" (15:39).

In telling the story Mark illustrates four important Christian convictions about Jesus:

(1) Jesus is the Messiah;
(2) His death was redemptive;
(3) God's plan was "fulfilled";
(4) Jesus died and "rose" from death.

Jesus the Messiah

Mark describes Jesus in ways that have clear associations with the ideas about the Messiah current in that time, or with work forecast for him in the Old Testament. In chapter 11, for example, nearly all the paragraphs have a direct association with the thought of the coming Messiah, and the first paragraph is the climax of the progression of events that began when Jesus left Galilee (10:1).

During the events of the last week Messianic attitudes may be noted. On Monday Jesus *acts* within the temple with an assumed authority that reveals Messianic conviction on his part. On Tuesday, his *teaching* is similar in tone. Mark says that the condemnation of Jesus on Friday morning turned on Jesus' assent to a question about Messiahship (14:61-64, see also 15:2-15).

The reader will bear in mind that this tension over the question of Messiahship seems not so much to have involved a questioning about *deity* as about *function*. The question was, "Is Jesus doing the work that the Messiah is intended to do?" It seems not to have been an issue of a general sort whether his nature was unique. Jewish thought seems to have been divided on the matter of the Messiah's more-than-human quality, but there was little doubt that he should show power over his enemies and the enemies of his people.

"Not to be served but to serve"

Reference to the redemptive quality of Jesus' death first appears directly in 10:45, but Mark, who tends to speak in a practical way about mysteries, has already recorded the paradoxical nature of discipleship (8:34-36): that self-denial in faith even if death results means not death but life in the ultimate sense. As this is a principle of response and obedience for followers, so it is also a principle that binds the Messiah: his obedience, even though it leads to death, will mean not failure but triumph.

We recall that Mark is writing as one who believes in the redemptive power of Jesus' death, and has seen the effectiveness of faith in him in Christian missions. No doubt he believed theologically more than he wrote in his Gospel. His point here is to show that *in the story of Jesus lies the evidence on which Christian theology rests.* He stresses the idea that *Jesus understood his death to be redemptive, not accidental, in its meaning for men.*

The references to redemptive meaning are less surprising than the simplicity with which they are recorded. The reader might reflect on what the pious Christian might have done in rewriting the parable of Mk. 12:1-12 in the light of the crucifixion.

Prophecy and fulfillment

Mark's story of Jesus is presented as a part of God's purpose in the world. There are numerous references to the Old Testament in the words of Jesus, for both he and his contemporaries agreed that the Old Testament recorded what God had done, and what he had commanded his people.

The major difference between Jesus and his associates in

understanding the Old Testament was that Jesus insisted on searching behind the specific words of the Old Testament for the purpose of God disclosed there (10:6-7). This point of view leads to a very active, vigorous kind of religious thinking. It thinks in terms of God's acts rather than in terms of stationary principles of truth. It tends to believe that God is still acting, and interprets the fulfillment of Scripture as completing purposes expressed therein, more than as carrying out predictions.

Perhaps we can make clear this basic distinction between views of fulfillment alluded to in the preceding sentence by drawing it out a little further.

Jesus seemed to believe that events connected with himself brought into fuller reality the divine purpose which had already been expressed in the Old Testament stories. These stories need not be predictive of the Messiah. The meaningful thing about them was that they conveyed insight into purposes of God which he intended to realize fully in later events.

As to his own place in relation to this purpose and its fulfillment, Jesus believed that all that God meant to do *came to completion in the time of the Messiah.* Thus, all expressions of spiritual principle, all partial accomplishments of what God wanted of his people, and all scattered experiences of men with God were to come into full flower when God established his Kingdom. Jesus connected this realization with himself. (On the nature of the Kingdom, see Chapter XVI; on Jesus' view of his Messiahship, see Chapter XXIII; the connection between his experiences and the past underlies such sayings as Mk. 7:6; 14:21; 14:27.)

This is not to deny that Jesus believed in specific predictions and pin-point achievements of those predictions. Mk. 11:1-10 should be compared with *Zechariah* 9:9 in this regard. But it would be well to associate with this literalistic illustration of fulfillment the view that John the Baptist fulfills the Old Testament prophecy regarding Elijah (Mk. 9:11-13).

Since this is a matter of some complexity, let us summarize the discussion in a series of sentences:

Jesus regarded the Old Testament as a record of acts of God which showed his long-range purpose.

He found in the Old Testament inspired statements of what the fuller expression of God's purpose would be, and a partial description of the way in which it would be realized in the future.

He did not regard the Old Testament as a schedule of predicted events which he completed and scratched off, one by one.

As for the attitude of Mark himself, it may be said that he shows no concern to document his story of Jesus with an abundance of references to the Old Testament. One has to look in *Matthew* for this Christian tendency. The references which Mark gives are sufficient to show the major lines of thinking about Jesus and about the Old Testament. They are also sufficient to show Mark's purpose of describing through his story the circumstances by which God's saving program is being carried out.

Death and resurrection

The tremendous point of arrival in *Mark* is the account of the crucifixion, the burial, and the discovery of the open tomb. Crucifixion fits, in all its aspects, into the principle of Jesus' complete obedience to God regardless of the outcome. It would be hard to decide where Mark senses the final crushing step of this obedience to lie: in the cry expressing the sense of separation from God in 15:34, or the wordless utterance of verse 37, or the act of dying itself (v. 37).

The striking thing from this point to the end is that the

"official" disciples are missing from the scene. The only follower of Jesus who prepared his body for burial whom we know by name was a certain Joseph of Arimathaea. He is not otherwise mentioned in *Mark*. The only visitors to the tomb are women whose names have been mentioned previously.

Mark's story is more quickly told than he intended, for the account breaks off at 16:8 and no one can say what the original ending of the Gospel was. The present text gives evidence that the author would close with a description of contacts between Jesus and his disciples in Galilee after the resurrection. If, in fact, this were ever written, it has been lost in the most serious accident to have befallen any portion of the New Testament. All trace of the original ending is now lost. It has even been conjectured that the author was interrupted and never able to finish his work.

The two endings printed in the notes of the Revised Standard Version represent two ancient endings to the Gospel, the longer of which appears in the Latin Bible and in the King James Version.

The result of this condition at the end of *Mark*, whatever its cause may have been, is that we lack Mark's evidence for the way in which the story of Jesus' resurrection appearances were told in his own Christian circle. Though he gives no interpretation and very little narrative, he says enough, nonetheless, to testify that the pathetic mourning of Jesus' friends was not the end of the biography; there was a unique event. Jesus rose from the grave.

But what did Mark mean? Were we strictly dependent on 16:4-7, very little could be said. Mark reports that the tomb in which Jesus was buried was found empty on the Sunday morning after Jesus' death. He names three women who saw the tomb empty and were shocked by its emptiness. He records their fear and implies on their part a lack of satisfactory explanation.

A "young man" inside the tomb, though not identified, seems to have more information than the women. He uses the Christian technical expression, "He is risen."

Mark also points forward (v. 7) to contacts between Jesus and his disciples which, described in other Gospels, are called "post-resurrection appearances." Recognition of Jesus and a renewed personal relationship with him are implied by Mark, but little more can be inferred from his words taken by themselves. As *Acts* 10:40-41 indicates, however, Mark's material is part of the Christian *kerygma*. It is possible, therefore, without trying to guess at what Mark may have once included, to discuss the problems he raises in his report of Jesus' resurrection. These problems are of different sorts, and may be divided into groups:

(1) The resurrection comes under the heading of miracle; what has been said about miracles, and the general problem of truthfulness applies here.

(2) The resurrection became the subject of the first Christian message. There can be no doubt of the fact that the original friends of Jesus believed something tremendous had happened to him, and that they had seen him alive after his death. They described their experience with Jesus, and their beliefs about it, in everyday language. What their experience was is hard for us to state in modern terms because when we do so, we must decide about its true nature. If one believes that in the experience of the disciples with Jesus there was a miracle involved, then it is impossible to state the essence of the event in modern technical terms because there is no way of establishing a terminology.

(3) The first Christians described the evidence for this reality in two major ways: *(a)* Negatively, there was the accumulated evidence to the fact of the empty tomb. This is directly found in *Mark* and the other Gospels, which do not depend on *Mark* at this point. The same point of view

is present *by implication* in *1 Corinthians* 15:1-11, a passage earlier in date of composition than the Gospels. *(b)* Positively, there was the accumulated witness to experiences of the friends of Jesus with him after his death. Paul stresses this in *1 Corinthians* 15 and lists six different appearances, three to individuals and three involving groups ranging from eleven to 500 people. Mark's Gospel was presumably intended to include similar accounts, and the others in fact do, although it is not possible to harmonize the various ones in an integrated narrative.

(4) The nature of the first Christian belief as to what happened to the physical body of Jesus is unclear. Paul probably believed in a miraculous transformation of the physical substance by or into the spiritual (1 Cor. 15:42-50). Mark offers nothing to explain the emptiness of the tomb save the words, "He is risen." Other passing references in the New Testament (as *Acts* 10:41) point toward belief in a more materialistic revival of the body and a mechanical transfer of it to heaven.

(5) The disciples' belief in the miracle of the resurrection was powerful in their lives not because they believed in it merely as a true fact, but because they saw it as *a fact with promise in it.* Their thinking seems to have gone something like this: since Jesus had triumphed over death, obedience to God was not doomed by mortal evil, and death was not final. Since the happening of this attesting miracle, surely men could believe that Jesus had the saving significance for his followers which he had claimed. Since this decisive act, Jesus was evidence of God's future program of salvation.

The power of this line of thinking in early Christianity, and its reality as "good news" (that is, "gospel"), is a particularly effective illustration of William James' remark that "Abstract considerations about the soul and the reality of a moral order will not do in a year what the glimpse into a world of new phenomenal possibilities enveloping those of the present life, afforded by an extension of our insight into the order of nature, would do in an instant." [1]

. . . . for further study and discussion

1. Prepare an outline of Mk. 10:1-16:8 similar to the outline of Mk. 1:14-9:50 on p. 123.
2. Read Mt. 19:1-27:54 with your outline of *Mark* as a guide. Prepare a supplementary list of *events* mentioned in *Matthew* but not found in *Mark*.
3. Read Lk. 19:28-23:49 and prepare a similar list supplementary to *Mark*. What events are found in *Luke* that do not appear in *Matthew?*
4. Many readers of the Gospels have asked, "Did Jesus commit suicide?" What reasons can you think of to support both an affirmative and a negative answer.
5. Write an outline of events related to the resurrection (Mk. 15:40-16:8) and compare this with the accounts in Mt. 27:55-28:20 and Lk. 23:50-24:53. What are the major points of similarity between the accounts? What are the prominent differences? How might the results of this comparison be interpreted (see Chapter VII)?

---

[1] *The Letters of William James,* edited by his son, Henry James; in two volumes (Boston: The Atlantic Monthly Press, 1920), I, 236-7. Permission to reprint granted by Paul R. Reynolds & Son, 599 Fifth Avenue, New York 17, N. Y.

XII
The Christmas story

$\mathcal{T}$HE stories of Jesus' birth in *Matthew* 1, 2 and *Luke* 1, 2 are among the treasures of Christian culture. As we have seen, they were not part of the earliest preaching, nor were they part of the oldest general teaching (in "Q"). They are, however, evidence of Christian interest in the beginnings of Jesus' life and in that regard have been followed by most biographers, from those who penned the "apocryphal gospels" of the second, third, and fourth centuries to modern novelists.

A problem for readers today is deciding the nature of the Christmas stories. There are three important kinds of interpretation. Are they historical, or fictional, or do they share in the qualities of both types of story? The traditional Christian understanding, of course, has taken them historically. The stories are admittedly incomplete, but preserve trustworthy memories. On the other hand, common modern views are that the stories are either completely fanciful or combine some memories about Jesus' family with a large measure of pious imagining.

It should also be said that, from the Christian understanding of Jesus, the Christmas story goes farther than the language of history may properly go: It deals with God's act in becoming man. Christian faith in the divine incarnation speaks here through a story; but wherein is the story *historical* and wherein is it attempting to describe what is

139

beyond history? (The name for a story that describes truth transcending human history is *myth*.) A decision here is one that rests partly on the evidence, and partly on the reader's faith.

To the extent that these narratives are biographical, they are the major contributions of *Matthew* and *Luke* (apart from the material in "Q") to our knowledge of Jesus' life. The present chapter is limited to the problem of understanding the stories of the birth of Jesus in the way they looked to the Gospel writers. We shall take up (1) matters of origin, (2) contents, and (3) the place that the story of Jesus' birth held in first-century Christianity.[1] I wish to point out by way of anticipation that Christian faith in the days these Gospels were written was based on convincing aspects of the life-death-resurrection story rather than on this more intimate and personal narrative.

Origins

The accounts given by Matthew and Luke stand alone in the New Testament. There is nothing else like them. These are separate narratives in the sense that they were preserved independently and do not stem from a common original source, either within Christianity or from outside it.

The narratives of Jesus' birth took their present forms in the latter part of the first century, and therefore circulated among Christians who knew the family of Jesus and Jesus himself. Each account shows within itself signs of having come through Aramaic-speaking Christian groups.

Contents

Matthew and Luke tell the story of Jesus' birth in distinct ways. The easiest way of stating the difference is to

---

[1] The date of Jesus' birth is discussed on pp. 113-14.

say that Matthew tells his story *as if* seen through Joseph's eyes, and Luke, *as if* seen through Mary's. This form of statement is open to misunderstanding in that it must not be taken to state as a fact that the accounts are connected directly with either parent. It is useful, however, in describing the point of view in each Gospel.

Matthew includes well-known features of the Christmas story, such as the birth in Bethlehem, the visit of the Wise Men (Magi), the flight into Egypt, the slaughter of infants in Bethlehem. He includes a genealogy of Jesus from Abraham, and reference to the miraculous conception of Jesus.

Luke tells a somewhat longer story. He includes reports of the conceptions and births of both John the Baptist and Jesus, the birth of Jesus in Bethlehem, the manger-cradle, and the visit of the shepherds. Luke includes three poetic utterances which became the texts of famous Christian hymns (the *Magnificat*, 1:46-55, the *Benedictus*, 1:68-79, and the *Nunc Dimittis*, 2:29-32). These may have been in church use before being included in the Gospel. (The names of the hymns are derived from the Latin translation.) Luke includes a genealogical list somewhat different from Matthew's and traces Jesus' lineage back to Adam. Luke reports the virgin conception of Jesus more circumstantially than does Matthew, and includes the only Biblical glimpse of Jesus as a boy (2:41-52).

It will be apparent that neither account is biographically complete. The dominant note is religious, and Luke's literary purpose was to provide background for the kerygmatic message. That is to say that behind the declaration of God's saving purpose in Jesus of Nazareth, the Messiah, lies the story of how God's Messiah came among men in great humility, in an atmosphere of worshipful obedience to God, and with attesting signs that puzzled and yet encouraged his family.

A second fact which closer inspection of the narratives

discloses is that they cannot be fitted together in detail. Because of use in the religious life of Christians, the historical relations, if there were any, between the accounts have been lost. We now have a series of testimonies pertaining to his birth. Christian piety has naturally fitted these together without concern for its lack of historical knowledge. Through the course of centuries popular Christmas observances have included other things as well, which have no Biblical basis whatever.

It may be said here, in order to be specific, that the miraculous conception of Jesus is an integral part of each Gospel. Neither one, so far as we know, ever existed without it. It is this miracle of virgin conception that is commonly referred to as "The Virgin Birth." It will be observed that this is not the same as the "Immaculate Conception" of Roman Catholic piety and dogma, which refers to the conception of Mary as preserved from the taint of original sin, and not to the conception of Jesus.

The importance of the nativity stories

Apart from the prominence which the nativity stories acquired in later Christian culture, they occupied a place of importance in the Christian thinking of the first century. This place, however, is somewhat different from what the modern Christian might suppose.

The stories give family background, and probably reflect Christian curiosity about Jesus' family, even though, at the same time, they are more significant in showing that Jesus had family background than in detailing it. They may have been prepared in reference to some early form of *Gnosticism*. Gnosticism was a philosophy of religion that was exceedingly widespread and influential in the Greco-Roman world in the second century. In Gnostic thought it would be impossible for a divine being to *come into* and *become* a *real part of human life.* It is just such an entry that the Gospel stories stress. Jesus was truly human and his origin is known.

In addition to the place these stories may have had in early Christian controversy with the Gnostics, they had a theological value as well. They are descriptive of the Christian doctrine of incarnation. That is, they describe the way (or "mode") by which God became integrally part of human existence. They are not, however, *ground* for faith in Jesus' meaning for men, since, as we have seen, the *kerygma* was first proclaimed without need of them. This means that the story of Jesus' birth with the miracle of the virgin conception was part neither of the first Christian evangelism nor of the primary instruction in Christian living.

The evidence of its actual place in the first-century Christianity is, therefore, more largely negative than affirmative. The miraculous conception is not mentioned in any of the New Testament letters that were written prior to *Matthew* and *Luke.* Chiefly these are letters of Paul who taught both the deity of Jesus and his Messiahship (see *Romans* 1:1-4). It seems clear then that this Christian leader either did not know or did not use as primary evidence the material now preserved in *Matthew* and *Luke.* We shall return to this point in a moment.

It should first be said, however, that the Christmas stories may not so easily be written off as Christian myths as is sometimes supposed. The doctrine of the incarnation is present in Paul's thought (as in *Galatians* 4:4, "But when the time had fully come, God sent forth his Son, born of woman, born under the law"). It is also present in Jn. 1:14 ("The Word became flesh and dwelt among us") although *John* is usually dated after *Matthew* and *Luke.* While in the Gospels and in Paul's thought account is taken of Jesus' family relationships (Mk. 3:31-35 and 6:3), his connection with David (Rom. 1:3), and the genuine quality of his

humanity, all this is so held that in the portrayal of Jesus
in our earliest texts he shows clear affinities with God and
clear distinction from the natural quality of human life.

Because of such references as these, the argument from
silence (appealing to the fact that the rest of the New Testament makes no mention of the virgin conception and con-
cluding that, therefore, it is not historical) is a risky procedure in the extreme. The rest of the New Testament shows
that the reality of Jesus' birth and the identity of his family
were facts of importance. It also shows belief in a miracle—
the incarnation. It hardly shows through silence what additional knowledge the several Christian writers had, or did
not have, about the family of Jesus. Nor does it show what
they thought about the *mode* of the incarnation.

The texts of *Matthew* and *Luke*, however, show that some
Christians of the first century did believe that the miracle
of the incarnation was effected by the miracle of Mary's
virgin conception. It is my feeling that both Paul and John
must have known that this belief was held. It is my opinion
also, though this can be only a guess, that had either Paul
or the writer of John's Gospel been dissatisfied with the narrative of virgin conception, they would have made their
opposition clear in materials now surviving. In the nature
of the case, it is hard to see how any other evidence to the
event of conception could exist than the word of the mother.
This testimony does not exist unless it be in *Matthew* or
Luke. Lacking certainty on just this point, many modern
Christians will continue to question the traditional *mode*
of the divine incarnation, to the reality of which they adhere
as essential to their Christian faith.

It may be remarked that in the period of the New Testament, Christian faith in Jesus was founded on the miracle
of his resurrection. This statement includes, as far as is
known, the faith of the members of Jesus' own family circle.
In later times some Christians, though holding in doubt the

reported miracle as to the mode of the incarnation, have confessed their faith in Jesus as the supreme Lord and Saviour of men, showing in their personal lives all the evidences of faith that Christian piety knows. Thus either in the past or the present there seems no necessary reason why the matter of the historicity of the virgin birth should become, as it appears in some Christian groups to be, the touchstone of faith.

. . . . for further study and discussion

1. Outline the contents of Mt. 1-2 and Lk. 1-2.
2. Prepare a statement of the specific points on which the two accounts agree. State the items recorded separately in each Gospel.
3. What does each account tell the reader *in addition to* the circumstances pertaining to Jesus' birth. (That is, how does each Gospel *interpret* Jesus?)

XIII

The wilderness temptation

*A*CCORDING to *Mark*, the baptism of Jesus, significant in the impress it made on him, was followed by a period of solitude, during which he worked over in his mind the clash between God's will and all other ways of thinking and living (Mk. 1:12-13). Mark gives no description of this experience beyond describing its setting, but the story he tells of Jesus' public life makes it reasonable. He frequently portrays Jesus as holding an attitude of devotion to God that conflicted with the more "practical" attitude of his contemporaries. That attitude is tested in the wilderness. He also shows us Jesus viewing Messiahship according to the same principle of devotion to God. Though Mark does not so speak, we could infer that if Jesus came to any new conviction in his baptism, it would immediately be tested in relation to the devotion by which he had hitherto lived. What Mark leaves unsaid Matthew and Luke write out in clear terms (chapter 4 in each Gospel): the wilderness temptation was a testing of Messiahship.

The narrative material in *Matthew* 4 and *Luke* 4 comes from "Q," and to the extent that it describes anything biographical, came from Jesus himself. Here we have Jesus' description of an inner experience of his own. This fact gives the stories of the three temptations an unusual quality of intimacy; there are very few expressions of Jesus' own

146

inner life surviving. These narratives also indicate the interest among the Christians of the first century in the sufferings of Jesus. As *Hebrews* 2:18 and 4:15 show, believers were zealous to point out that Jesus' experiences were in a way part of men's common life, and were real testings of character.

The temptations, together with the verse references, are as follows:

The temptation to turn stones into bread, Mt. 4:3-4, Lk. 4:3-4;

The temptation to jump off the temple, Mt. 4:5-7, Lk. 4:9-12;

The temptation to worship Satan, Mt. 4:8-10, Lk. 4:5-8.

How do the temptations tempt?

A careful reading of the two Gospel accounts should distinguish between the *content* of the narratives and the *appeal* lying in the solicitations. The problem for study is to decide in each case what made the suggestion of Satan a "temptation" to Jesus. To most of us, for example, the suggestion that we should turn stones into bread would be no temptation, no matter how hungry we might be. Such a transformation is beyond any power we ever assume for ourselves. To be tempting in any vital sense, a suggestion must in some way be possible, or be supposed to be possible, to the one entertaining it.

When we turn to the story of Jesus' temptations with this problem of "appeal" in mind, we notice in each one the assumption that Jesus is the Messiah. This is explicitly stated, in both accounts, in the temptations to turn stones into bread and to jump off the temple, the phrase "Son of God" clearly meaning "Messiah" (as in Mt. 26:63 and probably in Lk. 22:67, 70). The remaining temptation, to receive

the kingdoms of the world by worshipping Satan, is not introduced by the words "if you are the Son of God," but is
directly set on the level of Messiah's interest; the kingdoms
of the world are promised to him in the Old Testament.

Thus it may be suggested that these temptations, if they
are indeed tempting, presume some capability on Jesus'
part, or some interest in his mind about Messiahship. They
are temptations, if they test his view of Messiahship at
selected points, offering courses of action seemingly warranted by circumstances. Jesus' response in each case is to
reject the suggestion as out of harmony with a life of complete obedience to God and trust in him. It is wrong for the
Messiah, if it is wrong in principle.

As one studies these brief stories, it will be discovered that
many issues are involved. The following discussion is limited
to the *point of testing* in each case.

Stones into bread

In the temptation to turn stones into bread, the
apparent problem is Jesus' hunger. Satan's suggestion is to
use Messiahship to care for the Messiah's physical existence.
Jesus' answer, as far as it goes, is to assert that man's true
existence depends not on food alone. His argument seems
to be that in the same manner the Messiah does not depend
merely on material things. The real issue, then, is not hunger,
but the relation of the Messiah, in the fulfillment of his sense
of duty, to his own survival. May the Messiah use powers
which he had received in any other way than in carrying out
his Messianic task? Jesus' answer is in the negative. As men
should depend on God for the fullness of life, including life
in the body, so should the Messiah.

The descent from the temple

In the temptation to jump off the temple the immediate issue is uncertain. Jesus treats the suggestion as involving, if followed, a testing of God's promise in the Old Testament (*Psalms* 91:11-12). He insists that *faith* is the true basis of life. But, the question is, in what way is the proposed act of jumping a temptation to Jesus? *Why* test God? One answer could be that the testing was related to a question lurking in the mind of Jesus, "How do I really prove to myself that I am the Messiah?" If this were the issue, then the temptation was to try out a promise in the Old Testament and see if it worked.

A second suggestion is that this temptation applied to ways by which the Messiah might win men. Should he do something spectacular to make his entry and convince them? On this interpretation Satan proposes a misusing of divine promises for the Messiah's program, and again tests Jesus' view of Messiahship.

Either interpretation takes the Biblical quotation from *Psalms* 91:11-12 somewhat out of context, for in the psalm God's watchful care is promised to any man (not necessarily to the Messiah) whose life depends on God.

Worshipping Satan

In the temptation to worship Satan and so receive the kingdoms of the world, the point of difference concerns the principles by which the Messiah is to achieve his goal. Since Satan represents opposition to God, the suggestion to worship him is the suggestion to honor some other principle than that of trust in God alone. Jesus rejects it because men must honor and serve God.

What, however, makes this general truth a specific temp-

tation for Jesus? In *Matthew* there is nothing by way of
explanation, but in *Luke* the offer is expanded in what may
give a clue to the nature of the appeal. Satan says, "To you
I will give all this authority and their glory; for it has been
delivered to me, and I give it to whom I will. If you, then,
will worship me, it shall all be yours" (Lk. 4:6-7).

Whatever else these words may mean, they claim that the
world rejects trust in God in favor of rebellion against him.
The point, then, is this: is the Messiah to face this world
with the principle of obedience to God which it has already
rejected? Should he seek his success over the world by ac-
comodating himself to its standards? The tempting suggestion, therefore, lies in the prospect of immediate success,
should the tempted one become part of man's rebellion
against God.

What is the alternative prospect which, by its foreboding
quality, makes this temptation more attractive? Since the
thought of failure would be excluded by the assumption
that God intends that the Messiah shall succeed, the alternative appears to lie in experiences of delay, rejection,
and suffering on the Messiah's part. The solicitation once
again is that the Messiah take care of his own well-being
by compromising his duty to God.

If it is the case that the anticipation of suffering forms the
temptation here, Mk. 8:31-33 is a striking parallel. In the
latter passage the suggestion likewise is that the Messiah
avoid suffering. Jesus labels the speaker (Peter) "Satan,"
and rejects his plea, "for you are not on the side of God, but
of men."

In our study of Jesus' testing we have noticed that his
view of Messiahship allowed no suspension of the rule of
faith which bound his countrymen to God. His appeals to
the Scriptures are to passages which speak of *common* duty.
Rather than taking the Messiah's problems as something

apart, he seemed to insist upon a quality of obedience that avoids any reservation. Here, he seemed to say, is the Messiah's starting point. This attitude may be a little window into the progress of Jesus' personal development. It may be that *he progressed to the sense of Messianic duty from the earlier sense of filial relation to God.* In his public life he maintained his filial obligations in the difficulties of the Messianic task as he saw it. He trusted God to win the Messiah's victory through this obedience, regardless of its involvements, including his own death.

It is clear, from our study of *Mark*, that Jesus' filial view of Messiahship conflicted with popular, nationalistic hopes. In the realities of this conflict there were many moments when the appeal of these preliminary temptations reappeared. Thus these are less "The Temptation" of Jesus than they are a description of the true issues in *all* his temptations. Might it not be true to his mind to conjecture that the reason for his telling of these first struggles was to show his disciples that he had taken his position about Messiahship thoughtfully and prayerfully at the very beginning?

The possibility that Jesus shared with others his private experience of temptation makes it fruitless to ask whether *Matthew* or *Luke* preserves the true order of the temptations. The best that can be asked is, "In which order did he describe the conflicts?" Since these were experiences within the consciousness of Jesus, they had no discernible sequence in the external world. He may well enough have used both descriptive orders, neither mattering the more.

I personally believe that in studying the accounts of these experiences there is no need to objectify the figure of Satan. That is, I doubt that, could we have looked at Jesus in those moments, we should have seen *two* figures. This struggle and its conclusion, as far as the evidence of the Biblical texts is concerned, could have taken place *entirely within*

Jesus' conscious thought. Of course, this comment does not bear on the question of whether Satan is a real personal existence or not.

．．．． for further study and discussion

1. Give an event from the story in *Mark* to illustrate each of the temptations of Jesus. The point of comparison in each case should be the underlying temptation.

2. When material is available in the Gospels, compare the way in which Jesus met these later temptations with his responses in *Matthew* 4 and *Luke* 4.

XIV

The incarnate Word

*T*HE biographical testimony that remains to be considered is preserved in John's Gospel. The modern student finds himself in a perplexing position in relation to this Gospel. We may summarize the problem in a series of short sentences.

The contents of *John* are largely distinct from the Synoptics. The style of writing is different from that of the Synoptics, but it is all of a piece, words of Jesus and of the writer being indistinguishable in style.

The Gospel as a whole has less interest in biography than the others, but it gives a rather detailed outline of Jesus' movements prior to the beginning of the Galilean period.

The Gospel shows the results of long and severe meditation about Jesus, and was written to show that Jesus is the Messiah (20:30-31); yet it deals with religious issues quite different from those in the Synoptic Gospels.

One of the aims of *John* was to help the reader understand Jesus; yet at the present stage of modern study this Gospel is less useful for that purpose, at the beginning level at any rate, than *Mark* and "Q."

The date for the publication of *John* is at the end of the first century; yet there are textual evidences that parts at least of the Gospel originated within Aramaic-speaking Christianity, and presumably were written earlier in the

153

century. The text of *John* has the oldest manuscript evidence of any New Testament book; a single fragment survives which was penned between A.D. 125 and 150.

Its authorship is unknown now, yet was known and emphasized by the Christian circle which published it first (21:24).

Though an interpretation of the historical character of Jesus in *John* must seemingly wait on a solution of certain other historical problems in early Christianity, this Gospel has been more important than the Synoptics in influencing Christian piety toward the deeper spiritual life.

The upshot of these contrasts is the paradoxical situation that a Gospel written to help understand Jesus is not directly helpful for historical study, especially at the beginning stages. At the present time it is far easier to say of *John*, "This is what a group of Christians believed about Jesus in the later first century," than it is to say, "This is the way Jesus of Nazareth talked and acted at certain critical moments in his career." Many scholars, in fact, despair of extracting much biographical information from *John*. They describe Jesus in terms of *Mark* and "Q," regarding *John* as a later, theological interpretation of Jesus.

Whether this position is justified by the facts is a matter for discussion, a very difficult discussion as it happens, with many unanswered questions in it. Unfortunately, therefore, there has grown up the tendency to dismiss *John*, neglecting the fact that quite apart from *historical* matters there is a *spiritual* congruity of some sort between *John* and the other Gospels. Sincere and, I believe, perceptive Christians have felt a likeness between the figure of Jesus in *John* and in the Synoptics. This is evidence that the Fourth Gospel must be taken seriously in our search for understanding. In my own opinion it is evidence that all historical presentations of Jesus will be faulty until it is possible to include this testimony on a historical basis.

With all the facts in view, however, I prefer to start the study of Jesus with the Synoptic materials. This is the method we are following in this book. In the next two sections we shall take occasional glances at things in *John*, but we shall continue to keep the main focus on *Matthew, Mark,* and *Luke.* This will prepare us to read *John* and be able to appreciate its interpretation of Jesus, which, if I may say so, I believe to be theologically right and biographically warranted by evidence in the Synoptics.

The early Judean phase

Within the Fourth Gospel the historical interest in Jesus' career settles on his activities in Jerusalem, the conversation at the Last Supper, and selected episodes out of the first year of public activity. Since *John* is the only witness to Jesus' activities in the first months after his baptism, a brief summary of its material and a word on its relation to *Mark* is in order here.

In *John* 1-4 careful account is taken of Jesus' sojourns in both Galilee and Jerusalem. It appears that Jesus divided his time and attention between his home district (Galilee) and Judea, where the center of Jewish leadership was. If one looks at all between the lines, one gets the impression of hostility in Judea which may have caused him to center his activity in Galilee.

The series of geographical references in chapters 1-4 follows. In themselves they make sense and represent a possible situation at the very beginning as Jesus is making first contacts with his countrymen.

(1) After the baptism in southern Palestine somewhere, Jesus returns to Galilee (1:43).

(2) After a stay in Galilee (in Cana and Capernaum) he returns to Jerusalem for the Passover feast (April A.D. 27? 2:13).

(3) He leaves Jerusalem for the countryside nearby where he begins baptizing. This is mentioned in the same context with a reference to John's similar activity, implying the preaching by Jesus of repentance and judgment as well (3:22). This is prior to John's imprisonment and the beginning of Jesus' activities in Galilee (3:24 with Mk. 1:14).

(4) Jesus abandons this activity because it appears to the Pharisees to be in competition with John, and withdraws from Judea to Galilee (4:3, 43-46). As if to reinforce this display of unconcern for popular opinion, John describes his route to Galilee through non-Jewish Samaria, and his visit in a village that was completely unacceptable to orthodox Judaism (chapter 4). At this point Matthew and Luke pick up the story, describing a move from Nazareth to Capernaum and the beginning of Jesus' concentrated activity in Galilee (Mt. 4:12-13; Lk. 4:16, 31; also Mk. 1:14).

(5) In Jn. 5:1 Jesus goes to Jerusalem to an unnamed feast. If this is a Passover, then it is one year later than the feast of 2:13. Identification, however, is uncertain. There is no corresponding reference in the Synoptics, which ignore any journey south until the last one.

The period of about a year covered in these journeys and visits resulted in preliminary contacts which, it may be, prepared the situation for the widely spreading response Jesus later received in Galilee. The early, hostile reception in Judea, together with difficulties arising out of the prior appearing of John the Baptist in that area, possibly explains the location of Jesus' main activity elsewhere. The hostility itself is accounted for in the clash of viewpoint as Jesus called on the religious leadership of his time to heed his message. Thus his popular mission in Galilee followed from an informal but emphatic rejection in the south.

Jesus' message

It is probably fair to say that if *John* is not historically correct in the details of this period, then we know nothing of events between Jesus' temptation and the imprisonment of John the Baptist, nor can we estimate the length of the period. On the other hand, there is nothing intrinsically improbable about the underlying frame of narrative though the author's interest is in Jesus' teaching.

Taken from this point of view, the reference in Jn. 3:22 to Jesus' activity of preaching and baptizing is revealing. Since this seems parallel to what John was doing (v. 23), the stress of Jesus' activity, as was John's, would be on *the character of God's coming Kingdom.* If a difference is to be conjectured in this early period between the message of Jesus and that of John, we might wonder if Jesus described the *character of Messiahship,* as he had seen it in his temptation. The continuing work of John and the apparent similarity of Jesus' message to John's suggest in each a lack of stress on the Messiah's *identity,* a fact true also of the message of each in *Mark,* as we have seen.

Here, then, as elsewhere in our reading Jesus is represented as saying fundamentally:

(1) There is a new *activity* of God, the extending of his Rule to solicit the response of individuals directly to himself.

(2) The demand of God's Kingdom is for man's moral-spiritual submissiveness to God, so that God's power comes to dwell in individuals.

(3) The avenue to this new submissiveness is through one person, Jesus, who knows his own relation to God, and who, in obedience to that relationship, can assist others.

This content that we see in *John* 1-4 appears in the later discourses of Jesus in that Gospel also, but the problems raised by these long speeches are too complex for study at this point.

The Word

The Fourth Gospel begins with eighteen verses now commonly called the "Prologue." These verses describe Jesus' relation to God and the world through the use of an important philosophical term of the time, *the Word*. Jesus, according to the rhythmic prose of the Prologue, is the Word. This description is not directly mentioned elsewhere in *John* and may represent a philosophical meditation designed to associate Jesus in the minds of cultured readers with important contemporary thinking. Standing alone at the beginning of the Gospel, the Prologue seems to say that the person who walked the highways and visited in the cottages of Palestine was more than a man and to be understood more profoundly than as the Jewish Messiah, though he was truly both man and Messiah.

The philosophical meaning of the term *the Word* has a number of roots, both Jewish and Christian, which it is hard to summarize briefly and which belong to the study of John's Gospel rather than of Jesus. To call Jesus "the Word," however, is an obvious claim to understand him in terms of the philosophies that used that conception. We can see something of the meaning simply by noting the force of words in ordinary human contexts. Words are expressions of purpose; they are the vehicles by which intentions are shared and one man communicates his will to another. Therefore words have power to get things done. Words linked together voice reasons and give explanations.

Philosophical thought, of course, refined this superficial significance of the term *word*. In some discussions the Word was referred to God, and was thought of as the instrument, or possibly the agent, by which God worked in the world (e.g., Jn. 1:3). In other systems of thought the Word was the inner principle of reasonableness or purpose that held the universe together. But whatever the different philosophers meant by the Word that was at the heart of reality, the opening verses of *John* asserted that Jesus was this cosmic force incarnate in human form (v. 14). Jesus was to God what words are to men. He expressed God's purpose. He was God's power to accomplish his will. He was God's living communication with men.

Thus the Christian writer (whoever he was) who presented *John* to the Christian Church (see the veiled references in Jn. 21:24-25) wished to point to a threefold understanding of Jesus: biographical, historical, and metaphysical. That is to say that Jesus lived a natural life in Palestine, part of which he records and other parts of which were common knowledge. Jesus showed in his activities that he was the Messiah (20:30-31) and so was God's fulfillment in history of Jewish hopes and faith. But more than all else Jesus is the clue to the understanding of *all* life. All other solutions of life are partial; all valid solutions come to grand fulfillment in him.

. . . . for further study and discussion

1. As each Gospel begins the story of Jesus it connects him with some preceding person, or group of persons. Compare the association of Jesus and "the Word" in *John* with the connections described in the Synoptics.

2. Point out which associations of Jesus with others would be (or could be) acknowledged by his enemies, and which are matters of interpreting Jesus.

3. Read Jn. 12:12-13:30; 18:1-21:25. Compare this narrative with the outlines you have already prepared (Chapter XI), and make a list of events not reported elsewhere.

The teachings of Jesus

XV

Jesus the teacher

*J*ESUS was called "teacher" by friends and foes
alike. This title was based on his activities of
teaching rather than on any academic preparation or recognized position in Jewish society. After his baptism he devoted all his time to proclaiming his message about God's
Kingdom, and discussing with any who would listen the
meaning of God's truth for human lives. He was invited to
speak in the Sabbath services of synagogues in Galilee. He
attracted friends who became his pupils and accompanied
him on his travels. He publicly challenged the views of men
who by virtue of education and social position were regarded as "rabbis."

So far as we know, however, he never studied with any
of the prominent rabbis of his time. Beyond his intimate
knowledge of the Holy Scriptures he showed no sympathy
for the great body of tradition kept and handed on by Jewish teachers. In his own teaching he impressed his hearers
with his freedom from the established "schools of religion"
within Judaism (Mt. 7:28-29).

We can simplify the problem in understanding Jesus as
a teacher by discussing separately the *methods* he used in
teaching (the purpose of this chapter) and the *content* of
his teaching (Chapters XVI-XXIII). Under the first head-

163

ing belong all the devices of language and presentation by
which Jesus sought to "hook on" to the minds of his listeners. The second heading includes the subjects about
which he talked.

The discussion of his methods may be subdivided, since
it is helpful to distinguish between what was peculiar to
Jesus himself in matters of expression and ideas, and what
was in common acceptance at his time in Palestine. In his
manner of presenting his ideas he used ways of thinking
and speaking that gave him common ground with his hearers. Like his fellow countrymen he used (1) exaggerated
language, and (2) visual images for abstract thought. These
forms of expression, unusual to us, occasioned no comment
in his audiences.

Probably more noteworthy to those who listened to Jesus
was his choice of means to *illustrate* his ideas. People would
associate the use of these techniques with Jesus and use them
to recall his teachings. To be included here are (1) his illustrations drawn out of the daily life of common people;
(2) his references to the Old Testament; (3) his parables.
Jesus' use also of (4) Hebrew verse forms is probably a
device to make his teachings remembered more easily.

We may add at this point mention of (5) Jesus' use of
conversation in order to win a person's assent. Although this
is not a form of literary illustration, it is the way by which
Jesus preferred to mold men's thinking. Finally, (6) we may
mention briefly other bits of expression or ways of using
words and ideas that stuck in people's memories and were
retold as characteristic of him.

It would be mistaken, however, to assume that in describing Jesus' techniques of catching attention and communicat-
ing ideas, we had said all that was to be said about Jesus
as a teacher. It is important to notice that Jesus showed no
interest in ideas for their own sake. His techniques commonly seem designed to stir up doubts and questions rather

than allay them. He seems more concerned to persuade men
to make a decision than to educate men in understanding
facts. It is in this way that we can see a oneness between
his teaching and his message. Both put the hearer in such
a position that he must *decide* not merely whether Jesus'
words are true or false, but whether *he* is for them or against
them. This quality in Jesus' thinking which would force
decisions is the most important thing about him as a teacher.

Common speech in common ways

Jesus talked like his contemporaries when he used
exaggerated speech or visual images instead of abstract
language, and each form of expression may readily be illustrated from the Old Testament. The problem in understanding such expressions is to get at the idea within its clothing
of words, and restate it in the less vivid forms of Western
speech.

EXAGGERATED SPEECH. For example, when Jesus
says, "If anyone comes to me and does not hate his own
father and mother . . . he cannot be my disciple" (Lk.
14:26), we are probably in the presence of exaggerated
language (see also Mt. 19:11-12). Probably Jesus' meaning
is that the obligations of discipleship are so far-reaching that
life's most sacred natural relationships sink into second
place. If this interpretation seems to water down the pas-
sionate character of Jesus' words, it may be compared with
Jesus' attitude toward his mother and his brothers in Lk.
8:19-21.

Not all instances of exaggeration are as clear as this. It
is still uncertain what Jesus meant in Lk. 18:25 in reference
to the camel, a needle's eye, and a rich man. In Mt. 5:48
the words, "You, therefore, must be perfect as your heavenly
Father is perfect," are frequently taken as exaggerated language, although the present writer believes that they were

intended in the most literal sense. In such decisions there
is no easy rule to be followed. Readers will decide what
Jesus *meant* in a given case on a basis of their understanding
of his general point of view.

PICTORIAL LANGUAGE. The Semitic usage which expresses itself in pictorial rather than abstract expressions
causes more difficulty for modern readers. The sayings in
Mt. 7:1-11 illustrate the idiom. Verses 1-5 seem to deal with
humility (abstract term) in judging others, but Jesus, instead of using an abstract word for the attitude he has in
mind, *describes a specific condition* and warns against it.
Jesus' description can be "seen" or visualized as he presents
it; whereas had he used an abstract term such as *humility,*
the visual element would have come, had it appeared at all,
through the imagination of the hearer.

This analysis may be continued in the following verses.
Verse 6 seems to speak of caution in discussing religious matters. Verses 7-11 teach earnestness in prayer to God, but the
language is pictorial, "ask . . . seek . . . knock. . . ."

The principle of expression involved here is that Jesus,
*instead of using abstract terms to describe ideas or condi-
tions, presents his thoughts in language that employs visual
images.* It is important, therefore, that the modern reader
prepare himself to separate Jesus' thought from the *verbal
delineation* of it by becoming acquainted with the conditions of life at the time. This process of restating Jesus'
thought is necessary not because our way is "better" than
the ways of the ancient Jews, but because ours is a *different* inheritance derived from the ancient Greeks. Ours
is the more effective tool for expressing logical thinking
and for the analysis of ideas; the Semitic style of pictorial
expression is far more vivid and forceful. One of the very
important discoveries the student of Jesus can make is that
his thinking, within its pictorial guise, was logical in its
substance. It is to be regretted that much modern study

of Jesus, though expressing high regard for his "religious insights," has missed seeing the keenness of his intellect.

Common speech in uncommon ways

ILLUSTRATIONS FROM DAILY LIFE. Jesus' references to ways of life in his own time may obscure his meaning at first for modern readers. As a good teacher he illustrated his ideas in ways that his own hearers used and understood. His sentences are filled with references to all sorts of everyday things such as pieces of money, ways of cooking and eating, occupations, raising one's family, politics, and gossip. Intended to be illustrative, they may be quite the opposite unless the reader makes the effort to inform himself. While not every reference is easily explained, most are matters of practical fact which can readily be cleared up with a good Bible dictionary.[1]

USE OF THE OLD TESTAMENT. Jesus' references to the Old Testament sometimes are very important in interpreting his thought. It will be recalled that these writings were the sacred Scriptures of Judaism; and on their authority over human life both Jesus and his hearers agreed. Jesus differed from his hearers in the way he saw this authority in the written words. Jesus saw God working through the events recorded in the Old Testament, so that for him the Scriptures were records of God's will in action. His contemporaries, in an approach that had far different results, looked on the Old Testament as a mine of divine truth, whence they might bring to light, sometimes at great effort,

---

[1] Such as the *Westminster Dictionary of the Bible*, by H. S. Gehman (Philadelphia: Westminster Press, 1944); or Madeleine S. Miller and J. Lane Miller, *Encyclopedia of Bible Life* (New York: Harper & Brothers, third edition, 1944). Use of such tools will disclose the interesting fact that the "Good Samaritan," giving the hotel keeper two denarii (Lk. 10:35) left behind him two days' wages at going rates (Mt. 20:2). Even with a good dictionary at hand there is still need for perceptive imagination that can read about the Samaritan's donkey and see it as a business coupe!

precious help for human life. This analogy, that Jesus looked
to Scripture as to a description of God in action, and his
hearers as to a treasure mine, is an oversimplification, of
course. It has the virtue, however, of emphasizing that, for
Jesus, God was in action and had to be understood from his
acts. (These contrasting attitudes and the consequences of
them are discussed further in Chapter XVII.)

Many of Jesus' references to the Old Testament will cause
little difficulty. Many English Bibles (including the Revised Standard Version) indicate in footnotes or marginal
references the location of the important quotations and less
formal allusions. A Bible dictionary will be helpful when
names of persons or places are included. Ordinarily the *setting* within which the reference occurs should be read, since
Jesus normally quotes a text with an eye to its context. The
reader who desires help for the Biblical quotations that do
not yield their meaning by these methods will find further
material in such reference works as *The Interpreter's Bible*.[2]

In addition to the vivid and original way in which Jesus
used the Old Testament and the life about him to teach
men about God, there are three important techniques of his
which seem suited to his nature and his message: parables,
Hebrew verse forms, and interviews. The first two of these
are literary and are found in the Old Testament, parables
infrequently and verse often. The technique of the personal
interview, of course, is not a fact of literature but a way of
treating other human beings. The prominence of each of
these devices of communication shows that Jesus chose
them deliberately.

PARABLES. Without doubt the parables in the
Synoptic Gospels are the best illustrations of Jesus' thinking that we have. Usually they are brief, simple stories
drawn from everyday life. Nowhere in his recorded words

---

2 New York and Nashville: Abingdon-Cokesbury Press, 1951-54; Abingdon Press, 1954—.

is Jesus' observation sharper and his sympathy for everyday things more evident.

Jesus was a master teller of stories and used them in talking to the crowds, because they were easily remembered. They were barbed devices to fasten his points of view into the minds of the hundreds who milled around him. By a simple story he connected his view of God's work with the everyday life of everyday people, leaving them with truth to think over for long afterward.

The parables thus are *illustrations* of Jesus' point of view. They came from the practical experiences of his listeners, and were presumably self-evident to the farmers, housewives, and businessmen who heard him. The religious truths that Jesus illustrated by these references *were not self-evident,* so that it is very important to observe that *these stories are descriptive of some religious principle only because Jesus makes them so.* There is no connection, for example, between the growth of a crop from seedtime to harvest and the Kingdom of God (Mk. 4:26-29) except that Jesus says his hearers are to see in the natural process an illustration of the Kingdom.

Though Jesus used parables freely in public discussions, this fact does not always mean that we can understand them easily. It is sometimes a difficult matter for the modern reader to "get inside" the ancient illustrations and feel their bearing. Difficulty with Jesus' parables also stems from the fact that they illustrate a *message* that is hard for us to grasp. It seems also to have been difficult for Jesus' own hearers. The troublesome words in Mk. 4:11-12 make sense from this point of view. Here Jesus indicates that the parable is the form in which he clothes his message for the crowds. His message is difficult (v. 12 quoted from *Isaiah* 6:9-10), and hearers may reject it, as they rejected the prophet Isaiah. In fact, Jesus (as Isaiah) felt that rejection was inevitable; and, with sad irony, he could describe his

illustrative parables *as if spoken* to win not assent but
refusal!

In addition to this use of the parable to convey truth,
Jesus may also have used the device to conceal his meaning
from hostile ears. By speaking in this pictorial way he
avoided explicit statements upon which his enemies could
build a case against him. In Mk. 12:1-12 is a situation in
which Jesus' enemies sensed an application to themselves
and hated him for it, yet he had not laid himself directly
open to formal charges.

HEBREW VERSE. Jesus' use of Hebrew verse forms
is less apparent to the general reader than his use of parables, and less important. It is harder to illustrate because
its appearance has been changed by the process of translation, first into Greek and then into a modern tongue. It is
also less clearly poetic to us because it lacks rhyme and, in
translation, lacks metrical rhythm, too.

The principle by which Hebrew poetry was written, in
addition to rhythm, was the principle of parallelism. This
means that an idea was stated in one line and then restated
or expanded in a parallel way in the following line or lines.
The sense may be identical in the repetition (e.g., the quotation in Mt. 4:10), or the thought of the first line may be
varied by the second (Mt. 11:17; 12:18-21).

The reader will notice that the Revised Standard Version
prints poetic passages from the Old Testament in a distinct
form. This is easily done when the Hebrew form has been
preserved, for the poetry is easier to spot in Hebrew than
in English translation. The fact is, however, that a large
amount of parallelism may be seen in the words of Jesus
in our Gospels. The Revisers, for example, recognize it in
Mt. 6:9-13, though it is equally apparent in verses 19-20
and elsewhere.

As a device for teaching, the poetic form made for ease
of memorizing. In our understanding of Jesus this evidence

that he used verse shows not only his sensitivity to beauty of form but religious meaning, too. It suggests a sense of kinship with the prophetic writers of the Old Testament, whose prime concern was religious, yet who used poetry as well as prose to express their ideas. In fact, the Hebrew prophets intermingled the two forms just as Jesus did. Jesus' use of this language, then, shows the same sense of relation to the leaders of the past that he expresses in Mk. 12:1-12 and in Lk. 4:16-21.

The modern reader will understand that when Jesus or the Hebrew prophets used verse forms, the message was no less serious than when prose was the form of expression. The thought is not fanciful nor is it "poetical" (in the sense of being freed from the restraints of everyday life). It is merely expressed in a rhythmical way.

INTERVIEWS AND CONVERSATION. Jesus appears in our sources to have been as willing to talk with an individual as to speak publicly to large crowds. The recorded interviews are worthy of separate study and show the impress of his personality. His sympathy for human beings with problems appears repeatedly. He shows a readiness to meet people on their own level of interest or concern, and he must in some way have radiated an atmosphere of approachableness.

A purposeful technique for conducting interviews appears in the records. Jesus' method was to get people talking. Then he tried to lead them to think more deeply than they had thought before. As a final step he invited his questioner to make what was for him a new decision based on faith in God. Illustrations of this technique may be studied in Mk. 7:24-30; 10:17-22; Mt. 11:2-6, as well as in the extended interviews in *John*.

A single purpose runs through Jesus' interviews—he talked with men to bring them to a decision that included moral and spiritual steps. There is no sign that he was interested in debate as an intellectual pleasure. The interview was, for him, the climactic opportunity *to persuade* men to decision. For this reason he keeps his discussions in relation to actual rather than to theoretical situations. When, for example, in Mk. 10:2 the Pharisees ask his view on divorce in principle, he insists on introducing the second personal pronoun "you" (verses 3, 5). He similarly insists on treating a principle of ritual in personal relation to his questioners in Mk. 7:5-13. In Lk. 12:13-14 Jesus refuses to deal with a specific wrong on the ground that he is not a court of law. It will also be noticed that in this instance the responsible person is not present, whereas in the other two cases Jesus finds him represented in the persons of his questioners.

As we look at Jesus' use of illustrations, whether from daily life or the Bible, and study his technique for reaching men's minds, we see at least one feature common to all: he would help people "see" in order to decide; he would catch the mind in order to effect decisions in a man's personal relationships. It was his interest to provoke men to think in order that, out of a man's reflection, there might follow deliberate steps in faith, steps which also included changes in one's relations to one's fellows.

This attitude is significant. It means that though Jesus used poetic forms, he did not seek to satisfy aesthetic longings for beauty of expression. Though he told stories, he did not seek to be a story-teller. Though he loved to talk with men, he did not himself seek intellectual stimulus and satisfaction, nor did he desire to provide these for others. By his teaching he sought to lead men to new relations with God as they freely responded to his message.

OTHER WAYS OF SPEAKING. Still other recognizable ways by which Jesus seized attention and communicated ideas appear in his recorded words, although with less frequency than the foregoing. The following may be mentioned: the short, pithy saying (Lk. 9:57-62); play on words

(Mk. 8:14-21); reference to the Old Testament with the application left unstated (Mk. 12:35-37). Like the other techniques these are easily remembered and provoke reflection.

Conclusion: The aim of Jesus

Viewed in this way, our study of Jesus' teaching methods corroborates the other evidence of the Gospels about his activities. They all show that he had one purpose in life: to declare to men a new message about God's purpose (the Kingly Rule of God), to seek on men's part a willing response to God, and to explain in its manifold variety the application of the new message to all the complexities of human life. To achieve this end, Jesus had but one method, namely to appeal to the wills of his hearers, forcing them to make decisions for or against his message. He brought to the reinforcement of this "method," as devices to make the appeal, various ways of using language that would lead hearers to question, remember, and reflect.

He made this appeal also in two other ways which were psychological and emotional rather than intellectual. (1) Jesus' *message*, merely by being stated, was *an appeal to the wills of his hearers.* As we shall see in the next chapter, one of the deep hopes of the Jews was for God's Kingdom in Palestine. As a result of these national expectations his message could not be a neutral thing. The mere stating of it, that God's Rule really was present, called on men to take a stand for the speaker or against him. The emotional atmosphere surrounding Jesus, at least when he was in public, was never calm.

(2) Jesus' *life*, merely by being lived, was *a teaching device.* This is the way it looked to his followers *later,* and they recalled that he had used his own experiences as a guide for those with him (Mt. 10:24-25; Lk. 6:40; Jn. 13:13-16). It is

harder to show that *during his lifetime* his disciples understood him well enough to find guidance in his example of life. Indeed it is quite apparent that at important moments in their experience their thoughts were on themselves and their personal fortunes.

Yet it is hardly likely that men like Peter or John were completely insensitive to the winsomeness of Jesus' person. Even though we grant that their feeling of hero worship gained new theological dimensions and grip over their lives as they lived in the aftermath of his death and resurrection, it must have been present in rudimentary form during his lifetime. We may say, if we like, that Jesus' way of life was transparently consistent with his spoken words, or we may say that it had an indefinable quality that attracted many people. However we say it, we recognize that Jesus, as he was, made men wonder, drawing their thoughts to his message about God's coming Rule and so leading them to the threshold of acceptance.

. . . . for further study and discussion

The following questions illustrate points discussed in this chapter. In studying each Biblical passage state the point that is *chiefly involved*. Give another Biblical illustration of the same point drawn from your own reading.

1. What specific differences may be suggested in understanding Lk. 16:19-31 according as one understands it to be (a) a parable or (b) a straightforward historical account?

2. Compare Jesus' answer to John the Baptist (Mt. 11:4-6) with *Isaiah* 35:3-6 and 61:1 and state the implications of Jesus' words.

3. Explain Jesus' words in Mt. 10:34-36 from two points of view: (a) What does he say will be the effect of his words upon members of families? (b) What does Jesus mean when he speaks of his purpose as intended to provoke quarrels (v. 35)?

4. (a) Describe the illustration Jesus used in Lk. 12:54-56.

(b) What idea is Jesus illustrating? (c) What does he mean by "the present time" (v. 56)?

5. Read Jn. 4:3-26 and answer the following questions: (a) What does this story illustrate about Jesus' interest in people? (b) How, specifically, does Jesus influence the woman's thinking (vv. 7, 10, 13-14, 16, 21-24)? In each case state in your own words the woman's feeling about Jesus.

· · · · preparation for Chapters XVI-XXII

1. Read Lk. 4:14-19:27 and Mt. 4:12-18:35. Read each portion at a single sitting if possible.

2. Reread each of these more slowly. Jot down on seven separate sheets of paper references to words of Jesus that seem to you important in relation to these seven subjects:

(a) God's Kingdom;

(b) Man's sin and need of repentance;

(c) love (God's or man's);

(d) the calling of, and the responsibility of, disciples;

(e) family life (any aspects);

(f) prayer, sacrifice, and other acts of worship;

(g) future events.

XVI

The Kingly Rule of God

J ESUS' message about God's Kingdom [1] is the
key that unlocks his teachings. In his thinking
it is a "message" rather than a subject of instruction, because
he tells how God is beginning a new program of deliverance
among individuals. He describes this new activity and
shows its connections with earlier Jewish faith in God as
the sovereign lord of the world. He brings the "good news"
(that is, "gospel") that God is engaged in saving action.
Whereas faith in God's lordship was a subject of instruction
among teachers of religion, the Gospel was a message that
was Jesus' own.

Thus, if the modern reader would approach Jesus' religious thought from the same perspective that he held, the
beginning point is with his message about the Kingdom of
God. This is the reality that shapes his teachings and relates
them to each other. From the standpoint of the general
reader it is also enlightening to study Jesus' views about
God's Kingdom before other teachings, because we find
illustrated here with particular clarity the relation of Jesus'
thinking to that of his fellow countrymen. Furthermore,
all the points of method described in the preceding chapter
appear here.

---

[1] In *Matthew* the phrase "Kingdom of Heaven" carries the same meaning
as "Kingdom of God."

176

It must be added that the discussion of Jesus' views about the Kingdom of God includes matters of considerable difficulty on which expert students make differing judgments. It is not practicable to indicate these differences in detail, involving as they do matters of text, of history, of philosophy and religion. Our discussion proposes to show the main background of thinking in Palestine, in relation to which Jesus' words must be understood. Then we shall trace the main lines of Jesus' own thought, and indicate at the close of the chapter some of the variety of interpretation that exists.

How Jesus' hearers understood the Kingdom of God

Jesus' hearers had definite convictions about God's "Kingdom." Though a number of words or phrases were used in addition to the specific noun *kingdom,* the conception was one that bound together in a single bundle the faith, hope, and ambitions of Jews as individuals and as a religious group. It was the Jewish solution to the apparently insoluble problem of evil in human life. It furnished the clue by which history, especially future history, could be understood. It roused emotions. Because of the association of God's Kingdom with political freedom in Jewish thought, many people in Palestine in Jesus' day lived in a state of conscious anticipation. The fulfillment for which they were looking was the "coming" of God's Kingdom to be the world's dominant reality.

Jesus was aware both of the religious thinking about God's Kingdom and the widespread popular hope of what it would achieve. Though he uses many of the common words and ideas, he revises the thinking and largely rejects the prospective hope in its local, Palestinian form. To understand him we need to be clear as to what these convictions were, *and the ways in which they were expressed.* We may organize our study around three points:

(1) the meaning of the term *Kingdom;*
(2) the hope of the Kingdom;
(3) distortions of the Hope of the Kingdom.

THE MEANING OF THE TERM *Kingdom.* Primarily the Hebrew and Aramaic words mean "kingly power in action." God's "Kingdom" was the proper and characteristic activity of a king. The best translation seems to be "kingly rule" or perhaps simply "rule," but in the phrase "Kingly Rule of God" ("Kingdom of God") the word "God" is the important one. His Rule is his own ruling activity.

The kingly activity of God was specified in various ways in the Old Testament. He is spoken of as ruling the world of nature, for he was the creator and the one who controlled all natural phenomena. He ruled over the spiritual forces of the universe, being the only God whom men should worship. Especially he ruled in the affairs of the Hebrew nation. He had brought it into existence. He had kept it alive in the physical and national sense. More than this, he had given it its spiritual life, making it possible for frail, sinful men to find hope and satisfaction (see *Psalms* 103 or *1 Chronicles* 29:10-16 for examples). From the Old Testament point of view, therefore, the significant thing about God's Kingly Rule is that *he rules in order to do good to men by satisfying the needs of their lives.*

Out of this primary sense of *kingdom* as "kingly rule" there followed two natural applications of the same Hebrew-Aramaic word to the *effects* of the rule. Since in the nature of things a king hardly rules without subjects, his people who are *the ruled* may be spoken of as his "kingdom." (In *Revelation* 1:6 the subjects are directly called a "kingdom," and the meaning of "kingdom" in Mt. 8:11; 11:11; 13:43; 18:1; or Mk. 9:1(?) seems to have rather the ruled than the

Rule directly in view.) When the effects of the Rule are taken as a whole the word *kingdom* may refer to the *realm* or *sphere of the rule* (Mk. 3:24; 6:23; 13:8 or the figure of speech involved in the phrase "enter the Kingdom"). In many cases it is very difficult to say which of these three senses of the term *kingly rule* is chiefly in view, but apparent confusions in the Gospels will evaporate when this variety of meaning is kept in mind.

The reader will notice that the English word *kingdom* conveys only the third sense of "realm." Accordingly, it is necessary in reading Jesus' words in most English translations to make the mental substitution of the phrase "kingly rule" or occasionally "the subjects of the rule," in many cases in which the eye sees "kingdom."

In the words of Jesus' questioners the "Kingdom of God" was specially limited to God's activities toward the Jewish nation. This usage came from the Old Testament and is described in the next section. According to it the *ruled* are limited to the Jews and the Jewish nation is God's realm.

THE HOPE OF THE KINGDOM. The past, present, and future are implicit in the meaning of God's Rule. Jewish faith saw descriptions of God's *past* activity in the Holy Scriptures where are accounts of his creative and guiding power. In the *present* his Rule could be seen in the lives of those who obeyed his Law. God as ruler in nature was not denied, far from it, nor his power over Gentile peoples questioned; but it was more important that he had given his Law to Moses and established his sway in human relations among the descendants of Abraham.

The main point of interest, however, in the first century, and for some centuries previously, lay in what God meant to do in the *future*. There were several motives behind this concern. Faith in God, for one, yearned to see his righteous will vindicated and evil destroyed from among men. It was clear that his goodness was not yet established and so in a real sense his Kingdom had not yet "come." More than this, the Jewish nation had lived since the sixth century before Christ under various oppressors and had learned to dream of freedom and fulfillment when God would establish his Rule. Not to be minimized either is the incorrigible curiosity of man's spirit that asks about future events, and sometimes insists on black and white answers when none are rationally possible. In Jesus' day all these factors—religious yearning, personal need, and intellectual curiosity—were at work and can be seen reflected in the Gospels.

For the Judaism of Jesus' day, the basic statements about God's purposes were, of course, the words of the Old Testament. It should be added, however, that certain Jewish groups held the original conceptions of the prophets in modified form. In the prophetic literature itself the pictures of God's Rule were set down in relation to his way of dealing with Jewish (Hebrew) violations of his Law. The prophets pleaded with the nation to return to God's right way. They warned of the certainty of divine judgment if men rebelled against God, but described with equal certainty God's purpose to bless mankind and establish conditions of righteousness and fullness of life. Thus there were a number of elements in the prophets' messages: words of warning, and of judgment; assurances of blessing, and prosperity. About the Kingdom itself the following points were emphasized: (1) The coming Rule will rest on God's initiative; he will "bring" it. (2) It will be for human good. (3) It will satisfy the national significance of the Hebrews and yet be universal. (4) It may be described in terms of an unbelievable harmony and productivity in nature.

The following quotations, out of many that could be made, show both the spirit of the prophetic hope and form of expression that was used.

Amos, about 850 B.C., wrote:

"Behold, the eyes of the Lord GOD are upon the sinful kingdom,
     and I will destroy it from the surface of the ground;
     except that I will not utterly destroy the house of Jacob,"
                                        says the LORD.
                                             Amos 9:8-9

A later prophet wrote:

Break forth together into singing,
     you waste places of Jerusalem;
for the LORD has comforted his people,
     he has redeemed Jerusalem.
The LORD has bared his holy arm
     before the eyes of all the nations;
and all the ends of the earth shall see
     the salvation of our God.
                                        Isaiah 52:9-10

The prophets described in pictorial detail the blessings
of God's future Rule. The prophet Jeremiah said:

They shall come and sing aloud on the height of Zion,
     and they shall be radiant over the goodness of the LORD,
over the grain, the wine, and the oil,
     and over the young of the flock and the herd;
their life shall be like a watered garden,
     and they shall languish no more.
                                        Jeremiah 31:12

Isaiah 35, which begins:

The wilderness and the dry land shall be glad,
     the desert shall rejoice and blossom;
like the crocus it shall blossom abundantly,
     and rejoice with joy and singing . . .

should be read in its entirety.

Modern readers differ in the meaning they get from the
Hebrew prophets' words about the future. These differences
arise many times from a neglect of basic ideas and problems

in the writings. Since these issues reappear in the teachings of Jesus, let us summarize them briefly.

First, the prophets wrote about the future in *general terms* and dealt with *principles* that operate in human affairs. They described in broad outline what it would mean to obey God, and what it would mean to disobey him. They were preachers, however, rather than predictors. Though on occasion they became quite specific about future events, they usually did not set dates or prepare time schedules.

Second, much of what the prophets said had a *conditional element* in it. According to them both the warning and the blessings were certain, as far as God went, and yet they were both influenced by man's responses. These Hebrew thinkers presented God as accomplishing his sovereign purposes in the future notwithstanding this conditional element. If the Hebrews persisted in sinning against God, warned the prophet, God would punish them. If they repented and turned to God, he would bless them beyond measure and mankind through them.

Third, the prophets faced the difficult question of eschatology, namely, *the whole understanding of the future of the world and the relation of worldly history to God's ultimate Rule.* It is possible to hold the view that they expected the full realization of God's plan to develop *within* the progress of unfolding history of this planet (where, it will be remembered, God is at work). In this way of thinking the End of history toward which the prophets looked would be the *goal* of history.

My own feeling, however, is that in the faith of the Hebrew prophets about God's Rule there is an element that *reaches beyond this world.* This reach of faith certainly grew in Judaism after the Babylonian Exile, but when, for example, earlier prophets talk about the state of man's *unending obedience* to God, it seems as if they have faith in some *fundamental change in the nature of historical life.* I believe, therefore, that they looked for a climactic ending of all history as an act of God from the outside, an act that gathered together the hopes and goals of history and made them possible as the real nature of life in this world never could do. In this case the End is the *terminus* for history. Although it is the goal toward which historical life is directed, it comes itself from "beyond history."

Fourth, for a number of reasons I believe that the prophets' descriptions of God's Rule are by nature *figurative* rather than literal in intent. This view does not mean that we cut in size the meaning of the writers; it means rather that we regard them as describing in all the wealth of man's imagination the wonderful character of God's saving purposes.

This point of view means that when the prophets sought to describe the eschatological future, speaking as they did, not from knowledge of it but on a basis of trust in God, they used *symbols.* That is, they talked about the new kind of life by using the language of earthly life. They drew illustrations from agriculture, social relations, religion, and politics to explain aspects of the non-earthly, non-historical nature of the End. *They asserted the faith that some such meanings as these realities stand for here are to be found in the Rule of God in the future.*

We should notice carefully that eschatological descriptions *must* have this symbolic character simply because they reach beyond the kind of experience we know anything about. For example, unending fire is a familiar eschatological symbol for suffering beyond death. In our historical life "fire" refers to a definite process of combustion, and there is nothing that burns and yet remains unburnt. In eschatological contexts, of course, no process of combustion is intended. The word *fire* has been separated from its relations in nature, and only its painful, destroying quality is in view in the symbol.

This illustration also suggests the inadequacy of all symbols. Although they express faith and describe the hope that faith holds, they never measure up to the reality that faith foresees. The symbol never fully conveys the symbolized reality because it is drawn from this historical order and the latter is part of God's heavenly order.

This limitation is true of the word *kingdom*, which we are discussing in this chapter. It, too, is a symbol. It describes God's relation to this world by drawing on certain powerful realities within it. The ultimate meaning of "kingdom," however, is fixed by the dimensions of God's purpose rather than by the limits of the human authority that forms the symbol.

Let us summarize our discussion of God's Rule as the Hebrew prophets saw it. God's purpose is to establish the kind of life among men that is righteous and fully obedient to himself. It will satisfy the longings of all his creatures. He punishes his people by suffering and national loss when they sin against him, but the hope remains that he will bless them when they turn back to him. God shall achieve his purposes and man's rebelling shall be destroyed. The goal of world history blends into its terminus and into a gathering-up of historical life into the eternal order.

DISTORTION OF THE HOPE OF THE KINGDOM. The prophetic descriptions of the future, with their rather simple outline of coming events, were open to a natural process of expansion and application in the religious life of the Jews. For our understanding of Jesus the most important development is that which is called "apocalypticism." The term means "unveiling," and refers to the specific aim of apocalyptic thinking to unveil future events, particularly those attendant upon the End of world history. We need to look at this trend within Jewish religion because extreme forms of it were popular in Jesus' own day, furnishing a point of view against which many of his words were slanted. Though in general he followed the simpler eschatological faith of the prophets and used prophetic symbols, apocalypticism was pervasive enough for him to use some of its symbolic vocabulary also.

Essentially, apocalypticism distorted prophetic eschatology by changing the emphasis and exaggerating the hope for material prosperity and Jewish national power.

For example, apocalypticism emphasized the acts of God in bringing evil men to heel and history to its close. The paradoxical fact that God is acting *within* historical life as well as "beyond" it is lost sight of, or minimized.

As a consequence of this conception of God, apocalypticism created a sense of separation between men's daily lives and God's eschatological purposes. Many orthodox Jews were waiting in Jesus' day for God to act to introduce his ultimate Rule. They hoped this climax to history would be in their lifetimes. They hoped that they would be the beneficiaries in a benevolent program due to come. The emphasis thus shifted from the prophetic *warning* about what God would do to the two classes of men that apocalypticism recognized: those who obeyed and those who rebelled.

This form of thinking about the future, therefore, often became a dogmatic philosophy of history instead of an expression of faith in God's purposes. It showed the tendency to bring the various eschatological symbols of the prophets into a fixed program, dated by the historical calendar. It tried to draw what was eschatologically *beyond* history (according to the prophets) within the range of history. The various challenges to Jesus to prove his Messiahship illustrate this desire, as do the questions in Mk. 13:4 or *Acts* 1:6, or the warnings in Lk. 17:20-21.

One way of describing the result of apocalyptic thought is to say that it organized the warnings and encouragements of the prophets into a system which men believed they could understand. Though it was felt that God would at the End act from "beyond history," the aim of the expert of this sort was to explain God's designs beforehand according to the intellectual tools of men within history (for example, Mk. 12:18-23).

Due to the wide range of Biblical interpretation and theological speculation in Judaism, there was no single and widely accepted picture of God's future Rule. Hopes, however, were keen. Men looked for the appearing of a Messiah with worldly power who would make Jerusalem his capital, reward Jews handsomely, and subjugate the Gentiles. They looked forward to the eschatological happenings of the resurrection of the dead and the final judgment. They circulated descriptions of these events together with predictions about the kind of history that would intervene before the End, the date of which they tried to set. Through all this there was little of the prophetic sense of awe and humility as men contemplated the unveiling of the mighty works of God.

Jesus' message

In the history of Christianity there have been many interpretations of Jesus' teaching about God's Kingdom. This variety is due to a number of factors. As we have already seen, the subject includes the difficult conception of the End of history and the nature of the End. There is likewise a long Jewish tradition behind Jesus' teaching, and this may be interpreted in a number of ways that directly influence one's understanding of Jesus. When we turn to the words of Jesus, there are differing opinions about the way in which he read the teaching of the past, and differing judgments about which words in the Gospels show his eschatological thinking and which represent the faith and experiences of his followers. A further element of uncertainty also creeps into the discussion through the presence of a small number of sayings of Jesus which, though seemingly significant, are certainly obscure (e.g., Mt. 10:23; Mk. 9:1, 49; 13:30; Lk. 12:49-50).

The following description, though differing at some points from conventional Christian understanding of Jesus, gives the main drift of interpretations widely held by Protestant scholars. I indicate some important variations of opinion at the end of the chapter.

As an outline summary of Jesus' teaching we may say this: *God's Rule is his gracious activity in* (1) *realizing his ultimate purposes for his creation by* (2) *seeking and establishing a complete relationship between individuals and himself with* (3) *resulting effects—moral and spiritual, cosmic, and historical.*

(1) Jesus' message was that God was in action to accomplish for men all that he ever intends to do for them. This activity is his Rule. The pattern for God's intention was already set in the Old Testament. In application it involved freeing mankind from the consequences of sin, sickness, suffering, and death (Lk. 4:16-21 or Mt. 11:5). This means that in Jesus' eyes the miracles of healing were the direct expressions of God's Rule in men's lives. They were "signs," as they are called in *John,* because they show God's goodness and power to rule.

The Old Testament prophets, however, made clear that God's action in establishing his Rule was eschatological rather than historical *in quality.* I myself believe that Jesus held the same conviction. The power of God's Rule comes about because God is "coming" to, or bringing his Rule into, the stream of human, historical life. Men "enter" but do not "bring in" or "build" God's Kingdom. Its benefits are not the creation of history, either through natural causes or through men's choices alone.

Another way of describing God's activity is to say that

God is acting to establish in the lives of men the same condition of harmony between his historical creatures and himself that exists *outside* history between himself and the rest of his creation. The form of the Lord's Prayer in Mt. 6:10 states this explicitly: "Thy kingdom come, Thy will be done, On earth as it is in heaven."

In either form of speaking let us notice the need for using symbolic language. Jesus' faith was that *because God was acting*, men could find the fullness of life the prophets described. When, however, we speak of that divine activity, we are trying to describe non-historical realities in historical terms. The "coming" of God's Kingdom is symbolic language, as one can see if he tries to explain what the action of "coming" means, taken strictly by itself. The related phrase "to enter the Kingdom" is symbolic also. Though a different symbol, it may not differ greatly from the other, in its eschatological bearings. Either symbol speaks of God's power newly made available to men. Jesus' message was that God is realizing his purpose.

(2) What is that purpose? Jesus stressed the message that God's purpose is to bring men, as individuals, into personal relationship with himself. We have seen this emphasis already in our biographical study. Jesus appealed to his hearers to repent as individuals and wholeheartedly accept God's will. What this meant in detail we shall consider in the following chapters as we deal with Jesus' ethical teachings. We shall turn to these topics, however, in the right perspective, if we remember that Jesus solves the needs of human life, and describes our duties, in terms of permanent, personal relations between God and individuals. God is reigning when these relationships are right.

This emphasis on personal relations between men and God differed greatly from popular Jewish hopes about the Kingdom. Contrary to expectation, Jesus did not associate God's Rule with an increase in material prosperity, and solemnly warned against a dependence on money (Mk. 10:23-27; Lk. 12:15). He had no place in his thinking for the use of force by those who offered his message of the Rule. Men must receive it voluntarily.

There is a similar absence of any interest in Jewish national advantage of any political sort. Jesus did indeed see a need on the part of the nation, which he proposed to meet (Mt. 10:6), and gave this precedence (Mt. 10:5; Mk. 7:24-30), but not sole concern (the probable meaning of the parables in Mk. 12:1-11 and Lk. 14:15-24).

In matters of eschatology, Jesus shows little interest in programing events *beyond* history. Here there is scholarly uncertainty about the texts. Mt. 25:31-46 comes closest to providing a schedule of eschatological events, but even if it be taken as genuine (as it often is not), its main point is quite different. In this passage Jesus is not interested in eschatological events as such, but in the *character* of earthly life and its long-range consequences. *Mark* 13, which uses considerable apocalyptic (or eschatological) language, deals strictly with history up to the End, not with what lies beyond. The same general comment applies to parables of processes of various sorts. They bring the hearer through history to the End, and point to some eschatological consequence. They do not, however, portray interrelationships beyond history. Here again the genuineness of individual passages will be questioned.

Thus at the critical points of apocalyptic interest (material abundance, national advantage, and literalistic description) Jesus rejected the usual interpretations of God's purpose in favor of the conviction that *all other eschatological symbols must be understood in dependence on the fact that God's Rule means men may be directly related to God.*

This attitude is illustrated in Jesus' biography in the account of the temptation (Mt. 4, Lk. 4). In this episode

Satan tempts Jesus with symbols of various sorts connected
with the Messiah, each of which Jesus counters by insisting
on the Messiah's basic relation of trusting obedience to God.
Sensing this relationship, Jesus could think of the Messiah
(as we have seen) quite differently from the attitude of his
contemporaries, and yet quote the same Old Testament texts
they quoted. He could clearly see that suffering and death
were to be part of the Messiah's experience because of the
inevitable conflict between God's purpose and the wills of
sinful men. He could combine this in his thinking with faith
in the Messiah's triumph (using appropriate symbols) because he trusted in God's purpose to triumph over evil.

The priority of the personal relation to God over other
eschatological symbols is apparent in the first part of the
Lord's Prayer. Jesus taught that the proper form of prayer
is, "Our Father who art in heaven, Hallowed be thy name.
Thy kingdom come. . . ." Both *Father* and *Kingdom* are
symbolic expressions; but the former is of personal relationship, the latter, of will in action. Had Jesus taught instead,
"Our King . . . thy fatherhood come," he would have meant
that men must first subject themselves to God's arbitrary will,
and then seek to grow into a relation of love. In reality, he
meant that because his followers are related to God in dependence and love, they wish to see his will done completely
in all life.

(3) We can trace a number of effects that Jesus associates
with this new relation between men and God.

Some of these are *moral and spiritual.* Jesus taught a re-
interpretation of the meaning of God's Law according to its
inner purpose (see Chapters XVII and XVIII). He held that
the new relationship clarified but did not change basic principles in the Old Testament. He stressed the practice of
humility for himself and his followers (Mk. 10:42-45) in
contrast with popular expectations about the Messiah (e.g.,

v. 37). In his own activity he showed his humility by the
company he kept. He avoided the use of the term *Messiah*.
He carried out with extreme deliberation a Messianic symbol that expressed humility rather than pomp (Mk. 11:1-10
with *Zechariah* 9:9). In connection with his followers, some
of his best known sentences deal with the duty of humility
on the part of those under God's Rule. For example, vital
relation to it requires the humble trust of a child (Mk. 10:13-
16). It is intended for the unlovely and the needy (Mt. 5:3;
11:28-30; Mk. 2:17; Lk. 19:10). Neither wealth nor religious
station is sufficient (Mt. 5:20; Mk. 10:23).

There are a number of references to the need for self-
denial, and solemn warnings of persecution for those who
accept the Rule. There are explicit statements, though the
history of the first century shows that Jesus laid no major
stress here, that non-Jews were to be part of the Rule (Mt.
5:14?; 8:11-12; Mk. 12:9? [see the expansion of the idea in
Mt. 21:43]; Lk. 13:28-30; 14:15-24. Mt. 28:19-20 belongs
here, but its genuineness is frequently challenged.).

Jesus also emphasized *personal spiritual power*. He cites
his miracles, as we noted, as evidences of God's Rule. He
probably included his followers in this release of spiritual
force in such a saying as Mk. 11:23. This is the way his first
followers understood him (Lk. 11:13 in comparison with
Mk. 11:24 and Mt. 7:11); but the presence of Mk. 11:25 in
just this connection reminds us that Jesus had in view a *new
kind of spiritual vitality which comes out of a right relation
with God*. This could be said in another equally important
way: in the new relationship under God's Rule men receive
power to live up to the obligations the Rule lays on them.

Jesus also thought of the results of the Rule as reaching
out *beyond* the sphere of human life. An appropriate term
to describe these effects is *cosmic*. They are an integral part
of God's eschatological purpose. For example, references to

Satan and his defeat (as Lk. 10:17-18; 11:20) are symbolic
of the power of God's Rule beyond human kind, but it is
difficult to say exactly what Jesus meant.

We should group here the references to Jesus' suffering
and death. Mk. 9:12 or Lk. 12:49-50 seem to refer to conditions among men in the light of some larger scheme of
things. Mk. 10:45 certainly does so; Jesus speaks of his death
as answering the basic question, "How can men's sins be
atoned for?"

Jesus' sense of the importance of suffering (based on
Isaiah 53, at least in part) leads to profound problems, especially in suggesting that he saw some organic connection
between historical life and the eschatological order, and between his death on the one hand and God's eternal order
on the other. Could it be that Jesus avoided the language of
sacrifice in his public teaching about the Messiah because
he felt that sacrifices were symbols, and there was something
about his death that was not symbolic? This question is not
intended to deny the symbolism of sacrifice which his followers came to use freely about him, but the point is that
there runs through Jesus' words about his suffering a sense
of larger purpose. In some degree this seems to be true also
of the sufferings of his followers (Mk. 8:34-38), but Jesus
held a paradoxical faith: through suffering and death he
could achieve the triumph of God's purpose. Thus God
through his Rule in history is in some way reaching beyond
history.

This is likewise a discussion that is directly affected by
particular sentences in the Gospels we accept as coming
from Jesus.

A third result of God's Rule applies to the historical process
itself. Jesus' teaching is clear on this point: God's Rule is
master over historical life in the long run, and so may be
spoken of as having *historical* results as it has moral and
cosmic ones. The big question here is, "How did Jesus con-

nect developing historical events with the Rule of God? How did he connect the End of history with God's Rule?" The following paragraphs give the main points of the answer.

We can be quite sure of Jesus' general teaching that men should live trusting God's goodness and his final triumph. We can also be reasonably sure of some of his attitudes toward historical life. Other things he thought may have slipped beyond recall; and on many questions about events in the future, he may have refused to say anything.

Apparently Jesus foresaw conflict between those who accepted the Rule and those who denied it. Discipleship spelled suffering as long as man's life held its dual relation to God's Rule *and* the historical order (Mk. 10:29-31).

Probably Jesus was pessimistic about the inner character of history. He never taught that men by themselves can achieve the qualities of life that God bestows eschatologically. He saw no direct line of progress from man's history into the eternal order. He held that men, unaided, can never set up God's Rule. Those who respond to it shall always encounter opposition to the full expression of that Rule within human life. There is, therefore, something about the quality of human life that alienates it from God's Rule. In Jesus' view, it is just this alienation that God proposes to overcome.

Whether Jesus believed that human life in history would grow worse is uncertain. Our knowledge depends upon the genuineness of a small number of sentences. It seems not to have been particularly significant to him, because man's need of God was clear anyhow. Seeing the need, Jesus proclaimed that the Old Testament symbols about God's Rule had valid meaning. Men could have as a gift from God the life they needed and could not find.

Jesus spoke about the End itself in symbolic language, specifically disclaiming knowledge as to when (in terms of

history) it would take place (Mk. 13:32). He used Old
Testament symbolism in reference to coming events, but
interested himself principally in the problems of historical
men living in the prospect of the End and already under
the Rule.

Among the symbols that Jesus used, the following occur
a number of times in the Gospels: the coming of the Messiah (Son of Man); the coming of the Kingdom; the resurrection of the dead (*resurrection* meaning originally "rising
up" or "standing up"); the Judgment (with various details);
scenes in the "Kingdom of God" (the non-historical order).
When we refer to these terms as *symbols*, it is not their
reality we question but their comprehensibility. Jesus affirms
the reality; he refrains from talk about "when," "where," or
"how" in terms of history.

His message was that the prophets were right in seeing
the God of the Hebrews as the Lord of history. God, he declared, had taken a new step *within* history. He was bringing
his power to bear on the lives of men *individually* to over-
rule everything that spoils life. He invited men to accept
God's Rule voluntarily and, although maintaining obedience to God's loving purpose, join in his struggle against
evil. To live under the Rule is to accept the principles and
the power that shall make the long future, because God is
to conquer all evil and fulfill his purposes for human life.

In this summary of Jesus' message about God's Rule in
history, I have omitted one topic completely: the destiny
of individuals, as individuals. We shall take this up in Chapter XXIII. I may anticipate questions here by saying that
Jesus does not speak of individual death as the transition
from history to the life beyond history. Neither does he
pessimistically refer to physical death as an escape from the
historical life to the eternal order. Some readers may see a
gap here in the words of Jesus, as they have been preserved.

Is this an omission of what could have been said but was not remembered? Or does it represent the "edge" of historical life, where rational description ceases and symbolic language must take over? In any case, in the surviving texts, Jesus linked death with history and resurrection with eschatological life, making little or no effort to bridge the gap (whatever it may be) between death and history on the one side, and resurrection and the eternal order on the other.

Other ways of understanding Jesus' meaning

In the preceding discussion I have kept to the main lines of interpreting Jesus' words about the Kingdom as modern historical scholarship traces them. Naturally there is not now, nor has there been in the past, universal agreement among Christians either on the main points of the teaching, or on its meaning for human life. Though it is not desirable to describe the variety of viewpoints here, let me list several typical ones to show what the directions for thinking are.

(1) Traditional Christian theology has done a number of things with Jesus' words. Some forms of Christian thought have followed Jewish apocalypses rather closely, speaking of a literal, historical reign of Christ in Jerusalem, and arranging the other eschatological symbols in a "chronological" sequence. Suffice it to say that this arranging has been done on other grounds than the Gospel texts.

Some forms of Christian thought have missed the eschatological significance of Jesus' teaching entirely. As a result, the Rule of God has been limited to the sense of "realm" or the "subjects of the realm," and equated with the Christian group as a whole, or with some particular denomination. In the last century, under the influence of evolutionary forms of thought, the Kingdom of God was thought of as the grand goal to which God's purpose moved by its own inherent laws.

(2) A development out of Christian theology, but expressing human ideals and aspirations rather than theological thought, is the attempt to link God's Rule with a perfectly ordered state of human society. The Kingdom of God thus was transformed into the kingdom of man.

(3) Modern research with its reemphasis on the eschatological in Jesus' thinking has led to views more extreme than the general position described here. It has been held, for example, that Jesus expected the immediate End to history, and died cruelly disappointed when it did not take place.

Another view, known now as "realized eschatology," holds that Jesus taught the fulfillment of the eschatological hopes and blessings through his own experience of resurrection, and the lives of his immediate followers. He did not anticipate, it is held, the long centuries of church life.

There are variations of either of these views, the general effect of which is to make Jesus extremely apocalyptic in his teaching.

Conclusion

There is no way of avoiding this long and detailed discussion of God's Kingly Rule, if we purpose to understand Jesus' thinking. Perhaps some readers have, or will come to, conclusions different from those I have stated here. If so, may I suggest two steps that are commonly helpful in gaining understanding. First, when we find differences in ideas, it is always helpful to be able to describe these differences accurately. Second, it is always helpful to be able to state specifically the nature of our own (and the other fellow's) basic faith about life, and the principles of reasoning that convince us. For intellectual stimulation, especially when our own beliefs and thinking are involved, it is more important to know *why conclusions differ* than it is to know *that they do differ.*

For my own part I put the essence of Jesus' teaching this way: God's purpose for men is good; God's Rule is God in action to give men the fullest possible life in ways that go beyond both the resources and the limits of world life.

. . . . for further study and discussion

Reread the references you collected on God's Kingdom and draw on them in preparing answers to the following questions.

1. What did Jesus think about the *beginning* of God's Rule among men in the light of the following references: Mt. 11:2-6, 12; Mk. 1:14-15; Lk. 4:16-21; 10:9; 11:20; 16:16; 17:20-21?

2. What did Jesus think about the *process* of God's Rule among men in the light of the following references: Mt. 13; Mk. 4:2-9, 14-20?

3. Consider Mt. 5-7 (Sermon on the Mount) from the particular point of view of how men should live in relation to God's Rule. The discussion could group the materials under the following points which provide a rough outline for the sermon:

(a) Ideals of the Rule
(b) Standards of the Rule
(c) Practices of life under the Rule
(d) Difficulties to be faced

4. How does Jesus seem to *relate himself* to the Rule of God in the following references: Mk. 10:45; 11:15-17; Lk. 12:32; 17:20-21?

5. Discuss the question, "Where did Jesus get his knowledge of God's Rule?" The following is a suggested outline for this discussion.

(a) Give various theoretically possible sources for Jesus' knowledge. (Be sure to include suggestions of non-religious as well as religious thinking.)
(b) Test each of these possibilities by the Biblical references above and in this chapter.
(c) What view do you think Jesus held? What is your evidence for your conclusion?

XVII

Sin and repentance

J ESUS' daily difficulty lay in the resistance of men and women to God's Rule. His words show an anxiety that the people with whom he talked obey the laws of the Old Testament. To fail to obey the Law was sin. Beyond this concern that men obey God, Jesus talked about the new possibility to be found in relation to God's Rule. When life was tested by the standards of the old laws and found lacking in any way, then the message about the Rule became relevant. Sins are defined by the Law; sinners are saved by the Rule.

Repentance is the attitude of people by which they relate themselves to God's Rule. The Aramaic word Jesus probably used meant simply "to return." This was a standard term in Jewish religion carrying the meaning that the Jewish people had wandered away from God's path, and were invited by the prophet to come back to God's will and way. Jesus used it as the prophets did, but gave it a new vitality in his teaching about God's program. When men "returned" to the will of God that they already knew, that is, when they sincerely confessed their sins and sought to rebuild their lives according to what they knew, they met a new power and reality because God's Rule was *present* (Mk. 1:15; Lk. 11:20; 17:21). This is Jesus' meaning in Mt. 11:28-30, the word *yoke* being a recognized term descriptive of the Jewish

198

Law. Jesus, speaking from the perspective of the Kingdom, invites men who are heavy-laden (i.e., by the obligations of the Law) to find relief in a new way, the Rule of God.

The modern reader may find Jesus' thought hard to follow for several reasons, which we have already discussed in principle. One reason is his insistence that wrongdoing is a matter of the heart as well as the life. This is not necessarily an accepted principle today. Secondly, he seems to hold that God's claims to moral obedience are more rigorous than human nature at its best can attain. This conception is difficult on several counts. Third, he expresses himself in vivid images and parables more frequently than by abstract and technical terms. The language of Mt. 17:17-20, for example, is more characteristic of Jesus than that of Mk. 7:20-23. Finally, his discourses with his countrymen on moral matters are never very far distant from the ancient Law of Moses.

How Jesus' hearers understood sin

Circumstances in Palestine obliged Jesus to develop his description of human sin by reference to the Law codes of the Old Testament. This gave him many points of contact with his hearers. As they heard his words they found much with which they felt completely at home. In the interview with an unnamed man in Mk. 10:17-22, the two agreed that in describing a good moral life the Old Testament Law is the standard for reference (vv. 19-20). Jesus and his hearers similarly agreed in turning to Holy Scripture when defining basic principles of conduct (Mk. 12:28-34 or Lk. 10:25-28). He agreed with current opinion about the *authority* of the Law of Moses over men (*Mark* 7, note the several ways of referring to the Old Testament text in verses 9, 10, 13). Sin, therefore, was any failure to keep the prescribed Law.

Jesus and his hearers also agreed that men *ought* to keep

the Law. The practical question, however, came up: "What does it mean to 'keep the Law'?"

Jesus' hearers understood that keeping the Law meant to obey it in all particulars. This seemed an obvious and natural assumption. Perceptive minds, indeed, understood that within the Law there were degrees of importance (e.g., Mk. 12:28-34); but the assumption was that the differences in the Law were differences of *degree* and that the minute details of life were just as significant as murder or large-scale robbery, or the principle of love. This attitude is reflected in Jesus' critical words preserved in Mt. 23:23-24 and Lk. 11:42.

The result of this approach to moral discussion was that an important group of Jews in Jesus' day defined a man's relation to God in terms of his relation to the laws. When the legal side was taken care of, that was all there was. Out of this way of thinking, the important religious issue had come to be between man and the Law of Moses rather than between man and his God. God, of course, was *behind* the Law—but therein lay the key fact: *man dealt first of all with the Law.* He went to it as to a mine of truth, to dig out help in guiding all details of conduct and faith.

This attitude of regard for the Law which makes it the direct object of a man's concern may be called "legalistic." Jesus, in his famous parable of the Pharisee and the tax collector (Lk. 18:9-14), contrasts the legalistic emphasis with the attitude that is concerned for the God who is back of the Law. The penitent tax collector had read the Law as well as the Pharisee. The result, however, was that by the Law he saw that he had erred in relation to God. By confession he sought God's mercy.

It was out of the *legal* emphasis that the various efforts to find loopholes in the Law arose. The pious man of Jesus' day sincerely wished to know what the Law required and did not require. Since the Law forbade work on the Sabbath, for example, the problem was to define what was work and what was not work. The less sincere person, in a universal piece of human self-interest, likewise wished to stay within the Law, but only in order that he might serve his own advantage. In Mk. 7:9-13 Jesus cites a case of exploiting a legal situation. The meaning seems to be that a man could claim that all his property was "Corban" that is, *dedicated* to God. Since it was "dedicated" it was, therefore, not available to help one's parents. Of course, it is assumed here that the man in the illustration, though refusing to help his needy parents, is enjoying his "dedicated" property himself.

Jesus' message

(1) Jesus started with the plea to "repent" (Mk. 1:14-15). His meaning included such feelings as regret and remorse, but his language went deeper than that. As the word had been used by the Hebrew prophets and by John the Baptist, the sense was an appeal to Jews to return to the will and way of God, which by sinning they had left.

(2) Jesus frequently used illustrations involving the experience of being lost, that is, separated from the right way or the right place. His immediate solution to the problem of being lost was to return to the way of God (e.g., Mk. 1:14-15). But since this return might be beyond the capabilities of the one "lost," Jesus pictured himself as a seeker of the lost.

It appears from Jesus' words that all men are "lost" in the religious sense that they are separated from God's way until they respond favorably to the message about God's Rule. Numerous references in the Gospels illustrate this thinking. It appears directly in Lk. 19:10 or Mt. 10:6 and 15:24. It appears in different figures, though the thought is much the same, in Mt. 23:37; Lk. 4:18-20; and Mk. 6:34. Although Jesus spoke only of Jews, the limiting of range was strategic.

Partly his direct concern was with Jews, and partly he was attacking Jewish national pride and sense of privilege.

This sweeping description is puzzling, chiefly as Jesus applied it to the "best" people of his time. We may see his meaning more clearly if we reckon with two points of reference: (a) a man is "lost" until he has found the "way" of the Kingdom. (b) Jesus translated the state of being lost into moral terms which he applied to both the outward living and the inward self (Mk. 7:14-23 and Mt. 5:17-48). Presumably it is out of this second line of thought that Jesus could call his followers "evil" (Lk. 11:13). The point of view is not merely that men fail. Rather, Jesus held that men at their best never do all that God requires (Lk. 17:7-10 and 19:11-27 or Mt. 25:14-30).

(3) He took the true point of comparison for man's life to be *God's own actions* (for example, in the Sermon on the Mount, Mt. 5:45-48). While there is evidence of God's actions in the world of nature, the record of them and the way they apply to human life is found in the Old Testament (for example, Mk. 10:6-9 on marriage and divorce) where God's will is recorded.

(4) The Law, viewed as a code of laws, has a vital center, the command to practice "love" (Mk. 12:28-34 and the important clarifying sentence in Mt. 22:40). We shall discuss the meaning of love in Jesus' thought in the next chapter. Here we notice that the connection between love and the Law is that *the parts of the Law apply the attitude of love in specific (and sometimes ancient) situations in human life.* This view led Jesus to what seemed to most Jews a great freedom of application. (a) In the Sermon on the Mount (Mt. 5:17-48) he changed *older* applications of love for larger meanings without feeling that he was critical of the older (e.g., Mt. 5:38-39). (b) He could make *differing* applications as, for example, when he spoke to the "rich young man" his word was "follow me" (Mk. 10:21). But in Lk.

10:37 in another situation his precept was, in effect, "show neighborliness."

It should carefully be noticed that Jesus did *not* treat the command to practice love as one out of many legal requirements. He did not rank it "first" on some basis of measurement. For him it was the wellspring out of which all other duties come. Probably this distinction in thought underlies the conversation in Mk. 12:32-34.

(5) *True* obedience to the Law is *obedience to its central command to practice love.* The quality of this obedience must be tested in relation to specific conditions in which a man finds himself (Lk. 13:10-16). Jesus rejected the way of life that seeks merely literal conformity to the details of the legal text (Mt. 23:1-33). Since Jesus insisted on dealing with the Law as meaning the attitude of love, it was inevitable that he apply the same principle to a man's inward life and attitude that he applied to actual behavior. He joined inward attitude and outward action, bringing the law of love to bear on both (Mt. 5:21-48) as, of course, the Old Testament did (e.g., the quotation already noted in Mk. 12:28-34).

(6) Jesus associated himself with his message about repentance far more profoundly than as a mere bearer of it. The following material indicates the nature of his involvement. The Gospel text is a specific saying, usually illustrative, which is paired with a general attitude found in his teaching. In studying Jesus we can make serious mistakes if we limit our attention to *either* isolated sayings *or* general statements about his points of view. Our understanding of him may probably be measured by the degree to which we can articulate his vivid and sometimes highly pictorial remarks with general statements about his teachings:

(a) Mt. 11:13-14 with Mk. 1:15 and the teaching that the Kingdom is present.

(b) Mt. 23:37 with the idea of seeking the lost.

(*c*) Mt. 11:28-30 with the Sermon on the Mount.
(*d*) Mk. 10:17-22 with Jesus' general claim on man's loyalty.
(*e*) Mk. 10:45 with Jesus' general attitude toward his death.
(*f*) Mk. 11:15-17 with Mk. 2:23-28.

Conclusion

We may conclude our discussion by remarking on the pessimistic and the hopeful aspects of Jesus' thinking about human life. We have seen that, in part, he is negative and condemnatory. He is firm in denouncing any deliberate defiance of God. Not only is he opposed to *sins,* he traces *the principle of sin* deep into a man's inner life. He encourages men to obey God's will, but offers no easy assurance that they either will, or can, do so.

At the same time Jesus is optimistic and hopeful about men because he is utterly confident of God. He emphasizes what man can become through God's mercy. He points to the way of life which rests on love and which, instead of the fruitless efforts of legalism, is God's will for men.

In the next chapter we shall study in detail Jesus' meaning about love and the way of life resting on it. In Chapter XXII I shall summarize Jesus' teaching about the future destiny of individuals.

. . . . for further study and discussion

Reread the references you collected on man's sin and repentance, and draw on them in preparing answers to the following questions.

1. What common picture underlies the following?:
   (a) "repent"
   (b) "strive to enter by the narrow door"
   (c) "I am sent to the lost sheep of the house of Israel"
   (d) "enter the Kingdom of God"
   (e) "I am the way . . ."

(f) The strict meaning of the English words *transgression* and *trespass*

2. Describe the significance of the fact that Jesus identified *discipleship* and *repentance* in regard to:
(a) His own thinking about himself
(b) His own claim to know God's will
(c) The position he seeks to establish over human beings

3. Collect nouns that Jesus used when, to judge from the context, he could have used the noun *sinner(s)*.

4. Answer the following questions based on your study of Lk. 15 (dividing the chapter into four parables):
(a) Who or what is lost (four answers)?
(b) What is the proper place of each?
(c) Describe the way in which *each* is separated from his proper place.
(d) Describe the seeker in each parable. (Is there one in the third parable?)

5. In an ancient manuscript the following words appear in Lk. 6:4-5: "On the same day he saw a certain man working on the Sabbath, and said to him, 'Man, if you know what you are doing, you are blessed; but if you do not know, you are accursed and a transgressor of the Law'" (writer's translation). Consider this quotation in the light of your reading in the Gospels, and answer the following questions:
(a) What sort of circumstances would make the man "blessed" because he was working on the Sabbath?
(b) What is the meaning of the words that he is a transgressor if he does not know what he is doing?
(c) Does this quotation seem in harmony with the accepted Gospels?
(d) What, if anything, would it contribute to our knowledge, were this quotation proved genuine?

XVIII

Agape (love)

*T*HERE is a story of a Jewish rabbi who was asked one time if he could recite the Law while standing on one leg. Obligingly the rabbi took the required position and said in effect, "Thou shalt love the Lord thy God with all thy heart and soul and mind and strength; and thou shalt love thy neighbor as thyself. All the rest is commentary."

Jesus' attitude is phrased differently, but he and the rabbi make the same point: *the command to practice love summarizes the Law.* In Mk. 12:28-31 he is asked to state the "first" commandment of the Law, and answers (quoting *Deuteronomy* 6:5) that man shall love his God with all his heart, soul, mind, and strength. As a "second" he adds (quoting *Leviticus* 19:18) that a man should love his neighbor as himself.

He gives no indication in *Mark* as to how he understands "first," or what he understands to be the relation between these "first" and "second" points and the rest of the Law. Among a number of possibilities I believe that we have a significant clue in both "L" and "M" material.

In Lk. 10:25-28 Jesus agrees with a questioner who cites these same two sentences as the way to gain "eternal life" (that is, the Kingdom of God). This would mean that Jesus agreed in thinking of love for God and one's neighbor as a summary of ethical duty which expressed in brief what the Law wrote out at length. Mt. 22:40 is more explicit ("On these two commandments depend all the law and the prophets"), but the meaning is about the same: the Law in its details expresses the principle of love.

This conclusion that the command to love is the heart of the Law I find supported by considerations of the nature of love. Although we shall turn to the meaning of love momentarily, let me say here that it is a principle which includes all other human duties and fits into all of man's relationships. Because it must be expressed, as an obligation, in particular words like any other law, its formulation is found *in* the Law. This fact, however, may be deceiving. Love cannot be just another part of the Law because of its *nature*. Love is the essence of the Law. When the relation of love to the Law is lost sight of, as indeed it may be, the true meaning of love disappears also.

In the evidence that Jesus thought of love as man's central duty, one piece of material seems contrary. That is, that although the *verb* "to love" is fairly common in the Gospels, the related *noun* is virtually absent, occurring in Mt. 24:12; Lk. 11:42; and six times in *John*. There is much more about love, as a matter of fact, in the rest of the New Testament than in the Gospels.

Possibly this fact of linguistic usage suggests a way of understanding Jesus. When we take up the study of love in his thinking, we are studying an attitude, a living relationship, a self in motion. We are not looking at something fixed and separated from other things. Love is not a thing, it is not a "truth"; it is an attitude primarily of choosing and conforming to God's life-fostering will. Like sunbeams through a prism, this attitude is broken up by the practice of living into many different appearances, and is described by many different names.

It is difficult to supply a word in English for this attitude

which, says Jesus, is basic to all the Law. The older word
charity now has undesirable connotations, at least in the
United States. The usual word *love* is so encumbered with
associations drawn from use that it is hardly satisfactory.
Furthermore, it stresses, in English, either the value that
the one who loves sees in the beloved object, or the feeling
that the beloved object rouses in the lover. Neither emphasis is prominent in the religious-ethical usage of Jesus.

The same problem of translation, however, bothered
Greek-speaking Jews in the second century before Christ
when they sought to translate this Biblical Hebrew idea of
love into Greek in the Septuagint Bible. They selected a
Greek verb *(agapao)* that was in common use in a number
of senses, but chose as the associated noun *agape* (pro-
nounced *uh-GAH-pay*), which was either their own creation or was, at any rate, virtually unused in ordinary Greek.

This selection shows that they felt a force in the Biblical
idea that words for "love" in common Greek use expressed
only in part. The translators, therefore, made *agape* a technical term in Greek-speaking Judaism, and it appears in this
special sense in the New Testament. That modern students
may more readily feel the Biblical force and see its distinct-
ness, the term *agape* is increasingly used instead of *love* in
modern discussions.

How Jesus' hearers understood agape

Jesus did not travel about Palestine teaching agape
—at least, he did not if the surviving texts are representative
at this point. His preserved sayings in which agape appears
in discussion are all in private conversations with his own
disciples or with religious experts. In these conversations it
is the *scope* of the application rather than the nature of agape
that is in question. The same holds true of utterances in public. Lk. 11:42-43, for example, seems clearly to mean not

merely that the Pharisees "love the best seat in the synagogues and salutations in the market places" but they hold this attitude even though their Law said they should "love" the Lord their God and their neighbor. The same problem of application is under direct discussion in Mt. 5:43-48 and in Lk. 10:25-37.

With due regard for misunderstandings that may have arisen, it appears that Jesus' hearers understood references to agape in one of two senses. These may readily be distinguished by noting whether the attitude indicated is evoked by something within the object or not. If it does arise in this way, the one having agape is responding to something he sees in the beloved. This is the relation of affection and seems to be in view in Jn. 11:5 and in numerous references to natural human relations in the Old Testament (e.g., *Genesis* 25:27-28, "When the boys grew up, Esau was a skillful hunter. . . . Isaac loved Esau, because he ate of his game . . ."). This is the usual context of the English verb *love,* and no further comment is needed.

The other sense of agape is distinguished in that it rests on the determination of one person to act helpfully in behalf of another. Here although affection *may* be present, it need not be, and the English term *love* is out of place. The best known illustration of this non-affectional kind of agape is in Mt. 5:44, "But I say to you, love your enemies and pray for those who persecute you. . . ." Jesus speaks here of an attitude of determination to act well toward some hostile person. Affection, which is probably impossible in this situation, is not in view. Generations of readers have pondered the command to "love," and have unnecessarily searched their hearts to find the feeling that was lacking.

There are numerous instances of agape taken in this non-affectional sense in the Hebrew Bible. Reference to some of these will show both the non-affectional character of the ideal enjoined and further features of it.

(1) Jewish religion clearly understood that to "love" God could be *commanded,* as man's affection cannot (in the Old Testament, in Deut. 6:5 and Lev. 19:18, which are quoted several times in the Gospels).

(2) Agape toward God was connected with obedience to his Law. For example, in *Exodus* 20:6 God describes himself as "showing steadfast love to thousands of those who love me and keep my commandments." In *Deuteronomy* 10:12-13 occur these interesting words:

> And now, Israel, what does the LORD your God require of you, but to fear the LORD your God, to walk in all his ways, to love him, to serve the LORD your God with all your heart and with all your soul, and to keep the commandments and statutes of the LORD, which I command you this day for your good?

The two ideas, namely, that agape can be commanded and that it is connected with obedience to God's Law, are strikingly combined in Deut. 30:16:

> If you obey the commandments of the LORD your God which I command you this day, by loving the LORD your God, by walking in his ways, and by keeping his commandments and his statutes and his ordinances, then you shall live and multiply, and the LORD your God will bless you in the land which you are entering to take possession of it.

(3) In this last quotation the divine blessing is the result of agape toward God, and the exact point of this blessing is *rich, full life which comes from God.* The blessing, however, is for those who stay with God (Deut. 30:19-20):

> . . . . therefore choose life, that you and your descendants may live, loving the LORD your God, obeying his voice, and cleaving to him; for that means life to you and length of days. . . .

(4) Based on this typical passage we may speak of the *religious* attitude of agape as *man's free choice of God's will for himself and his neighbor in order to find life's fullness.* *Leviticus* 19:18 put the idea in classic form: ". . . but you shall love your neighbor as yourself."

(5) Similarly, God's agape, when it is spoken of in the Old Testament, is his free choice of men in order to bless them. God chooses because he wills to do so, and his choice is not based on any attractiveness in man. See, for example, Deut. 4:37 or 7:6-8; or the Hebrew prophet Jeremiah, Jer. 31:3, among many other possible references.

We may say then, as a general statement, that in Old Testament religion agape on man's part stands for a concern deliberately chosen which actively promotes the fullest possible life in accordance with God's will for life. On God's part agape is similarly his free choice of men in order to give them life and to promote the fullest possible life for them in accordance with his will for them. In either case, agape represents an act of will rather than a movement of feeling. It is choice of God's way in order to achieve life.

Jesus' unique approach

In Jesus' thinking, agape is the comprehensive concern for the promoting of life. It should govern man's relations with his fellowmen, and his attitude toward God. The reason why agape should be the supreme principle is not merely because it is commanded in the Old Testament, but because it is *what animates God's relations with men.* On this point Jesus' view differed from the prevailing interpretations of Scripture. He made agape the one grand clue by which to understand *all* the relationships in which men find themselves.

The following discussion gives the major evidence for the place of agape in Jesus' thinking, and points to some interesting applications.

The authority of agape

MT. 12:28-34 AND MT. 22:34-40, ESPECIALLY VERSE
40. Jesus quotes from the Old Testament to summarize man's
duty to God and his neighbor. That duty is agape. The statement in Mt. 22:40 that the rest of the Law *depends* on agape
means that any ethical failure as in murder, stealing, or
any denial of God's standard is a violation of agape.

This connection leads us to observe that whereas agape
may be described in such language as "life-fostering concern," the breakdown of agape, when it occurs, must (to be
meaningful) be stated in limited, specific terms such as
murder, adultery, blasphemy, and so on. This specific vocabulary of the failure of agape does not mention agape.
Hence, when these violations are discussed, it is possible
to do so in reference to specific prohibitions in Jewish Law,
or in reference to the underlying principle that they break.
Jesus discussed them either way, though probably he
thought primarily in terms of agape, shaping his conversation to the legal language in order to reach his hearers.

MT. 5:43-48. In this paragraph from the Sermon
on the Mount Jesus presses home agape as a duty contrary
to human inclination. He develops his thought in easy
steps. In verse 44 the general noun *enemies* is defined more
particularly in the words "those who persecute you." In verse
45 the reasoning offered is that to practice agape is to act
comparably to God who provides equally for the lives of
good and evil men. In verses 46 through 47 Jesus notes and
criticizes partial applications of agape. The essence of his
thought is that since God shows agape without limitation
the disciple must do likewise. (In the same logical way Jesus
appeals to God's acts in discussing marriage and divorce,
Mk. 10:1-9).

The principle of God's fostering concern for man's life

underlies Jesus' thought in Mt. 6:31-33. It is simple fact, he
states, that God is concerned for the lives of his children.
The man who dares to trust him and live by his Rule shall
not find himself deprived of life.

The trend of the whole section of discourse from 5:19 onward, however, suggests another way of expressing Jesus'
mind: the "non-agapaic" way of life does not and indeed
cannot work. Though a man may deny agape because of
its demands on him, it is only in agape that man can find
the fullness of life he seeks. The reader will find that many
of Jesus' sayings (otherwise unexplained) rest on this view.
Among many the following may be considered in this light:
Mk. 8:34-37; 10:23-31; Lk. 12:13-21.

The pervasive influence of agape

Apart from these two major sayings in which
Jesus asserts the prime authority of agape, the conception
molded his whole outlook on God, the world and human life.

(1) Impressive evidence of the way that Jesus read God's
nature in terms of agape is in his well-recognized use of the
term *father* in application to God. Although the term comes
out of earlier Jewish religion (e.g., *Isaiah* 63:16), it was
used there of the relation between God and the nation.
Jesus used it of God in the relationship in which he found
himself, and probably of the disciple's relation as well. The
Lord's Prayer, it may be noted, is set in the plural number
although it must finally be applied by individuals.

Jesus nowhere describes his feelings about fatherhood,
but his passing references show that we may use the life-
fostering concern of the parent for his child in our understanding of God. This faith in God's fatherhood in itself
seems simple to modern readers reared within the influence
of Christian thought. It is, however, a most serious affirmation about God and not common to man's religions.

Probably we shall not be far from Jesus' thinking if we think of the ordinary father's place in the begetting and growth of his child. The father worthy of our respect cares, plans, helps, sacrifices that his child may grow. It is a major parental achievement when a parent by his life brings his children to independent responsible maturity. All this, when done willingly, is agape at work; and it is difficult to believe that Jesus, in calling God "father," could have had anything less in mind.

(2) Equally impressive, though confessedly an argument based on scanty data, is the fact that although Jesus talks about God's Kingdom, he never calls God "king." This usage indeed is found in the Old Testament, but the Gospels always associate the word *king* with political leaders, or with Jesus as the expected Messiah. In Mt. 6:32-33 and Lk. 12:32 it seems that he used "father" when "king" would have been in order.

There is only one recorded instance in which Jesus used "king" of himself. This is in Mt. 25:34 and 40 where he uses it with "the son of man" (v. 31). Though the authenticity of this paragraph has been questioned by many critical scholars, it has many of the same elements as the striking and likely authentic saying in Lk. 12:32.

Can we suggest any reasons for this apparent avoidance of the term *king?* Or, to ask our question another way, why does Jesus speak of God's kingship in terms of fatherhood? If one may judge from the way Jesus refers to earthly kings, he wished to avoid a number of associations that limited its meaning. Kings, he thought, showed an arbitrary power without agape. Kings were political in their authority. Kings were petty and, when one got right down to it, they were limited in power. (The various references to kings in Mt. 11:8; 17:25; 22:11; or Lk. 22:25 serve as illustrations.) For such reasons Jesus saw no value in the term *king*. He chose to take the *conception of kingly rule,* and thinking of its power and authority, assigned it to God. In so doing he gives the idea of Kingly Rule a new *goal* (man's good) through a new (non-kingly) relation to the Ruler of the world.

(3) A third illustration of the pervasive character of agape in Jesus' thought is the way it underlies his language as no other conception does. This fact is related directly to what was just written about his uses of the word *king*. In the characteristic sentence in Lk. 12:32, for example, Jesus mixes metaphors, referring to (a) sheep in a flock; (b) the father-relation which implies sonship also, of course; and (c) the Kingdom. If we try to interpret these figures of speech, understanding "Kingdom" from the political sense in which Jesus used the word *king*, its meaning simply does not fit into the first two figures. A shepherd is not "king" over his flock in Jesus' teaching, nor is a father "king" over his son.

We notice, however, that while the concept of a secular king does not fit Jesus' thinking here, that of agape does. In fact it fits all three metaphors. The shepherd cares for his flock (e.g., the Twenty-third Psalm in the Old Testament or such New Testament passages as Lk. 15:3-7 or Jn. 10:1-18). The father's relation to his son is (ideally) one of concern for the son's life. Then if we are correct in seeing a chief redemptive purpose in Jesus' message about the Kingly Rule of God (above, pages 187-92), agape also is the burden of the Rule. God reigns not to take advantage of man but to promote man's fullest possible life. Thus in a sentence involving figures of speech, all of which were favorites with Jesus, the unifying idea is not the Rule nor the King, but agape.

While the same is obviously true of those instances in which Jesus speaks of sacrifice, of man's salvation or God's goodness, the question naturally rises whether agape similarly underlies his sayings about judgment, and about suffering which God may be said to inflict as punishment. In fact, many readers have seen such a conflict here between punishment and love that they have felt obliged to deny the authenticity of sayings about judgment. If Jesus thought of God as a loving God, they have urged, surely he could not think of him as causing pain, suffering, or death.

I mean to express myself with both humility and caution on a point that becomes more difficult as one reflects on it. I recognize in my own thinking unsolved problems in the relation of God, who is life-giving, to creatures of his who for varied reasons reject that concern. This, however, is not quite the same problem as the one to which reference was made in the preceding paragraph: how did *Jesus* reconcile his views about God's judgment with agape? To this question it may be said that if the analysis on which these pages have been written is correct at this point, two facts hold: *first,* that agape is not to be identified with affection; and *second,* that Jesus never described God as filled with emotional love for sinners and yet condemning them. That is quite the wrong conception.

What Jesus says, for example, is that "he makes his sun rise on the evil and on the good, and sends rain on the just and on the unjust" (Mt. 5:45). This is agape at work, offering to man gifts to meet man's need. It will be remarked, however, that men must receive these benefits in order to find them beneficial. Agape *offers* but cannot *compel.*

In Peter's famous question in Mt. 18:21-22 and in Jesus' equally famous answer, it is likewise assumed that agape can offer forgiveness without stint, but cannot *restrain* the hostile will so that occasions for forgiveness will never arise. Agape braves the hostility, and forgives to the extent that forgiveness will be accepted. In John's Gospel, where God's agape for men is spoken of directly, the pattern of thought is the same. In 3:16 God's agape leads him to give his son

for man's salvation, but this gift must be received in order
to be effective. In 14:21,23 God's agape is shown toward
those who obey him and it leads to a closer relationship because of man's acceptance.

Thus it may have reasonably followed in Jesus' thinking
about God that his agape forgave sin to the extent that forgiveness was accepted (the meaning in Lk. 18:14), but that
his agape could force forgiveness and its life-bearing consequences on no one. If this was Jesus' view, then he could
have viewed God's judgment as the effect on men of men's
denial of his agape.

Though Jesus preferred to discuss principles of the Law
in relation to agape, he seems to have chosen to describe his
own mission *in concrete terms* and often in reference to
the eschatological situation. This, at least, is the way the
Synoptic evidence points. It seems probable that the word
agape became current in Christian vocabulary during the
later first century. We have already noted that the noun
is not common in the vocabulary of Jesus. It did not displace
the specific language of the Synoptic narratives; but it could
and did offer convenient Christian summary and interpretation of Jesus, as the Fourth Gospel shows. It became possible for a Christian writing late in the century to say "God
is Agape" (*1 John* 4:8).

Conclusion

In studying Jesus' thinking about agape, the chief
difficulty, I believe, is in enlarging our sense of the word
love. It is more than a self-oriented gratification in which the
object of our "love" is meaningful because it pleases us.
Agape is also more than respect for ethical teachings describing our duty. Jesus seems to have thought that he who
would practice agape must foster life as God fosters it. In

the decisions of such a person about what life truly is, he
follows principles already exhibited in God's great acts of
love for men.

. . . . for further study and discussion

Reread the references you collected on love (God's or
man's) and draw on them in preparing answers to the following questions.

1. Look up the definition of *love* in an unabridged dictionary.
Can you suggest an English word or a combination of English
words that will express the meaning of agape?

2. How do Jesus' relations with Peter and Judas illustrate his
thinking about agape?

3. Would you agree that agape is man's "impossible obligation"? Consider each part of the phrase separately, finding parallels (if possible) in the words of Jesus. *Then* put the *two* ideas
together! (There should be plenty of material for this discussion
in references in this chapter and the preceding one.)

4. How may the quotation in the fifth question, page 205, be
interpreted in terms of agape? What must be assumed about the
work being done on the Sabbath in order to make this application?

5. The most famous description of agape in the New Testament is found in *1 Corinthians* 13. Is it possible that verses 4
through 7 are based on the writer's knowledge of the life of
Jesus which he thinks of as illustrating agape? In considering
this question use verses 4 through 7 substituting the name *Jesus*
for the word *love* (or *charity*) in the English translation. Can
you find an illustration of each of the parts of verses 4 through
7 in the stories about Jesus in the Gospels?

XIX
Jesus and his disciples

*J*ESUS had a faculty for finding friends and followers. According to the records he won the
adherence of twelve men known as "The Disciples," (later
on, "The Apostles"), or "The Twelve." In addition, there
was a larger group, probably also known as "disciples,"
which included individuals as closely associated with him as
the inner circle of twelve (see *Acts* 1:21-23 for the names
of two of these). Some years after Jesus' death we find that
the inner circle of disciples represents the leading force in
a new movement in Judaism known as "the way" and then
as "the church." The question naturally rises, "What did
Jesus have in mind in choosing or encouraging disciples?
What did he anticipate in the future?" To put the drift of
the whole matter succinctly: Did Jesus found the Christian
Church?

If we set aside, as far as possible, opinions that rest on
the Christian faith, or contrariwise rest on a denial of Christian teaching, the fact that disciples gathered round Jesus
will occasion no surprise. The grouping is natural in man's
religions. It happens when the religious faith or experience
of some individual is seen, by himself or by others, to have
values beyond his own life. It is worth sharing, men feel,
and in turning to it they find it sharable. Thus the man with

219

the insight and the experience becomes the center of a group
of inquirers.

The formation of the group is more rapid when the central figure himself desires to establish continuing personal
relationships. This was true of Jesus, according to our records. He sought conversation with individuals and guided
the talk to religious themes. He invited men to accept and
share a relationship with God which he himself knew.
Strictly by offering what he had to give, yet at the same
time offering something that must be accepted without compulsion, he made himself the center of a group of men called,
by Jewish custom, "disciples" or "learners."

The place of Jesus' disciples in Judaism

The presence of pupils with a rabbi was not unusual in Jewish religion of the period. The traditional lore
of the rabbis was transmitted orally from teacher to pupil.
The pupil's task was to memorize his teacher's views and
methods, and pass them on. On a basis of custom in Judaism it would be expected that Jesus as a religious teacher
would have disciples; the surprising fact in his career lay
in his unofficial status as a teacher and in the content of
his message. His disciples showed faith of an unusual sort
in accepting the teachings of a "carpenter" of whom the
official leaders of religion at the time strongly disapproved.

The relation of the disciples
to Judaism in Jesus' thought

Natural though it was for Jesus to attract and
hold disciples, his own thinking about them starts with the
assumption that they are part of the Judaism of the day, and
ends by asserting that they are the goal and climax of all
that God meant Judaism to become. Each of these aspects

of Jesus' thinking can readily be underestimated by modern readers. It is possible to look at the historical life of Jesus from the condition of the Christian Church after its membership became predominantly Gentile, and miss the *Jewishness* of the situation in the Gospels. Many readers, Christian and non-Christian, have thought of Jesus as leading a religious revolution against the Jewish faith. Though this attitude is not completely wrong, it was not formative of Jesus' thought. He meant to revive Jewish faith, not to revolt against it; and to complete it, not to cut it off.

As to the fact that Jesus thought of his followers within the context of Judaism, either his message regarding the Kingdom or his ethical use of the Jewish Law furnishes evidence. If when Jesus preached repentance he probably meant, as did John the Baptist and the Hebrew prophets, "to return" to God's will and way, this can only mean that the people being addressed (and spoken to not merely as individuals but as a community) had left God's way and should return to it. The idea of being lost and of "returning" when spoken by Hebrew prophets meant something more than an individual's sin and recovery. It was the story of the faith of the whole nation and its special relation to God. In the same way the discussions about the Law of God are in reference neither to a general moral law, nor to man's conscience, nor to principles imbedded in the world of nature, but to Jewish Law traced back over twelve hundred years of Jewish history to Moses.

These evidences are cited because they permeate the sources and show the direct Jewishness of Jesus' thought. His disciples are in and of Judaism.

However, they are something more. They were visibly distinguished within Judaism by their attachment to Jesus; the implication runs through the material just mentioned that *they, with him, are in the proper attitude of response to the God of the Jews and are properly obedient to his Law.*

The Gospels, of course, make a very careful point of the frailty of the disciples, their lack of understanding and their easy failures. At the same time, these are the men who purpose to follow Jesus in the path of God's will and look toward him for guidance.

Jesus' conviction that, being in God's way himself, he could bring men to God is paralleled by his teaching that the Jewish nation could lose its privileged position with God. The following from various sources are samples of numerous possible references: the parable of the vineyard, Mk. 12:1-12; the saying on the men of Nineveh and the Queen of Sheba, Mt. 12:41-42; the parable of the great supper, Lk. 14:15-24; the series of indictments in *Matthew* 23. He applies to his own people the principle that being off the road means ending in the wrong place (Mt. 7:13-14; Lk. 13:22-30).

If, however, it is inevitable that the wrong road means the wrong destination, it should likewise mean that the right road, to which Jesus invites men, should lead to the proper destination. This is the road that he and his disciples travel. Its goal may be very differently described (Mt. 5:3-11; Mk. 8:35; 10:35-45; Lk. 12:32; 23:42-43; Jn. 14:1-14) yet one general principle is clear: *Jesus offers his followers the fulfillment of the hope of Judaism; there is nothing else* (Mt. 11:20-30).

Here we see once again the clash of viewpoint between Jesus and most of his contemporaries over the purpose of God for the Jews. He stresses the simple relation between men and God, passing over worldly conceptions of earthly pomp and power. When he speaks of God's goodness and God's blessings for the disciples, he is asserting for his followers the realization of true Jewish faith in God.

It is a bold assertion. It means that in his view the disciples gathered round him are related to God as God's people ought to be related, and have in their foreview the realization of the promises of God to the religious heritage in which they have grown up. This would seem to mean, then, that for Jesus his followers are not a "new" group *within* Judaism, but are the "true" group of Judaism (see the distinction in Mk. 4:11).

Jesus and the church

In the light of this discussion of materials within the Gospels, we are ready to consider the question, "Did Jesus have any teachings regarding the Christian Church?"

Christians have answered this question in very different ways. In many cases these differences about Jesus' teachings have come out of historical developments, as Christian thinking about the Church has taken shape and then looked back to the words of Jesus for confirmation or, it may be, for authority. As a result, Christians have given great attention to the only two references in the words of Jesus to the word *church* (Mt. 16:18 and 18:17) and discussed from various points of view the way in which the Christian Church of later days was, or was not, directly derived from Jesus' teachings.

Many historians of Christian beginnings feel that there are serious questions about the genuineness of these two references. They hold that each is the product of Christian efforts to establish and clarify the Christian position in the early first century. On this basis, it is held that whatever genuine words of Jesus may underlie either, the original form was different and has been lost beyond recall. This opinion about the texts leads to the natural conclusion that it is extremely doubtful if Jesus used any Aramaic equivalent to *church*.

On the assumption that the words in Mt. 16:18 and 18:17 are substantially genuine, it is obvious that they would have had special interest to Christian followers concerned for

their Church. The surprising fact is that so little could be
recalled. These references, taken strictly by themselves,
give little that is factual about the nature of the Christian
Church. By the uniqueness of their reference in Jesus' teaching, and by their obscurity, they tend to confirm the point
many historians seek to make in denying their genuineness:
Jesus was not organizationally minded, and did not think
in terms of a new organization.

Although I agree basically with the principle that the
words of Jesus were open to modification by the use to which
the Christians put them, I remark that modern discussions
often have in them two unexamined assumptions.

(1) It is assumed that an understanding of Jesus' meaning
here will prove or disprove the truth of later Christian
conceptions of the Church. It is probably impossible to discuss the meaning of the references to the Church without
an eye being cocked to the later history of the Christian
movement. This tendency is manifestly true of those who
belong to it. The meaning of Mt. 16:18-19 has been the subject of intense controversy between Protestants and Roman
Catholics for other than historical reasons. As a result,
strictly historical judgments are blurred; and the questions
about Jesus' meaning, which would be difficult to answer
in any case, are, in a practical sense, beyond solution.

(2) It is easy to assume a larger element of newness in the
two references than is required by the texts themselves. In
Mt. 18:17, the clearer case, the background is thoroughly
Jewish. The "church" operates according to established principles with the exception that Jesus speaks with authority
regarding it. Since Jesus is teaching *within* Jewish society,
it *seems* the natural assumption that the "church" is a new
thing running by the old rules. This assumption would be
strengthened if the underlying Aramaic term were in some
way unusual. As nearly as we know, however, the word
church in *Matthew* presupposes the Hebrew term for "the

worshipping assembly" of the Jews. A clearly indicated interpretation of Jesus' words, then, is that he thought of his followers as being God's true people and following the principles already established. The shocking thing is not that he referred to those outside the "church" as "Gentiles and tax collectors." The shocking thing in his own situation was that he applied this Jewish terminology of exclusion from the people of God to those Jews who rejected him and his message. In so doing they left the religion of their fathers. Jesus' point of view, it may be concluded, is theological, not organizational.

The same interpretive principle applies to Mt. 16:18. Jesus applied to his followers one of the Old Testament words for God's people. He went on to assert for them not something new and unheard of before, but the same kind of spiritual prerogative and security that the religion of the Old Testament claimed (e.g., compare *Psalms* 23 with the last part of Mt. 16:18).

The meaning in Mt. 16:19 is obscure. The words *binding* and *loosing* mean, respectively, "forbidding" and "permitting" in Jewish usage in reference to doing things. The "keys" are a symbol of authority. Many Protestant scholars, seeing an origin for this sentence in the second-century authority of bishops in the Church, reject the verse as unauthentic.

Let us pause to summarize our thinking. We have seen that Jesus in gathering disciples was following patterns common to religions rather generally, and to Judaism.

He regarded his disciples as faithful Jews because of their willingness to follow him in devotion to the spiritual meaning of God's Law. He regarded those who rejected the spiritual meaning of the Law as rejecting God and being rejected by God.

He associated God's promises to the faithful nation with the future of his own followers who, therefore, may be thought of as the true Jewish community.

He may have used the Old Testament term *assembly* on two occasions recorded in *Matthew* as a way of referring to his followers. The English translation of the Greek translation of the uncertain Aramaic original is *church*. The genuineness of these passages is questioned by many historians, and the meaning of each is obscure. We must approach Jesus' relation to the Christian Church in other ways.

The disciples and the Kingdom of God

Even a superficial reading of the Gospels shows that Jesus refrained from pinning a name on his followers. Most frequently he used the second person singular or plural pronoun *you*. When he spoke in the third person he used descriptive words which related the disciples directly to God's will. Samples are the following, though each usage is infrequent: "He who has ears to hear," Mk. 4:9; "the wedding guests," Mt. 9:15; "laborers into his harvest," Mt. 9:38; "blessed of my Father," Mt. 25:34; "my brother, and sister, and mother," Mk. 3:35; "the elect," Mk. 12:20, 22. Mk. 10:42-44 is an interesting case in which a label is avoided.

The terminology of discipleship, it may be said, was practical and concrete. The important fact was not its terms but the relation men had to God's purpose. Although the term *assembly* (Greek, *ekklesia*) is frequently used by the Christians twenty years later, the mere fact that Jesus is represented as using it twice only is good evidence that he developed no special term for his followers.

One fact, however, does appear clearly from the study of Jesus' terms for his followers: he did not call them the Kingdom of God, and did not equate them with it. This linking was indeed made in Christian thought of a later time, but this is probably because the dynamic meaning of Jesus' word had been lost through translation. For Jesus, as

we have seen, the Kingdom of God meant God's kingly
sway, especially as God moved to overcome evil and man's
weakness, and win men to himself. The body of disciples
(called by whatever name) was the group that existed in
response to and because of God's power. The message about
the Rule created the possibility of discipleship; the response
made it a fact.

Organization and spirit

Just as Jesus gave no special name to his disciples,
so he was unwilling to involve himself in questions of organization by which they might live as his followers.

In Lk. 12:14 he rejects for himself the work of a secular
judge. The context in Lk. 12:13 is instructive. Jesus refuses
to act as a disinterested third party in a dispute, but, far
from being disinterested, he picks up the issue at its heart
with a solemn warning about the shortness of life and the
unreasonableness of greed. He refuses to deal in the ma-
chinery for solving disputes; he concerns himself with the
issues behind the disputes.

This limitation of concern does not mean, of course, that
disputes do not occur, or that they can be dissolved by
warnings against greediness. It means that Jesus left the
working out of what was necessary for organizing human
relationships to his followers, whom he gathered about himself *on a personal basis.* Something of an organization shows
itself among the inner circle of twelve even during his lifetime. Peter was often the spokesman, and Jn. 13:29 may
mean that Judas had a formal responsibility in the group.

There is no good reason to suppose, however, that Jesus
was indifferent to human problems involved in group living.
Quite the contrary—he himself gathered his disciples into
a group. One of his favorite illustrations involving sheep,
shepherd, and flock rests on organized group life. His mes-

sage about God's Kingly Rule presupposes an orderliness
in God's nature and the divine intent to establish an orderliness among men. It will be observed that his approach to
problems was not through matters of organization but
through the inner issues of human life. He sought to get
at people individually, and win them to God's way. He laid
before them the age-long duty of agape, encouraging them
to struggle in all their relationships to express it.

Thus the Christian Church, as it is known in history, came
from several interrelated facts in the life and teaching of
Jesus. It stemmed from his gathering of followers and from
their response to him, first as the Messiah, then as their
heavenly Lord. But it was rooted also in the ancient faith
of Judaism in one God, Creator and Lord of history, whose
purpose is to form within history a fellowship of men willing
to live in dependence on the Unseen and share the eschatological Kingdom.

Conclusion

Since agape is a living principle by which the
disciple is free to adapt his way of life to his changing situation, there arose no serious difficulty when the new way of
looking at the Jewish faith discovered independence from
Judaism forced upon it. This took place in the first century.
Christians then felt themselves free to adjust the ordering
of their human organization in accordance with a multitude
of conditions we cannot consider here. This was in no way
disloyal to the Master, it was felt; it was the effective way
to organize the impact of his message upon men.

If Jesus anticipated any such growth among his followers
as occurred during the three hundred years after his death,
his followers recalled no words of his about it. Neither did
they remember any specific directions on his part for organizing their group to face their new responsibilities. Whether

they did well or poorly in discovering how to meet changing circumstances lies beyond our consideration. Some Christians will feel that the later Church in all essential features had its origin in his words; other Christians will feel rather that the Church at its highest stems from his redemptive purpose, though at many moments in its life it reveals man's inadequacy to match that purpose. Most Christians are humbly thankful for the fellowship of that body which has brought them to God.

. . . . for further study and discussion

Reread the references you collected on the calling and responsibility of disciples, and draw on them in preparing your discussion of the following problem.

These points of view have been seriously held regarding Jesus:

(a) He never intended to organize a religious movement; "the Church" was quite contrary to his attitude of simplicity.
(b) The disciples were the first clergymen.
(c) Jesus established in principle the way in which the Christian Church later grew.
(d) Jesus taught the universal fatherhood of God and the universal brotherhood of man.

Prepare to discuss these points along the following lines:

1. Study each of these assertions separately. Gather specific sayings, parables, or sermons in the Gospels which seem to you to support or disprove each point.
2. Suggest reasons, with supporting evidence drawn from the Gospels, if possible, to explain how such widely differing assertions could be made about Jesus' purposes.

XX

Family life

THE relation of men and women in families is one of the significant things in human life. Since life in the family involves people in their most intimate associations, men's religions have commonly had a lot to say both by way of control of these relationships, and by way of interpreting the deeper meaning of them. This, however, is not so with Jesus. He treated marriage and its allied relationships as part of man's whole existence and as responsive to God's Rule in the way that all life should be.

His preserved words about things in the family circle apply three basic principles of his way of thinking that we have met before:

(1) He recognized conventional Jewish procedures (pertaining to engagement and marriage, for example) as the social expression of the Law of Moses.

(2) He judged human duty by God's intention for mankind, and saw that intention, as far as the episodes that concern us now go, in the Old Testament.

(3) He insisted, in an important discussion of divorce, on the *contingent* character of the Old Testament Law. That is, he argued *against* divorce partly on the ground that the Law regarding it was written for undesirable conditions that had arisen. Although it expressed God's will *within* the

historical situation that gave it rise, it was not itself all that God intended for man.

When one considers the broad range of problems and relationships involved in human family life, the fact stands out that Jesus dealt with principles that underlie all conduct. He refused to discuss man's family life as a thing apart from other spiritual issues. At a point deeper within man's being than any of its parts, he sought to unite men in a saving way with God.

Custom and tradition

Although we need not go into detail respecting Jewish practices in family relations, a brief word on certain of these will put Jesus' words in their natural setting.

In the Palestine of his day marriage was monogamous. Jesus in his sayings assumes monogamy, even though in earlier stages of Jewish religion polygamy was quite common, and is not directly opposed in the Old Testament.

According to the Old Testament, divorce was permissible (Deut. 24:1). The legal material is very brief, but appears to indicate the intent to regularize procedures and protect the wife from her husband's whims. Since the qualifying circumstances are not spelled out (as they were in certain other codes of the period), the rabbis of Jesus' day differed among themselves about the legal grounds for divorce. The question put to Jesus in Mk. 10:2 was intended to entangle him in controversy.

Marriage in Jewish life was economically necessary for the woman, and a widow was a symbol of extreme human need (Lk. 21:2-4). Marriage was considered desirable for all men, including rabbis and priests. In early stages of Hebrew religion, certain matters pertaining to sex are among the tabus requiring purification by special rituals.

In later times, celibacy had value only in certain small groups in Judaism.

Though marriage was considered natural, profound elements attached themselves to it in Jewish thought. According to the view in *Genesis* 2:23-24, marriage makes a unity of the human pair. The marriage relation could be used by the prophets to symbolize the ideal relation between God and his people. Two famous prophets, Isaiah and Hosea, used aspects of their own family life to reinforce their message.

Jesus' attitude

(1) In general, Jesus adopted the current practices as far as conventional arrangements went for establishing marriage. Regarding the relationship as God's creation, Jesus supported it by his presence at weddings, and in his teachings never spoke in a derogatory way of it.

(2) He interpreted the marriage relationship as a unity, following the Old Testament, emphasizing that this oneness was God's will as the physical union was. For this reason he refused to talk about legal grounds for divorce. The Law, he held, did not express God's will but man's will on the subject of divorce.

Yet Jesus does not condemn the legislation but the attitude that obliged it. It was God's will to regulate man's denial of God's full intention.

(3) Jesus regarded marriage as part of man's earthly historical life (Mk. 12:25). It is not necessary for an individual (Mt. 19:11-12) if the call of God presses in (see vv. 12, 29). Jesus exemplified this latter fact (e.g., Mk. 3:31-35), but we know nothing about his private life otherwise.

(4) In Mt. 5:32 and 19:9 he introduced an apparent qualification to his general pronouncement that divorce followed by remarriage was adultery. The point of the two texts, as

they stand, seems to be that unfaithfulness within a marriage dissolves the marriage. The words have frequently been understood by Protestant Christians to mean that if a marriage were broken by unfaithfulness, the innocent partner was permitted by Jesus to remarry. While that might be Jesus' meaning, a point to which we shall return, the reader will notice that it provides no lawful "escape" from the marriage relation. Unfaithfulness, in itself, is contrary to God's will and so provides no way out.

There is a serious question, however, whether the two references represent the best tradition of Jesus' words. Many scholars feel that, since the words "except on the ground of unchastity" do not appear in Mk. 10:11, 12; Lk. 16:18, or in Paul's quotation in *1 Corinthians* 7:10-11, they probably represent the attitude of Christians, who were forced (like Moses) to deal with violations of the unity of marriage. The text of *Matthew* raises the question whether Jesus, like Moses, was willing to legislate restraints, when abuses among his followers could not be entirely checked. While the particular issue of divorce makes the textual problem a thorny one, it is fairly obvious from the Gospels that law-making was not, as a rule, Jesus' concern. If he spoke in a legislative way in this instance, the pronouncement was unusual.

This reservation about the genuineness of the words "except on the ground of unchastity" should be distinguished (it seems to the writer) from reflections on the suitableness of the exception to the teaching of Jesus. The point can be made that the text of *Matthew* exemplifies Jesus' own effort to put agape into practice in cases where ideals have fallen down (e.g., Lk. 7:50; Jn. 8:10-11). Here is an answer to the question, "What course of action in the long run will mean most to the spiritual as well as the physical lives—but both aspects together—of all persons concerned?"

The reader must remember that, due to the complexity

of human relations, agape might be expressed more sincerely in a divorce (and a subsequent remarriage) than by maintaining an external unity after the wedding vows have been violated. It is true that from a standpoint of Jesus' requirement this understanding of agape in action represents a compromise between life as it has come to be in some particular case and the ideal unity of marriage. The questions may be asked, however, "Does not agape make the same sort of compromise constantly? Is not all of life, on Jesus' basis, marred by man's failure to meet God's will, and is it not the field of struggle where a man should seek to achieve the best he can?"

(5) Jesus took human sexuality as a fact of life *within* the larger consideration of man's nature as a whole. This point of view, of course, makes his approach to marriage sound very different from much modern discussion on the same subject. He appears to have taken no greater offense at sexual sins than at others. He distinguished various types of action he regarded as wrong, but seems not to have placed matters involving sex in a special category. This attitude of taking human life in one piece is revealed significantly in his recorded dealings with women; in none of these meetings is any change in his general outlook observable. The same observation, of course, applies to his contacts with children.

(6) There is lacking in the words of Jesus the element of exhortation against sexual sin that appears many times in the Christian literature of the first century. This would not mean (considering Mt. 5:28) that his disciples were not open to individual temptation. It seems to mean rather that Jesus dealt, as far as he could do so, with broad principles of conduct rather than with isolated issues. It probably also means that he included family relations under the words "you shall love your neighbor as yourself." (So did Paul in *Romans* 13:8-10).

Conclusion

Does the following generalization seem out of order? Jesus, in his references to family life, shows that he combined in his own experience an explanation of man's family relations that satisfied his intellect, with a way of conducting his own relations that was personally satisfying. He was able to relate both sides of his life harmoniously to God's will.

. . . . for further study and discussion

Reread the references you collected on family life and draw on them in preparing answers to the following questions.

1. Describe the way in which Jesus' view of family life illustrates the following:
   (a) His attitude toward Judaism.
   (b) His refusal to compromise God's standards. Can you find similar attitudes in other connections in the Gospels? What are some of these?
2. Does Jesus' apparent neglect of practical problems in marriage show a lack of sympathy on his part, or a firm belief in certain fundamentals? As you develop your answer, use specific quotations from the words of Jesus and refer to basic principles in his message.
3. Explain in your own words Mk: 10:13-16. Begin your answer by describing very carefully the childlike attitude intended in verse 15.

XXI

The practices of religion

*J*ESUS' attention to practices of worship is less apparent in the Gospel texts than are his efforts to shape the theological thinking of his followers, and influence their relations with their fellow men. Nonetheless, he had a continuing sense of dealing directly with God, which expressed itself in various ways. This activity was of such importance in his living that any biographical account of Jesus must include it. There is a paradoxical element in Jesus' devotional life, however. He showed both a willingness to use the conventional forms of his people, and the freedom of spirit to leave these forms when they seemed unserviceable.

Devotional practice in Judaism

The Gospels give many hints as to conventional religious practices among the Jews. These had been inherited from the past, and provided daily, weekly, and annual ceremonials of varying sorts. At many points in the ceremonies the way in which the worshipper conducted himself, and the words of the prayers he spoke, were determined by the religious laws and customs. This established way of doing things is called *ritual;* it has a fixed *form* in contrast to spontaneous, private prayers.

236

In connection with the temple were animal sacrifices with public ritual. There was also opportunity for individual prayers in the temple.

In the synagogues the Sabbath services included readings from the Scriptures according to a regular sequence, written prayers with responses by the people, and a talk or sermon by the leader.

Each of the festivals had its own series of ritual procedures. These had a strong commemorative element, as each recalled some great event in Hebrew history. All able-bodied men living in Palestine were expected to go to Jerusalem three times yearly, at the feasts of Passover, Pentecost (Feast of Weeks), and Tabernacles (modern *Succoth*).

In everyday life, in close association with these distinctly devotional practices, was a number of ritualistic acts taught in the Jewish Law. These too might be termed "religious practices." They included rules about food, and the whole realm of the "clean" and "unclean" (see above, pp. 54-55). These practices, however, were by way of preparation for the acts of *public worship*. According to the Law of Moses, if a man was "clean," he could offer sacrifice; if he was "unclean," he could not. Jesus' attitude of freedom toward the idea that any material realities separate a man from God has already been mentioned (p. 55), and in this chapter we are considering only acts and activities that in some way mark the conscious, personal approach of men toward God. These are the religious practices that may be called "devotional."

In addition to the religious practices that were binding on the Jewish group as a whole, there were other prayers and rituals which the devout followed in their homes or in the temple. The result was that the devotional practices of Judaism, with the necessary preparations, could be very demanding of time and money. In this sense (though some provision was made for the poor) the rich could best be re-

ligious. This fact illumines Jesus' encounter with the "rich
young man" (Mk. 10:17-22). Whoever he was he had the
resources to practice the religious devotional life in Judaism,
and wished to know what he should *do*. Jesus' answer is
simply that he should dispose of all that *appeared* to make
possible an approach to God and did not because used
wrongly. Then Jesus invited the questioner to a life of simple personal devotion to God through discipleship with
himself.

Jesus' participation

Jesus' devotional attitude may be divided into
several parts:

(1) Since he shared in the common practices of his time,
we may begin with *the practices he accepted as useful*.

(2) Although our sources are not sufficiently detailed to
show his devotional life in perspective, it is likely that private prayer was *the practice he stressed above others*.

(3) Although he shows no concern to change the devotional *forms* of Judaism, he appears to have begun *a new
practice* among his followers. This slowly took the place of
the festivals and rituals which related to events in the history of the Jewish people.

In what follows we shall look at each of these parts in
some further detail.

PRACTICES HE ACCEPTED AS USEFUL. These included
his participation in the annual festivals under the leadership
of the priests, and involved animal sacrifices. Our texts do
not make clear the degree of value Jesus found in these
rituals, but they do show that he was not opposed in principle to inherited ways of worship.

In the act called the "cleansing of the temple" (Mk.
11:15-19) Jesus' objection is not to the system but to its

misuse (v. 17). The temple was intended by God as a help to prayer. Jesus acts in such a way as to show how this purpose may be restored—namely, by eliminating practices that hindered prayer.

In Mt. 5:23-24 Jesus recognized that ritual had an acceptable place in the worship of his followers. He insisted, however, that ritual is secondary to human relationships. A man may approach God (through ritual) only when his relations are right with his fellow men. Clearly Jesus sees a problem in worship, but one that lies *within* the worshipper, not in such external circumstances as those described in Mk. 7:1-4.

The Gospels are slightly more specific respecting Jesus' attendance in the synagogues. The reference in Lk. 4:16 seems borne out by Mk. 1:21, though it will be noted that the latter, and possibly also the former as well, represents him in a position of leadership rather than as a private worshipper. References to Jesus' activities in the synagogues seem to come from the early part of his career, and fade out of the later story. However this observation is to be understood, at least there is no recorded protest by Jesus against worship in the synagogue, and no intimation in the activities of his immediate disciples that he held any such attitude.

It appears, then, that Jesus accepted the devotional practices of his time, subject to the condition that they be part of a sincere approach to God. When we see him opposing any common practice, it is on the ground of insincerity (Mt. 6:1-7, 16).

THE PRACTICE HE STRESSED. We can understand from the above that Jesus would stress any acts of worship that bring men directly to God. The preeminent practice of this sort is prayer. In Jesus' own prayers, as far as these have been transmitted, the tone is comparable to conversation with God, though, of course, only his part of the relation has been preserverd.

According to our sources, prayer is the only devotional practice on which Jesus' detailed teachings have been preserved. It is likewise the aspect of contemporary devotions that he stressed most in his own living. For example, before each of the crises of his life he spent hours in prayer (see the following, all from *Luke:* 3:21; 5:15-16; 6:12; 9:18, 28). Luke also gives us an interesting collection of prayer-words of Jesus (10:21; 11:1-4; 22:39-46; 23:34, 46). These offer insights into his religious attitude, and give material for analyzing his specific conception of prayer.

One way in which to study these and other prayers of Jesus would be this: (a) After reading each one, suggest an identifying label based on something in the prayer or in its context in Jesus' life. (b) Point out in each prayer words expressive of religious attitudes such as: adoration, confession, thanksgiving, petition, intercession, acceptance of God's will, commitment to God's will. (c) Explain in each prayer the evidence of Jesus' sense of dealing directly with God.

Some readers may have questions about the reasonableness of prayer. In that connection it will be useful to observe any sentences of Jesus that suggest his own understanding of it. Probably he had no *philosophical* explanation of prayer, but rested its reasonableness in his view of God as "Father." This fact will not be directly helpful to readers whose acquaintance with modern scientific methods has brought into question the traditional conceptions of prayer, and who are groping after a fresh sense of reality. Might not a questioning about prayer be really a questioning about one's basic faith? May not our ultimate conviction about prayer rest on some fundamental attitude which makes the effective reality of prayer probable, or possible in varying degrees, or impossible?

Jesus clearly belongs with those who see the reality of personal relations between men and God, in which the self-conscious communication of prayer has its place. His concern, therefore, is not with the philosophical reasonableness of prayer but with the practical reasonableness of praying (Mt. 7:7-11) and the proper attitudes (Lk. 11:5-8; 18:1-8, 9-14).

THE NEW PRACTICE HE BEGAN. The Christians maintained, as early as twenty-five years after Jesus' death, that he inaugurated the new devotional practice of a special meal. (1 Cor. 11:23-26 was written a decade earlier than Mk. 14:22-25.) A meal with religious overtones was not new in Judaism, but this meal had in it a unique feature: It commemorated Jesus' death, speaking of it as sacrifice.

In modern Christianity this meal is known variously as the "Lord's Supper," "Holy Communion," the "Eucharist," the "Mass." The form by which it is observed varies greatly, and Christians interpret both the nature of this rite and its meaning very differently. So great are these differences that it is easy to remark that the religious practice by which Jesus apparently sought to express the common faith of his followers has become the chief instrument in dividing them! In part, these differences rest on our uncertainty regarding Jesus' intentions, and on disputes over the relation between his intention (as far as his followers understood it) and the physical form in which it should be expressed. These matters are far too complex for examination here, and it is, of course, the fact that if the last meal had in it any *unique* devotional qualities, these rest *on Jesus' death* and so belong beyond the rim of his own historical life.

If we may think of Jesus' possible approach to the last meal solely in relation to his devotional attitude, several common points appear that, at any rate, show the consistency of his mind.

(1) He used a conventional ceremony (a meal with religious meaning) to convey a new religious value.

(2) He combined the individual and social aspects of worship. Eating is one of the peculiarly individual acts that men do, as prayer may be. Jesus fits this individual act into a group fellowship, as corporate prayer becomes a group fellowship.

(3) He takes the historical moment of his suffering as his point of reference, and sets up a ritual that is to have historical, commemorative features. Admittedly, the *form* of what Jesus did at the table the night before his death was lost sight of as Christians retold the story and reflected on its devotional character. Yet what he did *in principle* has remained an effective part of Christian devotional practice. In associating a historical event of religious import with a ceremony to be repeated, Jesus followed the forms of the great festivals in Judaism. As it was characteristic of Judaism at its best to move from remembrance to devotion, it would appear that Jesus felt a devotional force to what he did. With the simplicity of a meal he bound together the past and the future, the individual and the group, and, as history shows, men with God.

Conclusion

When we consider Jesus' devotional practices in conjunction with his forming the group of disciples, is it not apparent that he taught organized group religion as well as individual practices of religion? Is it not likewise apparent that organization and form were, for him, *practical arrangements* by which men lived together and came to God?

. . . . for further study and discussion

Reread the references you collected on prayer, sacrifice and other acts of worship, and draw on these in preparing answers to the following questions.

1. Compare the form of the Lord's Prayer in Mt. 6:9-13 with the form in Lk. 11:2-4. Are there any religious attitudes present in *Matthew* that do not appear in *Luke?*

2. Find in the prayer recorded in *John* 17 as many as possible of the religious attitudes mentioned on page 240. State the basic petitions of this prayer in your own words.

3. On a basis of Jesus' teachings about prayer and anything else, how do you think he would state the reasonableness of prayer? Write an outline of this discussion.

XXII
Human destiny

*W*E ARE now in a position to summarize the vital perspective in which Jesus saw individual life. Much of this material we have already seen in our discussion in Chapter XVI about the future of God's Rule and in Chapter XVII about sin and repentance. The nature of the individual's future is an issue in Chapters XVIII, XIX, XX, and XXI, which treat problems of duty and relationship among those who would be disciples. Here in the background of discussion sounds the irreversible beat of passing years. All the religions that have caught and held the attention of men have talked about our earthly life and the way it affects men's experience after death. Jesus too saw a connection between life here and life hereafter; but though he looked to the future with confidence, his teachings on the destiny of individuals are not extended.

Contemporary thinking

In the Palestinian Judaism of Jesus' day there were varied teachings about the hereafter. Because the Rule of God was thought of in national terms, righteous Jews, as we have seen, desired to be alive *in this world* when the final kingdom arrived. It was an obvious fact, however, that

244

this could not be the case for most people; though the Old
Testament gave rather little guidance, some religious writers
in Judaism dwelt on the mysteries of the way in which God
would enable the righteous who had died to share with
the living in his Glorious Age.

The general solution was that the souls both of the righteous and the wicked survived death. God determined the
soul's quality, basing his judgment on his mercy and with
reference to his Law. If, however, a man was a Gentile, his
first step should be to become a Jew in this life, since God's
Rule was to be established from within Judaism.

It was believed that the souls of the dead went to *Sheol*
(literally, "the grave"). Here in a state of limited existence
they waited the time of consummation when God's Rule
would prevail in the world and the righteous dead would be
revived ("raised") to share in it. (The wicked dead come in
for little or no further attention in the descriptions.) In
some of the writings which date just before or just after
the beginning of the Christian era the restoration ("resurrection") of the righteous is linked with other eschatological
beliefs—the appearing of the Messiah with great power,
God's final judgment, and his future triumph over evil.

There was no single form of belief, and, it may be added,
the emphasis was not on the destiny of individuals by themselves, but as they were a part of God's purpose for the
whole nation.

The tendency in Palestinian Judaism was to take the
prophetic symbols in a very literal and historical way, and
separate the present world from the future world. The
present *might* (by an act of God) become the Kingdom of
God; but if it did not, now was the time when individuals
should devote themselves to obedience to God that they
might be fit subjects of his Kingdom later on.

Jesus' teaching

As we have seen, Jesus used the same general run of eschatological symbols as did his contemporaries; in the case of the destiny of individuals his words about the hereafter largely coincide with common Pharisaism. This is not surprising, since in general it was not so much in his terminology as in his meaning that he differed from his contemporaries. This principle appears here. He differed from others in two important insights which change the whole thrust of his words.

First, he refused to literalize eschatological descriptions (see above, Chapter XVI). This meant that in talking about the hereafter he was concerned with the forces at work in the present and the future, but not with giving a guidebook description. There are many questions about the future life that he did not attempt to answer.

Second, he declared, as we have seen, that God's saving Rule was already in operation. Men might become part of the future Kingdom in the historical present. This double quality of life is referred to in Mk. 10:30. In this sentence the important fact is that "eternal" life is not so much unending life as it is the kind of life that belongs to the eschatological order. (Duration, it will be remarked, is a quality of history and of time, rather than of the heavenly world). In Mk. 10:30 the same Greek root provides the noun *age* and the adjective *eternal.* The first impression one gets from the English sentence is one of temporal contrast, "this time" being set over against "the age to come." This need not be Jesus' meaning. Since the phrase "the age to come" is a symbolic expression for God's Rule, Jesus' point is that the "age to come" already *is.* Hence he contrasts two kinds of life, both of which exist, and which *may,* if one responds to God, be experienced together.

Scholars differ on the question of whether Jesus expected an immediate end to history. In any case, the fact of death was present in the experience of men around him, intervening between their historical lives and the achievement of their hopes in God's Kingdom. I am inclined to think that Jesus spoke in a way that he meant to be applicable to men who hope for God's Kingdom in its fullness, but who face death. The following paragraphs summarize his attitude:

(1) Human destiny rested on a living relationship with God, and not on racial origins, social acceptability, or participation in the religious life of the Jewish group. While it is true that the people mentioned by the Gospel writers are almost always Jewish and that Jesus did not emphasize the human potentialities of Gentiles, it seems clear that he allowed no eschatological advantage of Jewishness, and only limited historical advantage. The reader should be able to illustrate these comments from the Gospel texts without difficulty.

(2) Men living in history are in opposition to the Rule of God unless in humble repentance they subject themselves to it. Jesus does not so much theorize about this as state it: Men are in rebellion against God and have been so throughout Jewish history (Mk. 10:5; Lk. 11:47-48). Whether sin is the sympton or the cause of this disconnection Jesus does not say; but there are a number of texts that relate specific sins to an inner quality of human life (e.g., Mk. 7:14-23; Mt. 7:15-20) which Jesus probably thinks of as evil (Mt. 7:11) and as separating from God (Mt. 5:8).

(3) Men who persisted in living outside the (eschatological) Rule had no way at their disposal, when history should dissolve round them (by death or by the End), of passing over to eschatological life. Jesus developed a number of parables on this point. The opportunity, therefore, lies before men in history of accepting the Rule of God now,

and subjecting human existence to it in the faith that life
which seeks God's will here leads to life's fullness eschatologically. On the other hand, men may continue in denial
of God's Rule and survive (eschatologically) in "hell."

(4) Jesus phrased the transition from merely historical
existence to eschatological life in several ways. The reader
should be able, from his familiarity with the Gospels, to give
illustrations for the following ideas: repentance; obedience
to the will of God; discipleship; faith; state of being saved,
entering the Kingdom of God, or inheriting eternal life.

Conclusion

For the modern reader the dynamic quality in
Jesus' thinking is especially noteworthy. He believed that
human life is on the move in directions that determine destiny. Individuals, though they have no choice over the fact
that life does progress, may determine the direction and the
goal. They do this by choosing, on the terms established by
God, to live in fellowship with God, a relation which will
last through death into the eternal world, or by refusing this
fellowship.

. . . . for further study and discussion

Reread the references you collected on future events and
draw on them in preparing answers to the following questions.

1. On a basis of the distinction between the *historical* and the
eschatological divide your references into three parts: (a) references certainly eschatological; (b) references certainly historical;
(c) references which seem to be either or about which you are
uncertain.

2. Lk. 16:19-31 uses much Jewish symbolism and its genuineness as a saying of Jesus is frequently questioned. Does this story
state any causal connections between the experiences of its two

figures before and after death? In the light of your observation about Jewish life in Jesus' day, can you make any suggestions about causal connections? Explain the *point* of the story (vv. 29-31).

3. State in your own words Jesus' ethical and religious criticism of the Pharisaic leaders in Mt. 23:1-33. From your reading give illustrations of attitudes that Jesus *favored*. How do these differ in relation to God from the conditions described in *Matthew* 23? What is the final destiny of people holding either set of attitudes?

4. In the episode in Mk. 10:17-22, what does Jesus mean by the words, "You lack one thing" (v. 21)? Does the last part of Mk. 1:15 suggest Jesus' meaning?

XXIII

Jesus' teaching about himself

*I*N THE development of Christianity, Jesus himself has held a place of importance greater than
any of his teachings. It has been the basic Christian assertion that in Jesus of Nazareth God became incarnate, bringing the Rule into history and effecting, by the Cross, a
cosmic salvation beyond human language to describe.

There is no dispute that officially organized Christianity,
for the most part, holds this faith now and has held it from
ancient times. It is found, for example, in the letters of one
Paul of Tarsus who died between A.D. 63 and 67, and whose
writings are in the New Testament. It is found in the Gospels
which in written form come a few years after Paul. It appears, in most essential features, in the surviving evidences
of Christian life and preaching in the days before Paul.

Christian faith, of course, traditionally asserts that what
the Christian Church taught, Jesus himself taught, or at
least thought. Our problem, having surveyed the teachings
that seemed important to Jesus, is to ask, "What did *he* teach
about himself?"

The answer in one sense is very simple. It is that if we
take "teaching" in the sense of comunicating factual knowledge, he taught very little indeed about himself. If we take
it as an effort, based on his own inward sense of who he was
and what he stood for, to evoke commitment to himself,

there is somewhat more material. The *message* of Jesus, our study has shown, dealt with the eschatological situation and man's new possibilities in it. Jesus' first effort was to gain man's voluntary response, and his second to guide men in fashioning a new understanding of life and its duties. In this setting the question about his *nature* ("Who is he?") was less important than the question about his *place in history and eschatology*. Since the latter question was also phrased "Who is he?"—though it meant, ultimately, "Is he the Messiah?"—an ambiguity arises. It seems to most careful readers that the Gospels preserve much more evidence intended to bear on the second question than on the first. In either case, the over-all concern is for God's Rule.

Decisions respecting this problem are obviously tied to views about the sources of the Gospels and the genuineness of specific sayings of Jesus. The discussion in this chapter draws only on the two earliest sources, *Mark* and "Q," leaving out of account materials in "M" and "L." This is done because of widespread agreement that *Mark* and "Q" are the oldest existing compilations of Gospel material and so take us in a direct way a little nearer to the lifetime of Jesus (see Chapters VI and VII).

The evidence for Jesus' teaching about himself that we shall consider is of two sorts: (1) There is what may be called the *direct evidence* to be found in the names Jesus applied to himself. (2) There are *sentences* of Jesus *that in one way or another imply a claim* on his part. It is possible, of course, on technical grounds, to question the genuineness of individual texts. When the body of evidence is taken as a whole, so it seems to the writer, it is found to be sufficiently imbedded in the sources to come from Jesus himself. It may be added that from this point of view the implied claims of Jesus are, if anything, more convincing than the direct ones.

The result of this study is a fairly impressive collection of evidence that Jesus of Nazareth thought of himself as having a unique relation to God, and occupying a unique eschato-

logical position both toward men and toward God. We shall
consider the relation of this view to other views about Jesus
in Chapter XXV. The reader will recognize it as basic in
the Christian view that is widely held in the churches today.

Jesus' self-designations

MESSIAH. We have seen already the historical
background of the word and the place it held in first-century Judaism (pp. 55-56). It was not a term that Jesus
used. In Mk. 8:29-30 and 14:61-62 he is represented as *accepting* the term, though his responding words in either case
use "Son of Man." In Lk. 7:19 the words *he who is to come*,
which Jesus again accepts in reference to himself, are a Jewish equivalent for *Messiah*.

Out of the scarcity of this evidence, and for other reasons,
it has been argued that Jesus never claimed to be the Jewish
Messiah. The force of the *implied* claims seem to run in the
opposite direction, however, and an alternate explanation
is that Jesus deliberately *avoided* the use of the term *Messiah*. Possibly he did so because of its emotional overtones
and the popular misunderstanding of it.

SON (OF GOD). These words form one of the great
Christian claims about Jesus, referring to some inner relation of his nature to God. It is important, therefore, to notice that in Hebrew-Aramaic the words *son of* have two
meanings. They may be used in the filial sense, of course;
a son is the offspring of his father. But they are also used
in the qualitative sense, the "son of" something or somebody
sharing in the quality of the thing or person named. Thus
in the Gospels we have "son of lies" meaning "a liar," or "son
of righteousness" meaning "a righteous person." On this
idiomatic basis, therefore, *Son of God* carries the meaning
of "God-like person" and, similarly, the phrase *Son of Man*
the meaning of "man-like," or a truly human person.

In *Mark* and "Q" the phrase is infrequent. In the temptation and in the trial of Jesus (Mk. 14:61) it is used of the Messiah, in which connection, in Jewish thought, the direct filial relation to God was not in view. More significant references are in Mk. 12:1-9; 13:32; and Lk. 10:21-22.

Mk. 12:1-9 is interesting because it uses natural sonship in a parable with Messianic overtones. Since the parable is built up from *Isaiah* 5:1-7, the owner in the parable, as in *Isaiah*, is clearly God. This owner, says Jesus, has an only son who suffers at the hands of his father's rebellious servants and dies, trying to gain from them that which properly belongs to the father. Though no hint is offered as to the identity of this "son," it seems evident that Jesus *intended* to leave in the minds of his hearers a private claim.

In Mk. 13:32 and Lk. 10:21-24 the Messianic note is less apparent, the *relation* of sonship stronger. In Mk. 13:32 three types of personal existence are mentioned: the angels, the Son, and the Father. The first and third terms suggest some unusual meaning for *the Son* but no identification is offered. Though the sentence is eschatological, the use of *Father* for God gives filial force to the words *the Son*. Mark certainly understood Jesus to mean that he was the Son but did not know the eschatological End to history. Unless Jesus meant to distinguish between himself and the Messiah (a view not commonly held today), this interpretation seems the natural sense of the words.

That Jesus felt a sense of individual sonship toward God seems supported by Lk. 10:21-22. Here, in a description of his own religious life, Jesus unequivocally speaks of God as "the Father" and of himself as "the Son," distinguishing this kinship from the relation of all other men to God.

There are reasons for thinking that if Christians had been creating these citations to demonstrate from their Master's life that he claimed to be God's Son, the evidence would have been more like the Christian language of the later first century. The very peculiarities of the passages quoted argue that Jesus himself thought he had a unique relation of sonship, and that this carried with it a unique duty of Messiahship. The infrequency of such language in the Gospels confirms other evidence that Jesus' main concern was to proclaim God's Rule and gain men's allegiance. Men's attitudes toward himself were not his first problem (Mk. 9:38-40 and, of course, explicitly Mt. 7:21 and Lk. 6:46).

SON OF MAN. Jesus' use of the term *Son of Man* seems to bear out what we have seen about his lack of use of other terms. As a Hebrew-Aramaic phrase the words meant one who was human. They appear in this sense in the Old Testament. As they were used in Jewish religion, they acquired a specific application, referring to the coming ruler and judge of the world. This Messianic figure appears once in the Old Testament and is commonly mentioned in apocalyptic literature of a slightly later date.

When Jesus' hearers heard him use the term *Son of Man*, they had good reason for hesitating over his meaning. Their sense of language would suggest the equivalent of "human being," or "mere man," yet that must have seemed inadequate to the intent of Jesus' words. On the other hand, any eschatological reference must have seemed ridiculous. He spoke from a set of human circumstances—poverty, humility, and eventually death—which did not at all fit the picture of the apocalyptic Son of Man.

Yet it may have been that Jesus intended to provoke this conscious deliberation over his real meaning. The phrase *Son of Man* served to express his Messianic intention in relation to Jewish religion; but just because the popular sense of the words did not fit his own way of life, he was able to give them meaning drawn from his own faith and experience. In using them he forced men to decide for or against his message.

The indirect evidences

When a person speaks with serious intent, what he says rests on what he thinks or believes. One often reveals more about himself and his attitude toward life than he is aware of. This general fact leads us to consider a number of remarkable claims that Jesus made about his relationship to men. The fact that he said these things, or something like them, is reasonably clear. The question, therefore, is, "What did he mean by them? Who did he believe he was?"

Among such claims that carry further implications may be listed the following (each with a sample reference from *Mark* or "Q"): to forgive sins (Mk. 2:5); to have disciples (Mk. 2:14); to relate himself to man's final destiny and offer a secure basis for life (Lk. 6:46-49; 12:8); to die for others (Mk. 10:45); to subordinate everything to himself (Lk. 14:26-27); to fulfill the Old Testament (Mt. 11:2-6).

In this listing we might mention such an act as the "cleansing of the temple." This was an action that made a specific claim to unusual privilege (p. 131). It was not the sort of act that a Hebrew prophet felt free to do, but the act of a person who claimed some personal authority with respect to the building.

The implication of these claims clearly is that Jesus believed he had the authority and power to act on behalf of men's salvation. The likelihood that he thought of himself in this way is strengthened, I suggest, rather than otherwise, by the evidence of his own self-consciousness. In the stories about him in the Gospels no traces appear of a sense of fault or failure, of guilt or sin. Were there such evidences at one time? Did the first followers remove them from the records? I doubt it. Since Jesus' claims to a superior station are present in the texts, it seems unreasonable to suppose that had there been any attendant signs of violated conscience or violated spiritual relationship with God, these could have been eradicated completely. The evidence is that Jesus, with a completely good conscience, saw himself to be the answer to man's spiritual needs.

Therefore the evidence of the extreme claims and the evidence of Jesus' peaceful conscience support each other. Whether a sense of undisturbed harmony with God *must* accompany claims to such authority and power over men, who can say on any human ground? But on the other hand, the fact that this sort of claim does recur throughout Jesus' career, leaving behind no traces of bad conscience or violated spiritual relationship, puts Jesus in a class by himself. How did he think of himself when he talked in this way?

It is the writer's suggestion that these indirectly expressed claims to occupy a place of religious significance and authority are the extension of the direct claims to know God as "Son" and serve him as "Messiah." They corroborate other evidence that he personally did assert these associations about himself. Yet the reader will notice that these are indeed "indirect" claims to special position. They appeared as Jesus went about his main concern: proclaiming God's Rule in deed and in word.

Ways of understanding Jesus

But even if Jesus so understood himself, how is the modern reader to take him? A number of lines of solution are logical possibilities. Perhaps he intended deliberately to deceive his followers. If that is incomprehensible, it may be suggested that he spoke as the sources indicate he did, without understanding the serious import of his own words. Or possibly he was mentally unbalanced. Or, as his followers have commonly felt, he was a unique person, with unique self-awareness and unique relationships. Finally, it may be affirmed that in some obscure way our sources for our knowledge of Jesus are untrustworthy as they stand and need editing. This solution would hold that such claims as we have noted are by nature scientifically impossible and, therefore, must be historically improbable. Hence the Jesus of history was quite different from the picture of him in the Gospels.

Some of these proposed solutions are rather easily disposed of, and need not be discussed here. The final decision probably lies between the last two, namely that Jesus was in some way unique in his person and his relation with God, or that he was not. In the latter case it must be said that the testimony, including his own, to his uniqueness was mistaken at the start or was misunderstood by those who preserved it. Although matters of literary and historical evidence are involved in reaching the point of decision, I believe that the final determination which becomes the pattern for our understanding of Jesus lies in the sphere of faith as well as of reason. I shall describe in Chapter XXV the way Jesus appears according to each of these interpretations of him.

Conclusion

As far as our two oldest sources go, however, Jesus thought of himself in a way we may properly call "unique," and for which the best single word in his own vocabulary is the word *Son*. The fact that the phrase *son of* had two senses in normal use, and that in the history of the phrase *Son of Man* a specific Messianic application had developed in addition to the common meaning, quite suited Jesus' manner of stirring men's curiosity and forcing them to decisions on their own.

I personally feel that this sense of sonship is the connecting link in Jesus' experience between two unchanging convictions of his:

(1) that God is to be obeyed above all other considerations; *(2)* that the Rule of God is present, available to men, and fulfilling God's purpose for human lives.

The sources give insufficient evidence to show us how, in Jesus' personal life, these aspects of divine power, personal obedience, and sense of sonship linked together to make him what he was. Biographically, the fact is impressive that Jesus taught not so much himself as the Rule that he could share with men.

. . . . for further study and discussion

1. Name aspects of Jesus' thinking about himself that you see in the following references. How would you state possible claims in each case?   Mt. 5:21-48 (use of pronoun "I"); 11:25-30; Mk. 14:21, 24; Lk. 22:27; Jn. 13:13.

2. Discuss possible bases for Jesus' sense of certainty about the Kingdom of God.
   (a) What made him think the Kingdom of God was "at hand?"
   (b) How does he know what the Kingdom is like so that he can give parables about it?
   (c) Does he mention any possible sources? Are these available to others? To what extent may these not be available to others?

3. Compare Peter's words in Mk. 8:29 and Mt. 16:16. What are the key words in Peter's view of Jesus? What are the key words in Jesus' response (Mk. 8:31; Mt. 16:17)? State possible differences in meaning or emphasis between the texts of *Matthew* and *Mark*.

4. Read Jn. 5:1-17:26. Collect references to Jesus' direct teachings or *implied* teachings about himself.

5. On a basis of your reading summarize the similarities and the differences between the words of Jesus in *John* and in the Synoptics. Refer especially to matters of *expression* and *content*.

SECTION FOUR

Who is he?

XXIV

The four portraits

$\mathcal{A}$ NY reader who sets out to answer the question, "Who is Jesus?" joins an innumerable company. No man forms his conclusion alone. We modern readers, indeed, are dependent for our knowledge of Jesus entirely on records preserved to communicate certain specific understandings about him. The four Gospels give four somewhat different views of Jesus (see Chapter VII), each, as I have noted earlier, having its own individuality, unity, and purpose. In the work of this book we have given less attention to the Gospels than to the sources underlying them, both because of the demands of historical method and because we wished to share with the early Christians in their efforts to understand Jesus.

The Gospels as portraits

The Gospels are the four oldest accounts of Jesus. They show us how he was understood in the first century, and may be thought of, for practical purposes, as four portraits. When we recognize this fact, it helps us understand the Gospels, and illustrates the problem of understanding Jesus. Every person's understanding of Jesus has in it the virtues and the limitations of a portrait.

261

A PORTRAIT IS THE REPRESENTATION OF A LIKENESS. It shows the lineaments of its subject. If it does not show him as he seemed to others, it loses its value *as a portrait,* whatever other artistic merit it may have. It is a fact that we may stand before the portrait of a person dead for centuries and, because of the skill of the artist, feel the character of the man portrayed.

This observation, however, does not mean that merely the *surface* likeness of the subject is portrayed. The task of the artist is to *see* the person before him and cause others to see him through portrayal by color, line, and shade. The artist does not say, "These *are* the wrinkles, and the moles, and warts, and so on, that are on the face of my subject." He says rather, "Look at my picture, and see the man himself."

In this freedom in reproducing its subject, the portrait created by the artist may be contrasted with the photograph from the camera of the average man whose concern is solely to capture an appearance. The one mechanically reproduces what is "there," the other would help others "see" what he "sees." The fact that a man may be an artist with his camera need not spoil the essential contrast between the principle of interpretation and the process of duplication.

It seems to the writer that the four Gospels are more like portraits than photographs, *presenting Jesus as one who is seen and understood in order that others may see and understand also.* As the writer of the Fourth Gospel tells us, this means deliberate purpose and selection (Jn. 20:30-31), but, the reader will notice, this does not itself imply that the chosen details are of themselves untrue. It rather means (as we saw in Chapters VI and VII) that the basic insights and understandings of those who first sought to understand Jesus come into question. Were they right in seeing him as they did, and so portraying him?

A PORTRAIT VIEWS ITS SUBJECT FROM A FIXED POSI-
TION. This is a limitation it shares with the photograph. It
means that no picture can show all sides of a subject or all
phases of his character. In a similar way each Gospel looks
at Jesus from a specific viewpoint and cannot fully depict
him. This is simply stating an underlying fact about the
selective process that operated on the Gospel materials as
described in Chapter VII.

The result, however, has importance. Just as a picture of
the left side of a man is no more "true" than a picture of the
right, so one balanced portrayal of a rich personality is no
more "true" than another. One or the other may be more
interesting, attractive, or helpful, but hardly more correct.
Here, then, is a psychological reason for several accounts
of Jesus; he was too complex a figure in himself and struck
men's understanding in too many ways to be squeezed into
one narrative.

EVERY PORTRAIT IS AFFECTED BY THE VIEWING AND
INTERPRETING MECHANISM. It is readily apparent that the
kind of camera and photographic equipment has much to
do with the photographic results, as do the kinds of colors,
brushes, and so on bear on the finished portrait. Although it
is true that the artist may be greater than his equipment, he
can never be independent of it. Neither can he be independent of himself. He is limited by his own technical skill,
his physical well-being, and by the insights or blindnesses
in his own character. He sees what he sees and records what
he can.

The same observation holds true of the Gospels. They are
the work of the Christians of the first century, who spoke
in the intellectual and religious forms of Judaism in that
time. The Gospels show men struggling to fit conceptions
larger than human life to the language of human experience. They reveal their authors gripped by a faith in one

who awes them and whom they feel they do not fully understand.

Thus, if we see the process of understanding Jesus in the
Gospels, we understand something of our own process. It is
true that opportunity for individual observation of Jesus is
lost to us. We can no longer, as did his contemporaries,
"look" at him. In what material has survived, however, we
have the task of reading character rather than describing
the surface details. We may work selectively within the
scope of the Gospels. We too must decide on the point of
significance from which we shall seek to understand Jesus.
Should we not, moreover, soberly estimate the limits of our
own qualities of intelligence, observation, sympathy, and
moral insight? Should we assume that because our horizons
are different from those of the evangelists that they are
wider? Or can we see more profoundly because through
the work of historical science we can see, in some ways,
more clearly?

The Gospels as interpretations

The Gospels as we read them now present in detail the key aspects of Jesus which we see in essence in the
oldest underlying sources. Jesus was the hoped-for Jewish
Messiah ushering into history the eschatological period. He
was genuinely human in his relation to historical reality. He
was genuinely the heavenly Son of the Father. He exercised
miraculous power over the natural world and over evil
spirits. He was crucified; and died, in some way acting on
sinful man's behalf. All four Gospels describe the last week
of his life in considerable detail. He left his tomb alive and
made reassuring appearances to his friends.

Within this general frame of understanding, each Gospel
makes its own detailed emphasis.

MATTHEW stresses Jesus' Jewishness. It shows

Jesus in relation to Jewish hopes and prophecy as the one who meets the Messianic expectations. This Gospel emphasizes Jesus' deity, not only by including the Christmas story, but by omitting details of the human life of Jesus to be seen in *Mark*. It presents detailed evidence of Jesus' teachings, roughly three-fifths of the text being devoted to words of Jesus.

MARK, which we have studied in detail, is the Gospel of action. Especially is this the activity of God's Messiah directed toward the saving of men's lives both historically and eschatologically. The humanity of Jesus shines clear here, both in his reactions to conditions around him and in the force of his personality on others.

LUKE portrays Jesus especially in his human sympathy for people of all sorts. There is less that is distinctively Jewish in this Gospel, the author seeing instead Jesus' underlying connection with the human race as a whole and with God's world-wide purpose. As we noted in Chapter XXI, Jesus is portrayed as a man of prayer in the crises of his life and in his daily experience.

JOHN depicts the paradox of the human and the heavenly in Jesus. Though both realities are factual in the biography, the more meaningful one is that Jesus is the divine Son of God, who takes away sin and transforms man's life, giving him the life of the eschatological age to come.

The study of the portraits

The description just given in brief of the portraits of Jesus in the Gospels is the product of detailed comparisons of the texts. It is difficult to carry on this study extensively without special tools, including, for exhaustive work, the use of the Greek texts. The reader whose appetite has been whetted for further reading will find suggestions at the end of the next chapter.

. . . . for further study and discussion

1. Collect evidences from the text of each Gospel to illustrate the special emphasis of each one. Distinguish for the sake of clarity between (a) words or acts of Jesus, and (b) comments made by the writer or others about him.

2. What differences of emphasis may be described in the following parallels:

The Christmas story: Mt. 1:1,16,18-2:23; Lk. 1:26-56; 2:1-40.
Preaching in Nazareth: Mt. 13:53-58; Mk. 6:1-6; Lk. 4:16-30.
The "cleansing of the temple": Mk. 11:15-19; Jn. 2:13-22.

XXV

The alternative views today

$\mathcal{T}$wo interpretations of Jesus commonly claim attention today, and either may become part of an individual's religious thought and experience. We may call these the *naturalistic* and *supernaturalistic* views of Jesus, taking our names from the basic issue in either case. The former sees Jesus as a figure in and of history, the product of the same natural forces that give life to all mankind. The latter, through many variations of statement, sees Jesus as the coming of the divine into the human, the sharing of the life of God in the life of men. Modern thinking is concerned directly with the problem of Jesus' person, therefore, and this issue forms a common link joining together other interpretations of his life which have followed other emphases.

These "other" interpretations have little immediate value for us in seeking to understand Jesus, although we may think of them all together as exhausting the range of possible explanations.

About the beginning of the twentieth century, for example, it was proposed that Jesus was a fictional character— he never existed; he was the creation of his "disciples." This view has not commended itself to many readers, for there are too many traces of the actual and the historical about the Gospels. As a further consideration, the evidence for Jesus' existence is at least as good as for the existence of many other figures of history who are never called into question. This modern denial of Jesus' historicity had an interesting parallel at the end of the first century when the view was going round that he was a heavenly being in disguise, and not a genuine human being at all. This view likewise failed to commend itself on the twofold ground of its weakness in the face of historical evidence, and its unsatisfactory philosophical assumptions.

In an effort to account for some of the things that Jesus said (as, for example, that he could forgive sins or had a unique relation to God), it has been suggested that he was mentally unbalanced. This view had some currency in his own lifetime, though for slightly different reasons (Mk. 3:21; Lk. 11:15 carries further meaning). It must be said, however, that most readers are impressed by the sanity of Jesus' words rather than by any lack of balance on his part.

An equally desperate suggestion to account for the character of some of his sayings is that he was intellectually deficient. The point is that he talked about life, sin, salvation, God's Rule, and so on, with no good appreciation of what he was saying. Although this suggestion would account for some unusual things in the words of Jesus, the evidence is available that he had a good mind and used it well, in accordance with Jewish ways of expression.

We need not consider separately descriptions of Jesus as a prophet, or rabbi, or carpenter, or religious enthusiast. These speak only of parts of his life and personality. They have been valuable emphases in the study of Jesus, but they do not interpret the basic issue: what was Jesus' relation to our world? Was he, on the one hand, *part of it* in the same sense that all men are part of nature? Rising above the moral and spiritual attainments of his time, was he nonetheless the child of humanity, as the swamp flower blooms from the muck? Or was Jesus something more, the representative of life that lies beyond nature?

Ultimately, all interpretations of Jesus come to the question, "Who is he?" and all the answers are either naturalistic or supernaturalistic.

These two attitudes toward Jesus have produced two characteristic modern interpretations of him which we may review briefly here.

Jesus, the great teacher

A sketch of Jesus and his meaning according to the naturalistic point of view would go somewhat as follows:

Jesus was the natural son of two Jewish peasants, born, it is thought, at Capernaum in Galilee about the beginning of the Christian era. He was the oldest son of a large family, but nothing is certain about his youth and young manhood. As he matured, he showed a great sympathy for human suffering and a marked sensitivity to natural beauty. He absorbed the religion of his parents, and in his simple but reflective mind made it deeply his own.

Although a number of things happened in Palestine during the years of his maturing that might have stirred his religious zeal, he was a man about thirty years of age before he came to public attention as a religious leader. At this point in his life he came in contact with a young priest known in Christian and Jewish history as John, who with passion and conviction was calling for religious and social reforms.

Jesus began a similar mission. His interest was less eschatological and more devotional than John's (perhaps it was not at all eschatological). He wanted men to recognize God as their Father, to search out each his own hypocrisy, and live toward one another as citizens in God's heavenly Kingdom of love. Though Jesus had little formal training, he began to give all his time to preaching and teaching his new insights.

For a few months he wandered with a small group of followers about his native Palestine. He became the object of great popular interest because of the political and social unrest of his time, and his challenge to it. Out of the winsomeness of his personality, the crystal honesty of his words, and the unbending character of his criticism of hypocrisy, stories began to circulate about him, including stories of miraculous powers. This development was quite the opposite of the moral emphasis he intended, but he struggled against it in vain.

The combination of great popular interest in him and his criticisms of his people's leaders led to a series of plots to take his life, one of which ultimately came off. He was executed as a common criminal by the Romans. He left behind him memories which led his followers to assert that in some unknown way he was still alive. They made a deity out of him, quite missing his own interest and purpose. Though this deification has led to a distortion of almost all the stories told about him, his image still shines forth from the disjointed texts in a way that for centuries has fired human imagination. Who can explain why one of mankind's choicest spirits was born in that time and place? Why was he as far ahead of his time as he was? Why is he still ahead of the spiritual attainments of Western men, who for centuries have been exposed to his influence?

The preceding summary can only suggest the general scope of this naturalistic understanding of Jesus. The view is widely held today by interested readers outside Christianity. It appears within the movement in Protestant groups holding what are called "liberal" theological positions. Though this view is distasteful to many Christians, the fact should be recorded that it is the result of serious study and thought, and is held by many men in combination with great moral earnestness and religious zeal. It proposes to find, as best it can, lasting values in the story of Jesus, and to assert them over against the supernaturalism of earlier Christian faith on the one hand, and the emptiness of modern materialism on the other. Whatever our own position may be, we should recognize that this interest in Jesus' human experiences and his moral teachings has enriched all contemporary understanding of Jesus.

PROBLEMS. This presentation of Jesus has two fundamental difficulties in it, one historical and one philosophical. The latter, which questions details of the Gospels on the ground that "this sort of thing is impossible," raises problems which we looked at earlier (in Chapter V) about the relation between historical evidence and our philosophical presuppositions.

On the historical side there are two serious difficulties. Many of the methods of studying the Gospels have changed since this naturalistic portrait of Jesus was drawn. I doubt if it would be drawn with either the same detail or the same certainty today. There has also been considerable change of attitude regarding Jesus' religious interests. It is clear to most scholars now that we cannot limit his concern to matters of moral relationships, or to men's devotional relations with God. Eschatological issues were not drawn into his sayings at a later date by the writers of the Gospels. We can no longer, for strictly historical reasons, think of him as a simple-minded peasant teacher. Neither is it as evident as it once appeared that Jesus was the *natural evolutionary* culmination of religious Judaism.

It is true that the portrait of the Jesus of liberal Protestant thought still shines clearly in secular and religious literature. But if we may use an analogy, we might compare this description of Jesus to the pigments of a portrait from beneath which the canvas has been taken. The picture still exists in its beauty, but there is the pressing necessity to provide it with new support. Whether this can be done in the case of the naturalistic picture of Jesus remains to be seen.

Jesus, the divine Lord and Saviour

The alternative view of Jesus, at its heart, is supernaturalistic. It holds that Jesus is not only to be understood by the operation of natural forces (though these need not be ruled out of consideration), but by the article of faith that he is the unique appearing of God within the sphere of man's life. According to this view, Jesus is a unique person embodying reality that is otherwise beyond man's experience. Thus what Jesus *is* must be spoken of partly in symbolic language. He himself reveals God.

In describing Jesus, therefore, the symbols vary with the speaker and his world of thought. The symbols of the Gospels have set the standard and served as points of reference; but they raise the question, "What in the Gospels is symbolic and what is historical?" The narrative of the birth of Jesus is a pertinent case. In Christian circles where the matter is regarded as open for discussion at all, there is no common agreement at present.

The supernaturalistic view of Jesus runs steadily through Christian faith from the beginning. We have seen it in such primitive sources as "Q" and the apostolic *kerygma*. It is clear in the texts of the New Testament as these now stand, dating from the latter part of the first century. It is the view, consequently, that we examined in detail in *Mark* and need not recount here. It received further theological formulation (though not additional historical details) in the traditional doctrines of the Christian Church, in which Jesus is spoken of as the eternal Son of the Father, "begotten not made," and the "second person" of the Trinity. This is the view that allows Roman Catholic piety to speak of Jesus unequivocally and commonly as "God," and many Protestants (who, incidentally, do not object to the Catholic doctrine on the point), to revere him as their divine Lord and Saviour from sin.

PROBLEMS. This view, in the philosophical problems it raises, takes us back likewise to the discussion about the place of faith in human experience, and its relation to natural science. It insists that our reasoning about the world as a whole must include the evidence about Jesus that cannot be reduced to merely human dimensions. In so insisting, it raises the problem of how to speak of supernatural acts in scientific terms.

Beyond these basic problems related to faith and the

world, Christians who hold the supernaturalistic understanding of Jesus differ greatly in their thinking and in the
problems they recognize. The result is that although we
should say something about these problems in order to
maintain the proper proportions of our discussion, it is extremely hazardous to frame general statements. The following, I trust, are fair in the present circumstances:

Some Christians have no problems at all in connection
with their faith in Jesus. They accept some form of traditional Christianity without reflection, and permit themselves
to ask no questions about it.

Other Christians find problems as they encounter modern
thinking in relation to Christianity. In some cases this means
that the Christian believers are primarily concerned with
fending off direct attacks on their faith by people who are
outside it, and whose interest is in disproving its essential
claims. This encounter may take place with very little appreciation on the part of Christians for the intellectual problems of men on the other side. This separation of minds is
not always the rule, however, and is not necessary. There are
Christian believers who are seeking to understand the meaning of their faith in relation to modern thought, and to state
what they see in modern forms.

Since this last way of thinking is the outlook from within
which this book has been written, it will not be amiss to
speak of its problems more specifically. It is engaged in
new and serious efforts to describe in modern terms the
transhuman reality it sees in Jesus of Nazareth. It is pains-
takingly probing the relations between eschatology, symbolic language, and history in the Gospels. It has seen in recent times far-reaching developments in our knowledge of
early Christianity, together with an increasing sense of uncertainty in some areas of study. It is trying to incorporate
all of these into a harmonious view of Jesus that also includes

Christian experience with him as Lord and Saviour. Though there are unresolved difficulties and vigorous conflicts of opinion that make generalizations difficult, we probably should be wrong if we either expected or desired inquiry to cease.

Here, then, are two descriptions of Jesus. Each is "religious" rather than "academic" because each is held as part of conscious religious life. Each is held wholeheartedly by many of its adherents, and with varying degrees of certitude by others. From the rational standpoint, strong arguments can be given for each, and weighty difficulties must be acknowledged.

But the final decision about Jesus is not entirely a rational one; it also includes religious commitment. As we have seen before, there is in us as human beings a fundamental connection with life that must express itself in some kind of acceptance and response to things about us, whether we understand them or not. I have previously called this response "faith"; it is the expression of man's religiousness.

Does not our attitude toward Jesus relate itself in a peculiarly direct way to this religious attitude of ours? If we are reflective at all in our thinking about this great person, is not our decision toward him a part of our larger religious attitude *because we believe that our particular decision offers in principle the solution to understanding him, and life as well?* Understanding Jesus, like understanding Tennyson's "flower in the crannied wall," means at last understanding ourselves, the world, and God.

This comprehensive significance that Jesus has for our thinking raises an interesting question. If, at the point of decision about Jesus, men divide, some of us seeing him in a supernaturalistic way as heavenly Lord and Saviour, others of us seeing him naturalistically as one of earth's finest products, which group understands him more completely?

Naturally, each group will maintain that its own view

about him fits more of the facts and is burdened with fewer difficulties than the other. This conviction is to be expected. Furthermore, many individuals in each group will very likely testify to the satisfactory religious experience they enjoy. Some people will be tempted to argue that one religious experience is *more satisfactory* than the other. This line of argument is indeed convincing in individual cases, but it has not carried the whole field. The two points of view about Jesus remain.

However, there is one consideration that seems to me commonly lost sight of in efforts to understand Jesus. This fact is that Jesus is indeed at the center of historic, traditional Christianity in theory, and in many Christians' lives he likewise is in personal religious practice. This is an experience involving Jesus that is religious rather than intellectual in nature. Naturally, only Christians share in it. Does it yield a larger understanding of Jesus than can be gained by rational methods alone? Is it a valid analogy to this question to ask if a man who *plays a game well* finds something in it that the spectator, even though he *knows the game well*, cannot find?

Christian believers, of course, will answer, "Yes," to both questions. It is our experience that Jesus of Nazareth, whether we will or no, is part of the larger, present reality we face. We have found that we understand him most as we relate ourselves to him, the symbol and representative of God's eternal order. We have found that through his person that order meets us, that through him men find God.

. . . . for further study and discussion

1. Prepare in parallel columns the *points of similarity and difference* in the two basic interpretations of Jesus, drawing your materials from your general reading and the descriptions in this chapter. Do not become detailed in this but deal with major items.

2. Select (a) any story of Jesus in action, (b) a teaching or assertion of Jesus, and (c) a story from the Gospels about Jesus, and show in each case the points of similarity and difference that the naturalistic and supernaturalistic views of Jesus might introduce into the explanation of each.

Suggestions for
the next step in reading

For studying the content of the Gospels, A. M. Hunter's *The Work and Words of Jesus* (Philadelphia: The Westminster Press, 1950) is a little more advanced than this book. As the title of the book suggests, Hunter keeps the theological importance of Jesus in view in his discussion.

Hunter's very brief *Introducing the New Testament* (Philadelphia: The Westminster Press, 1946) places the Gospels in the fuller perspective of the whole New Testament. It provides practical suggestions for further reading on pages 118-120.

For readers with a historical bent, Dwight M. Beck's *Through the Gospels to Jesus* (New York: Harper & Brothers, 1954) will repay careful study. In addition to some difference in theological point of view from Hunter—Beck characterizes his viewpoint as "liberal"—this book discusses the texts of the Gospels more extensively than Hunter and in greater technical detail. Although there is no collected bibliography, the footnotes point the way to further reading in more specialized writings.

The Westminster Study Edition of the Holy Bible (Philadelphia: The Westminster Press, 1948) represents the same general approach to the Bible that is followed in this book and used by Hunter. The text of the Bible is paragraphed, and provided with introductory articles and footnotes. There is a concordance that doubles as a Bible dictionary, and a set of maps. The Bible text is the traditional "Authorized" or "King James" Version.

Help in studying the key ideas of the Gospels is available in *A Theological Word Book of the Bible* (New York: The Macmillan Company, 1951) edited by Alan Richardson. Though the entries are necessarily brief, this is a valuable dictionary of *ideas* in the Bible, and should be more widely known by general readers.

For the study of Jewish religion in the days of Jesus many books are available. *The Interpreter's Bible* (New York and Nashville: The Abingdon-Cokesbury Press, 1951-54; Abingdon Press, 1954—) is a convenient and up-to-date source book for checking specific Biblical passages in this connection, and for general reference as well. The standard reference work is George Foot Moore's two-volume *Judaism in the First Centuries of the Christian Era, The Age of the Tannaim* (Cambridge: Harvard University Press, 1927).

Index of Biblical references

---

* Discussions of the meaning of the more important references are indicated by **boldface** type.

Index of subjects

---

* The main treatments of the more important topics are indicated by
boldface type.

285

288   INDEX: Subjects

Mary, 141, 142, 144
Matthew:
  interpretation of Jesus, 264-65
  (*see also* Gospel, Gospels)
Messiah:
  defined, 55-57
  in Jesus' thinking, 131, **190,
    191**, 252 (*see also* Temp-
    tation)
Messianic Age, 88-90 (*see also*
    Kingdom of God)
Messianism, 53, 55-57
Micah, 44
Miracle, problem of, 59-60, **67-
    73**, 105
Miracles of Jesus:
  expressions of God's Rule, 187
  in Gospels, summarized, 127-28
  in *Mark*, 125-26
  (*see also* Miracle, problem of)
Moses, 39, 40, 41, 45, 46, 51, 53,
    179, 233
Myth, 140
Nazareth, 126, 156
Old Testament, origins, 37-38,
    40, 44, 45 (*see also* Holy
    Scriptures, Law [of Mo-
    ses])
Oral Gospel, 75, 78-79, 94 (*see
    also Kerygma*)
Parables, 164, **168-70**
Paul, 30, 52, 116, 137, 143, 233,
    234, 250
Pentateuch, 40, 45, 46 (*see also*
    Law [of Moses])
Peter, 90, 116, 150, 216
Pharisees, **51-52**, 53-55, 156, 246
Philosophy, 65-66 (*see also* Faith,
    Religion)
Pictorial language, in Jesus' teach-
    ings, 166-67
Prayer, 126, **240-41**
Priests, 42, 50, 52, 231, 238
Prophecy (*see* Jesus, fulfilled Old
    Testament prophecy)

Prophets:
  attitude to ritual, 47-48
  illustrations from family life,
    232
  origins, 41, 42, **43-44**
  use of poetry, 170-71
  view of future, 179-86
"Q," 78, 92, 127, 139, 146, 153,
    154, 251, 272
Religion:
  definition, 16-18, 20
  difficulties in defining, 14-15
  forms of expression, 15-20 (*see
    also* Worship)
  Philosophy of, 8
  prevalence, 19-20
  problems, 5-8, 16-18, 27
Religions, History of, 8, **22-34**
Religious life, 18-20, 33-34
Repentance:
  defined, 198-99, 201
  in *kerygma*, 89
Resurrection:
  of Jesus, 4, 5, **134-38**, 144
  evidence for, 136-37
  in Jesus' teaching, 194, 247-48
  in Judaism, 245
Revelation, 46 (*see also* Inspira-
    tion)
Revised Standard Version, 135,
    168, 170
Ritual, 47-49, 236
Roman rule, 44, 55-56
Sabbath, 47, 50, 53-54, 237
Sacrifice:
  death of Jesus as, 132, 192, 255
  in Judaism, 47-50
Sadducees, 52
Samaria, 156
Satan, 147-52, 190
Saul, 41, 42
Science, modern, 6, 59-60, 63-66
Scientific knowledge, compared
    with historical knowlege,
    100-102